The Problem of Wealth

The Problem of Wealth

A Christian Response
to a Culture of Affluence

Elizabeth L. Hinson-Hasty

ORBIS BOOKS
Maryknoll, New York 10545

ORBIS BOOKS
Maryknoll, New York 10545

Fathers and Brothers
MARYKNOLL™

Founded in 1970, Orbis Books endeavors to publish works that enlighten the mind, nourish the spirit, and challenge the conscience. The publishing arm of the Maryknoll Fathers and Brothers, Orbis seeks to explore the global dimensions of the Christian faith and mission, to invite dialogue with diverse cultures and religious traditions, and to serve the cause of reconciliation and peace. The books published reflect the views of their authors and do not represent the official position of the Maryknoll Society. To learn more about Maryknoll and Orbis Books, please visit our website at www.maryknollsociety.org.

Library of Congress Cataloging-in-Publication Data

Names: Hinson-Hasty, Elizabeth L., author.
Title: The problem of wealth : a Christian response to a culture of affluence / by Elizabeth Hinson-Hasty.
Description: Maryknoll : Orbis Books, 2017. | Includes bibliographical references and index.
Identifiers: LCCN 2017003637 (print) | LCCN 2017025296 (ebook) | ISBN 9781608337033 (e-book) | ISBN 9781626982383 (pbk.)
Subjects: LCSH: Wealth—Religious aspects—Christianity. | Poverty—Religious aspects—Christianity. | Economics—Religious aspects—Christianity. | Catholic Church—Doctrines.
Classification: LCC BR115.W4 (ebook) | LCC BR115.W4 H56 2017 (print) | DDC 261.8/5—dc23
LC record available at https://lccn.loc.gov/2017003637

For
Garrison Douglass
and
Emmeline Dunbar,
two people who remind me
that hope and love
are possible and real

Contents

Part IV
Increasing the Theological and Moral Imagination of the US Middle Class

Part V
Additional Resources

Acknowledgments

This volume was significantly shaped by my role serving as a research consultant for the ecumenical and interfaith dialogues sponsored by the Poverty, Wealth, and Ecology (PWE) project of the World Council of Churches held between 2010 and 2014. The PWE dialogues focused on identifying the root causes of poverty, dramatically increasing inequalities in wealth in different regions around the world, and the impact of the current dominant forms of wealth creation on our natural environment. I am deeply indebted to two economists, Rogate Mshana and Athena Peralta, for their careful planning of those events and to the many colleagues who became conversation partners during hearings and forums that were part of that project.

The first hearing that I attended was in the fall of 2010 in Budapest, Hungary. At the time, I was living in Debrecen and teaching as a Fulbright Scholar at Debrecen Reformed Theological University. Making the train journey within Hungary to the European dialogues, and then (after returning to the United States) traveling over the next three years to take part in hearings and forums held in Jamaica, Canada, Indonesia, Switzerland, and Tanzania, enabled me to situate my own theological perspective and US white middle-class experience within a larger global context. While I was conscious of my privileged social location before participating in PWE, these dialogues challenged me in a new and much more critical way to confront my dependency on the very systems and structures that are accelerating the wealth divide and increasing poverty around the world.

Each dialogue began with an immersion experience to enable participants to make a significant connection between our conversation and the local context. In Hungary, we visited the Roma Parliament and met with a family of musicians living in

Budapest's Eighth District. The direct and undeniable impact of overconsumption in the United States and our ecological debt to other nations was most palpable in an Indonesian fishing village near Bogor where goats stood knee-deep in the trash that had gathered in the water of a canal and tried to nuzzle their way through the garbage to find edible food.

What I found most empowering in those dialogues were the visions of new community and economic justice that emerged out of the experiences of people who were most vulnerable in the world's economy. Our charge was to listen, learn, and write out of our experiences. Memories from and bonds of friendship pushed me in this book to confront an ancient question: "How can I say to anyone else, 'Friend, let me help you get rid of that speck in your eye,' when you can't see past the log in your own eye?" (Luke 6:42). For this reason, I am writing out of and reflecting on my white middle-class US experience, although I hope that people who live in many different regions and circumstances find the work helpful for interpreting their own.

This book began as the Thomas White Currie Lectures on "Grace-Filled Economy" delivered at Austin Presbyterian Theological Seminary in February 2013. I am grateful to seminary president Theodore J. Wardlaw for his support for the project and for the dialogue that was fostered in that community. Katharine and Charles Henderson provided another special opportunity by encouraging me to be a Coolidge Fellow and take part in the 2013 Summer Colloquium sponsored by *Cross Currents* and Auburn Theological Seminary. The Summer Colloquium allowed me access to the libraries of Columbia University and Union Theological Seminary in New York, which greatly aided my research. Being in conversation with incredibly creative colleagues and spending the summer in a city that has inspired several generations of Social Gospel theologians stimulated my theological imagination. The article on "The Problem of Wealth" that I wrote in the weeks following the summer colloquium and published in *Cross Currents* outlined the framework for this book. Additional research for the manuscript was completed when I was invited to give the George and Jean Edwards Lecture in Peacemaking at Louisville Presbyterian Seminary in Louisville, Kentucky, in November 2013 and the Tollefson Lectures at Buena Vista College in Storm Lake, Iowa, in November 2015. All of these conversations and the support were profoundly helpful to me.

I would be remiss if I did not acknowledge the significant debt of gratitude I owe to my colleagues at Bellarmine, in the larger academy, and in the church. Hoon Choi, Joseph Flipper, Greg Hillis, Justin Klassen, Deborah Prince, and Mil Thompson all supported me in innumerable ways by helping out with departmental projects so that I could continue my research while serving as chair of the department. Greg, Justin, and Mil offered exceedingly helpful comments on portions of the manuscript. Friends from the Society of Christian Ethics, Social Ethics Network, and ecumenical advocacy groups—Gloria Albrecht, Edith Rasell, and Laura Stivers specifically—improved my arguments with their careful and critical reading of different chapters. James Calvin Davis, Mark Douglas, Roger Gench, and Doug Ottati, members of the Reformed Theological Ethics Writing Group, offered their insights during our regular manuscript exchange at the Society of Christian Ethics. There were also friends and pastors engaged in advocacy work outside the academy who are skillful teachers and imaginative writers and preachers who joined my commons and entered into conversation about parables to increase the theological imagination of the middle class. I am especially thankful for the contributions made by Cory Lockhart and Christephor Gilbert.

There is no doubt that my family is an enduring and seemingly bottomless well of support and inspiration. Lee, my partner in life, frequently reminded me to finish the book because he had met so many people "ready to read and hear it." While they may not be aware of this, my two children, Garrison Douglass and Emmeline Dunbar, are two of the main reasons for me to put so much time and energy in this project. When they were born, I hoped that they would grow to see themselves as agents of change in the world. They are named after three great reformers of the late nineteenth and early twentieth centuries—William Lloyd Garrison, Frederick Douglass, and Emmeline Pankhurst. In recent years, however, I have realized what an uphill battle life will be for them if the direction of the economy and our patterns of consumption in the United States remain on their present course. What options will US society offer for them to be good and to act justly? I dedicate this work to them in hope that they will find a way to make a difference in movements of resistance and play an active role in the nonviolent revolution of love for which this volume calls.

Part I

THE PROBLEM IS WEALTH, NOT POVERTY

CHAPTER 1

Introducing the Problem of Wealth

The quality of life and our lives may depend upon the extent to which citizens understand those who shape attitudes and actually control institutional structures.

—*Laura Nader*[1]

Jackylyn Segarino immigrated to the United States from the Philippines with her mother and three siblings when she was five years old. Now in her twenties, she is the first person in her family to graduate from college. Most of her aunts, uncles, and cousins continue to make their home in the Philippine cities of Cebu, Manila, Angeles City, Toledo City, San Miguel, and others. They are among the 20 million people living in the slums of the Philippines, what outsiders to these communities call "slum dwellers."[2] Ramshackle housing built primarily from wood and corrugated steel that teeters over polluted canals reveals the quality of life in Filipino slums. Tight corridors between houses create the only space available for people to exchange greetings and conduct business, and for children to play. Modern skyscrapers provide the backdrop for the slums in cities like Manila. Their multistoried frames tower over dilapidated dwellings and punctuate the visible contrast between wealthy and poor districts of the city. Jackylyn gets emotional when she talks about her family. She sent money

---

[1] Laura Nader, "Up the Anthropologist—Perspectives from Studying Up," in *Reinventing Anthropology*, ed. Dell Hymes (Ann Arbor: University of Michigan Press, 1972), 285.

[2] For some powerful images of slum life in the Philippines, see "Quick Guide: Manila Slum Life," BBC News, news.bbc.co.uk.

to them even when she was a student living on a tight budget because she knows the true value of rice. Every few years, Jackylyn travels with her children the great distance from the home she has made in Kentucky to the Philippines. Maintaining a connection to her family and her roots is of great value to her. Perhaps more important is that she doesn't want her kids to allow geographical distance to create a social and attitudinal barrier between them and those who live in extreme poverty.

We live a world of contrasts, though we seldom want to examine carefully and name the root causes of deep inequalities in access to resources, opportunity, income, and wealth in the United States and around the globe. Forbes.com reported in 2015 that the list of the richest people on the planet "expanded to a record 1,826" billionaires; the majority on the billionaire list are from the United States, but Chinese entrepreneurs made serious inroads.[3] You might expect the largest economies on our planet to be the most highly industrialized and technologically advanced nations, but 58 percent of the top 150 largest economic entities in the world today are transnational corporations.[4] Energy giants such as Royal Dutch Shell, Exxon Mobil, and BP and the discount superstore Walmart consistently make it near the top of the list of the largest economic entities.

Serious questions have to be raised about whether the ability for individuals and corporations to amass this kind of wealth has increased the well-being of the whole global community. For example, direct connections can be made between sweatshops in Asia and wealth and the ability to consume in the United States. Factories in Asia make many of the garments for stores and brands that US residents favor. A 2006 National Labor Committee report estimated that "200 children, some 11 years old or even younger, [were] sewing for Hanes, Wal-Mart, J. C. Penney, and Puma at the Harvest Rich factory in Bangladesh."[5] These children were denied an education, exploited, underpaid, and beaten while working in

[3]Kerry Dolan, "Inside the 2015 Forbes Billionaires List: Facts and Figures," Forbes.com, March 2, 2015.

[4]Tracy Keys, "Corporate Clout Distributed 2012," *Corporate Trends*, www.slideshare.net.

[5]"Children Found Sewing Clothing for Wal-Mart, Hanes, and Other European Countries," Labor and Worklife: The Labor and Worklife Program at Harvard Law School, www.law.harvard.edu.

the factory. A survey of factories in the Philippines, Sri Lanka, and Indonesia done by the International Textile Garment and Leather Workers' Federation found that "not one of them paid a living wage to their combined 100,000-strong workforce. Many of them didn't even pay the legal minimum wage."[6] The poverty of Jackylyn's family in the Philippines described in the story at the beginning of this chapter in this way is directly connected to the wealth and consumption patterns of people living in the United States through the clothes we wear on our backs.

There are about 1.2 billion people in the world who live in extreme poverty.[7] Poverty is considered extreme when people are forced to live on less than $1.25 per day. Half of the people in the world are living on less than $2.50 a day. Eighty percent of the world's people live on less than $10 a day.[8] A large majority of the world's people live in countries where income gaps are widening. Poverty is also widespread throughout Asia, Latin America, and Africa. About 1 billion people in the world live in slums, with the vast majority of them in Asia. In Latin America, 80 million people still live in extreme poverty, half of them in Brazil and Mexico.[9] More than half of the people on the continent of Africa live in poverty.[10] The living conditions of people living in poverty in these regions are often made worse by the high levels of debt taken on by their governments from loans given by multilateral institutions like the International Monetary Fund. Theologian Daniel Groody points out that while there has been some debt relief, the world's poorer countries can "spend as much as thirteen dollars in debt repayment for every one dollar they receive in new loans, making it all the more difficult to break the spiral of poverty."[11]

The US economic outlook appears at least on the surface to be quite different, but wealth in the United States is more of a thin

---

[6]Madeline Bunting, "Sweatshops Are Still Supplying High Street Brand," Poverty Matters blog, *The Guardian*, April 28, 2011.

[7]World Bank, "The State of the Poor: Where Are the Poor, Where Is Extreme Poverty Harder to End, and What Is the Current Profile of the World's Poor?" and Where Are the Poorest," documents.worldbank.org.

[8]Global Issues, "Poverty Facts and Statistics," *www.globalissues.org.*

[9]"Poverty in Latin America: The 'Yes, But' Syndrome," *The Economist*, January 2, 2014.

[10]Daniel Groody, *Globalization, Spirituality, and Justice* (Maryknoll, NY: Orbis Books, 2007), 5.

[11]Ibid., 6.

veneer than a solid core. A country often characterized as a "land of opportunity" is seeing some of the highest numbers of people living in poverty on record since estimates have been published.[12] There are 46.7 million people living at or below the federal poverty line, according to US Census data gathered in 2014.[13] Of that number, 19.9 million US Americans live in extreme poverty, meaning that their family's cash income is less than $10,000 per year for a family of four.

Poverty in the United States is not colorblind. In 2013 the poverty rate among blacks was 27.2 percent, 23.5 percent for Hispanics/Latinos, 10.5 percent for Asian Americans, and 9.6 percent for whites or people of Anglo-European descent. The US Office of Minority Health reported in 2012 that 26 percent of American Indian and Alaskan natives lived in poverty, as compared to 11 percent of non-Hispanic whites.[14] Native Americans have the shortest life spans in the United States, along with higher illness rates, exceptionally high teen suicide rates, and higher than average school dropout rates.

US Americans are also deeply in debt. The US national GDP grew between 2000 and 2014, by about 51 percent. But during that same period, the national debt outpaced economic growth and "increased by more than 200 percent."[15] Forty percent of US Americans have absolutely no retirement savings.

Nonpartisan, nonprofit organizations researching social and economic trends consistently report that the middle class is also losing ground. A Pew Forum study concluded, "From 2000 to 2014 the share of adults living in middle-income households fell in 203 of the 229 US metropolitan areas . . . The shrinking of the middle class at the national level is to the point where it may no longer be the economic majority in the U.S."[16] The Brookings Institution also reported in 2013 that the lower middle class is

[12]2014 US Census Bureau Statistics, www.census.gov.
[13]Ibid. The 2015 federal poverty line was $24,250 a year for a family of four. See aspe.hhs.gov.
[14]"Profile: American Indian/Alaska Native," US Department of Health and Human Services, Office of Minority Health, minorityhealth.hhs.gov.
[15]Sheldon Filger, "The US National Debt: Can the Federal Reserve Perform Fiscal Alchemy Forever?" Huffington Post, May 28, 2014.
[16]Pew Social Trends, "The American Middle Class Is Losing Ground," December 9, 2015, www.pewsocialtrends.org.

struggling as one-third rely on income support from a government program, and 40 percent of children in lower-middle-class homes are food insecure.[17] According to the National Bureau of Economic Research, "over half of the population of the United States would not be able to access $2,000 in thirty days to respond to an emergency."[18]

These statistics represent a deep polarization evident across US society and around the globe. Within the US context, few people understand the connection between the growing financial portfolios of the minority at the expense of the impoverished majority. Furthermore, within the United States, the extent of poverty is concealed by our nation's high incarceration rate, because prisoners are not counted among the unemployed while they are incarcerated. Keep in mind that the United States has the highest incarceration rate of any country in the world; one out of every thirty-two US Americans are either in prison or supervised by a correctional officer on parole. African Americans and Hispanics make up about one-fourth of the total US population but comprise 58 percent of all prisoners. African American men are particularly vulnerable; one in six will be incarcerated at some point in their lifetime.[19]

Serving time in prison leads to impoverishment. *New York Times* journalist John Tierney reports that "a stint behind bars tends to worsen job prospects that weren't good to begin with."[20] Sociologists studying the impact of incarceration point out that prison almost inevitably leads to poverty, not only for the person incarcerated but for children of prisoners as well. Spouses and partners experience what sociologist Megan Comfort calls "secondary prisonization."[21] Wealth inequalities and the influence of for-profit corporations are evident in prisons and jails as well.

---

[17]Benjamin H. Harris and Melissa S. Kearney, "A Dozen Facts about America's Struggling Lower Middle Class," The Hamilton Project, Brookings Institution, December 4, 2013, www.brookings.edu.

[18]Mehrsa Baradaran, "How the Poor Got Cut Out of Banking," *Emory Law Journal* 62 (2013): 485.

[19]See National Association for the Advancement of Colored People, "Criminal Justice Fact Sheet," www.naacp.org.

[20]John Tierney, "Prison and the Poverty Trap," *New York Times*, February 18, 2013.

[21]See Megan Comfort, *Doing Time Together: Love and Family in the Shadow of Prison* (Chicago: The University of Chicago Press, 2008), 13-19.

Men and women who are convicted of misdemeanors and who have the ability to pay can buy "prison cell upgrades" to stay in "newer, less-crowded facilities."[22] Many US prisons are owned by private, for-profit corporations.

The inequalities in wealth and poverty described above are extremely evident in the city where I live. Louisville, Kentucky, prides itself on being a large metropolitan area made up of vibrant neighborhoods. Fourteen beautiful, well-shaded, tree-lined parkways designed by Frederick Law Olmstead, the famous landscape architect internationally known for his work on New York's Central Park, physically connect neighborhoods in different parts of the city. However, seldom are these parkways used for more than access to different areas or as a means to build relationships that reach across lines of social class and race.

Louisville Magazine conducted a study in 2013 of the divide between the west and the east in the city and concluded that it was not just geographical. The image below was taken from a vacant parking lot under the I-64 overpass that exits onto Ninth Street in downtown Louisville. The West End is 79 percent African American with an unemployment rate of 13.4 percent and a median household income of $21,733. A larger percentage of households in the West End are headed by single mothers, whereas Louisville's East End is 91 percent white with an unemployment rate of 3.9 percent and a median household income of $59,600.[23] These income and wealth inequalities translate into lack of access to a wide variety of community services, such as supermarkets, banks, pharmacies, doctors, dentists, and more. According to the *Louisville Magazine* report, the West End can boast of having more of one type of business: liquor stores. Significant disparities exist in levels of education as well. Louisville ranks third among cities where the wealthy are most geographically segregated from people living in poverty, particularly people of color who live in poverty. The rest of the top ten cities with similar patterns of segregation of the wealthy were:

---

[22]Claire Groden, "Want a Jail Cell Upgrade? That'll Be $155 a Night," *Time*, July 31, 2013.

[23]Mary Chellis Austin, Dan Crutcher, Jenni Landman, Josh Moss, Cary Sternli, Kane Webb, and Jack Welch, "The West End and a Tale of Two Cities," *Louisville Magazine*, March 2013, 30–31.

1. Memphis, Tennessee
2. Birmingham-Hoover, Alabama
3. Louisville, Kentucky
4. San Antonio–New Braunfels, Texas
5. Cleveland-Elyria-Mentor, Ohio
6. Detroit-Warren-Lavonia, Michigan
7. Nashville-Davidson-Murfreesboro-Franklin, Tennessee
8. Columbus, Ohio
9. Charlotte-Gastonia–Rock Hill, North Carolina and South Carolina
10. Miami–Ft. Lauderdale–Pompano Beach, Florida[24]

Figure 1.1 A View of Downtown Louisville from a Vacant Lot in the City's West End

Image of a vacant parking lot underneath the I-64 exit ramp onto Ninth Street in Louisville showing the visible difference and contrast between East and West Louisville. Photo by Lee Hinson-Hasty. Used with permission.

---

[24]Richard Florida, "The US Cities Where the Rich Are Most Segregated from Everyone Else," *The Atlantic Citylab*, April 2, 2014.

Like Jackylyn, I am deeply concerned that geographical distances not be used to create economic, social, and attitudinal barriers between people living in my community. More recently, reporters with *Louisville Magazine* interviewed residents of Beecher Terrace, a public housing project in the West End. Bernice Taylor told reporters, as she talked about her experience living at Beecher Terrace, "I just want a better way of life."[25] Who doesn't want a comfortable life with access to healthy food, good schools, and health care, as well as other community services?

People of faith are facing the most pressing theological and moral problem of our time as we confront the problems of wealth inequality and poverty. I am not referring to discerning how best to distribute wealth once we make it. Rather, I am referring to popular US attitudes toward the unlimited right of white individuals to their wealth and to the ways in which our current dominant forms of wealth creation are increasing poverty and accelerating the wealth gap within the United States and between nations around the globe. *The world has enough wealth right now to end extreme poverty and satisfy everyone's needs.* According to a report released by Oxfam International in 2013, the "world's top 100 billionaires added $240 billion to their wealth . . . enough to end world poverty four times over."[26] What we need to do is radically alter our attitudes, systems, and policies that support and justify the increase of one's individual wealth at the expense of a larger commons and to learn to distribute wealth and money more justly.

Why the Problem Is Wealth, Not Poverty

Political scientists, economists, sociologists, philosophers, and ethicists have written a great deal in recent years about wealth inequality and poverty, most frequently beginning the debate by focusing on poverty as the root issue.[27] However, gathering data

[25]Mary Chellis Austin, Arielle Christian, Dan Crutcher, Dylon Jones, Anne Marshall, Josh Moss, and Amy Talbott, "The West End, Part II," *Louisville Magazine*, March 2015, 45.

[26]"The Cost of Inequality: How Wealth and Income Extremes Hurt Us All," *Oxfam Media Briefing*, January 18, 2013, 2.

[27]Two examples include David Brady, *Rich Democracies, Poor People: How Politics Explain Poverty* (Oxford: Oxford University Press, 2009), and Jeffrey Sachs, *The End of Poverty: Economic Possibilities for Our Time* (New York:

about the lives of people in poverty assumes that the investigator holds a position of social and economic privilege. The term *privilege* refers to a special right or system granted to a particular people or group and comes from the Latin words *privus*, referring to an individual, and *lex*, meaning law. Nonfiction writer Eula Biss in an article on white debt points out that privilege is a "system in which not everyone is equally bound."[28] Sociologist Dalton Conley observes that "social scientists very seldom ask the question: 'Why are the rich wealthy?' in the same way [they] often ask why the poor are poor."[29] At issue here is the fact that people who are wealthy or even those who have just moderate wealth have the political clout to shield and protect themselves from social inquiry. Biss's and Conley's observations ring true with my own experience serving at a social ministry during the years Bill Clinton led the movement to reform public assistance programs.

From 1995 to 1998 I served as the grants coordinator for a social ministry called Interfaith Outreach Association (IOA) in Lynchburg, Virginia. IOA was supported by local churches and synagogues and provided help with furniture, food, prescriptions, energy, and emergency rent relief. My work at the association consisted of writing grants, offering educational programming for people needing financial assistance, and sometimes conducting home visits. One of the projects was called Super Cupboard, which helped individuals and families seeking assistance to develop the skills necessary to survive with low wages and on the Supplemental Nutrition Assistance Program (SNAP, more commonly called food stamps). Super Cupboard was a version of television's *Cutthroat Kitchen* for people living in poverty. You won the game despite social sabotages by becoming the most skilled in working with cheap ingredients that you could afford on food stamps—usually large amounts of beans, rice, pasta, and processed American cheese.

The years of my service at IOA were significant because in 1996 the US Congress reformed the federal public assistance program and turned the money over to the states to implement new models

---

Penguin, 2006).

[28]Eula Biss, "White Debt: Reckoning with What Is Owed—and What Can Never Be Repaid—for Racial Privilege," *New York Times Magazine*, December 2, 2015.

[29]Dalton Conley, ed., *Wealth and Poverty in America: A Reader* (Oxford: Blackwell, 2003), 2.

as they saw fit. In Virginia this new policy meant that people who had once been dependent upon public assistance had to prove that they were applying for jobs in order to access benefits. That aspect of the program was billed by politicians as "welfare to work." The welfare-to-work program focused on what people in poverty could do to resolve their situation.

IOA adopted a slogan from the 1960s War on Poverty, "A Hand Up, Not a Hand Out." Sargent Shriver, the man President Lyndon Johnson's chose as head of his 1964 task force charged with drawing up antipoverty legislation, used the phrase to emphasize policies "intended to help the poor to improve themselves, so that they could take advantage of an expanding economy."[30] Interviewed in 1995 by Terry Gross on National Public Radio's *Fresh Air*, Shriver made this observation about legislation to fight poverty: "The way out of poverty was through human effort. People had to have motivation to move out of poverty. Then we'd help keep the motivation alive and aid it. But we didn't just hand out money to people who had no motivation."[31] "A Hand Up, Not a Hand Out" conveys the understanding that people in poverty can move up an invisible social and economic ladder if they have the right opportunities.

If my memory serves me correctly, when welfare reform began in 1996, people seeking help had to show documentation that they applied for as many as forty jobs a month. Most of the applications were for jobs at local fast-food restaurants, as clerks in grocery stores, or cleaning at the hospital—all jobs that could potentially contribute to downward mobility. From my own experience of working with IOA, I have concluded that neither the politicians at that time nor those involved in the practice of social ministry asked the right questions about the root causes of the problem. The application process for assistance at Interfaith Outreach included a fairly intense interrogation of the income and spending patterns of individuals that was intended to distinguish between those "deserving" or "undeserving" of help. Questions posed to the clients were about their sources of income, how they budgeted

---

[30]Maurice Isserman, "Foreword," in Michael Harrington, *The Other America: Poverty in the United States* (New York: Scribner, 2012; reprint of 1962, 1969, 1981, 1993 editions), xvii.

[31]"Sargent Shriver: A Man of Public Service," KQED News, January 19, 2011.

and spent money, and whether they were applying for jobs. At that time, discussions of client's needs were not driven in the office by concerns about why employers weren't paying a family-sustaining wage, why clients didn't have the technical training they needed to find gainful employment, or why affordable housing was in such slim supply. Not pursuing those issues was largely due to lack of time. Although charities and social ministries provide essential emergency relief, their work is in too high demand and they are all too often understaffed and underfunded. Therefore, charities and social ministries cannot undertake the kind of advocacy needed to really change the systems and structures creating poverty.

A popular social narrative that informed the policy shifts regarding public assistance in the 1990s held onto the belief that the majority of people who were fully employed were playing by the rules and the people who were living in poverty were more likely to game the system. In addition, the popular assumption at that time, still held today by the majority of US residents, was that people in poverty could be upwardly mobile.

Recent studies prove that these assumptions are far from the truth. For example, sociologists Joe Soss, Richard Fording, and Sanford Schram show abundant evidence in their book *Disciplining the Poor* that, as a result of changes in policy related to public assistance, states created a racially biased system of welfare fed by stereotypes that people of color were more likely to be on welfare rolls.[32] Another example is found in a study conducted by the Brookings Institution in 2013 that concluded, "While social mobility and economic opportunity are important aspects of the American ethos . . . data suggest[s] they are more myth than reality. In fact, a child's family income plays a dominant role in determining his or her future income, and those who start out poor are likely to remain poor."[33] I suspect that people living in poverty have always been aware of this fact.

In this book, my primary aim is to reorient the conversation, challenge long-held yet faulty assumptions· about why people in

---

[32]See Bill Moyers, "How Bill Clinton's Welfare Reformed Created a System Rife with Racial Biases," billmoyers.com.

[33]Michael Greenstone, Adam Looney, Jeremy Patashnik, and Muxin Yu, "Thirteen Economic Facts about Social Mobility and the Role of Education," Brookings Institution, June 2013.

poverty are poor, and offer an alternative perspective by beginning the debate with the problem of wealth. To begin the discussion with the problem of wealth is not to say that I am unconcerned about the circumstances of people living in poverty. Clear questions of justice and the fair distribution of wealth in the United States and around the world must be raised from the standpoint of the people who live without daily access to basic material resources—food, water, housing, education, sanitation, and so on. However, I don't think that people in poverty are the main cause of their lack of access to these essential resources. The problem, particularly for US Americans, is how we think about self in relation to others and the prioritization of an individual's right to make money over against the needs of a larger community, the whole interdependent web of life. There are two key reasons why I want to reorient this debate by beginning with the problem of wealth.

The first is to frame the right questions so as to enable us to understand better power dynamics that are part of the debate over wealth inequality and poverty and to underscore the critical role that wealthier people, especially the middle class, must play in eliminating social distance and reducing our levels of consumption. Laura Nader was one of the first anthropologists to direct the attention of scholars in her field socially upward. She suggested, in her article "Up the Anthropologist—Perspectives from Studying Up," that "studying the colonizers rather than the colonized, the culture of power rather than the culture of the powerless, the culture of affluence rather than the culture of poverty" would raise new and difficult questions, underscore power dynamics, and bear the potential to engender a sense of responsibility.[34]

Nader wrote, "Studying 'up' as well as 'down' would lead us to ask many common sense questions in reverse. Instead of asking why some people are poor, we would ask why other people are so affluent? How on earth would a social scientist explain the hoarding patterns of the American rich and middle class? How can we explain the fantastic resistance to change among those whose options appear to be many?"[35] What Nader outlined in her essay was a way of reorienting the field of anthropology. The ideas she

---

[34]Nader, "Up the Anthropologist," 289.
[35]Ibid.

laid out in her paper suggested to me a new set of questions to engage in debates about poverty, wealth inequalities, and the human misuse and exploitation of the environment. Nader pointed out that there is "relatively abundant literature on the poor, the ethnic groups, the disadvantaged; there is comparatively little field research on the middle class and very little firsthand work on the upper classes. Anthropologists might indeed ask themselves whether . . . such dominant-subordinate relationships may not be affecting the kind of theories we are weaving."[36] Considering whether the focus on poverty as the problem to be solved has affected the theologies we are weaving is a question worthy of the attention of theologians, religious leaders, and people in the pew.

Most of my attention in this book is directed toward the growth of wealth inequalities and poverty in the United States, but it will be impossible to discuss these issues without making some comparisons between the United States and the larger global economy. The ways we create wealth and the US patterns of consumption need to be carefully interrogated and examined to understand how they accelerate the wealth divide, arguably create poverty, and lead to ecological destruction.

The second reason for beginning my debate with the problem of wealth is theological. Religious traditions offer a radically different way of entering into a conversation about wealth inequality and poverty by identifying the problem as *wealth*, not poverty. For example, in the ancient Roman society in which Christianity emerged, 90 to 95 percent of people lived in poverty. Logically, due to the makeup of society, members of the earliest community of faith were predominately found among people living in poverty. Thus, early Christians responded to wealth inequality and poverty by looking socially upward.

Early Christians did not condemn wealth per se, but saw greed as an "obstacle to salvation." In the Sermon on the Mount found in Matthew's Gospel, Jesus is remembered as saying that the poor are "blessed." For centuries, isolated and particular movements of Christians have interpreted Jesus's sermon as the heart of a Christian social ethic. Since the rise of industrialism, Jesus's ethic articulated in the Beatitudes has been seen as running directly counter to

---

[36]Ibid.

capitalism. That interpretation of the Beatitudes led Social Gospel theologian Walter Rauschenbusch to describe riches as "narcotic soul poison." Moreover, from the perspective of Christian faith, wealth is not defined in money form or found in the accumulation of material things, but in the discovery of community, shared partnership, gifts of reciprocity, and love embodied in acts of justice.

Consider the story of civil rights activist Fannie Lou Hamer. Her faith kept her involved in the struggles for justice, life, love, and dignity in the segregated Jim Crow South. Singing kept her going, and she used her musical gift as the means to inspire others during meetings, gatherings, and demonstrations and to calm other civil rights activists when they were afraid of white police or while they were sitting in prison. One of her favorite songs was "This Little Light of Mine," a musical reflection on the Beatitudes.

Fannie Lou was the youngest of twenty children born in Ruleville, Mississippi, to Lou Ella and Jim Townsend. Mississippi was known as one of the most repressive states in the Jim Crow South. Her parents made their living as sharecroppers. The sharecropping system perpetually held the Townsends in the bondage of debt. They often had to borrow money during the winter just to survive. Historian Beverly Mitchell says that the "one year Hamer's father was able to make a little money, he was sabotaged by a white man who poisoned the mules the family had purchased in hopes of earning enough to become solvent."[37] The family never recovered financially.

Fannie Lou began working in the fields alongside her family at the age of six. By age twelve, she was forced to drop out of school. Her formal education ended with fourth grade. When she married Perry Hamer in 1944 she began working for the W. D. Marlowe Plantation—in the cotton fields, as a house cleaner, and later, because she was the only worker who could read or write, she became the timekeeper for the other workers. Hamer joined the civil rights movement in 1962 after learning that a doctor performed a hysterectomy on her without her consent when she thought she was undergoing a much more minor surgery to remove a small uterine tumor. As a result, she and Perry never

---

[37]Beverly E. Mitchell, "The Vocation of Fannie Lou Hamer, Civil Rights Activist," *American Baptist Quarterly*, June 1, 2004, 180.

had their own biological children, but they adopted four children.

Hamer is well-known for her activism, but she never profited financially from her work in the civil rights movement. In Mississippi, African Americans who joined the civil rights movement were threatened by physical and economic intimidation intended to instill enough fear to maintain the power and control of whites. After trying to register to vote for the first time in 1962 she was dismissed from her position as a sharecropper. She believed that being kicked off the plantation set her free so that she could work for others. Hamer went on to found the Mississippi Freedom Democratic Party, advocate for African Americans' right to vote, and ran for Congress in Mississippi in 1964. In 1969, Hamer collaborated with the National Council of Negro Women to found the Freedom Farm Cooperative of Sunflower County, a county where as many as five thousand families survived on less than two thousand dollars a year.[38] The farm began with a project called the pig bank that enabled black farmers to breed, raise, and slaughter pigs. Later she also founded Head Start in the Delta and acquired federal funding for housing projects. Vincent Harding, another prominent civil rights activist, reflects on the witness of Fannie Lou Hamer in his Foreword to the 1996 reprint of Howard Thurman's *Jesus and the Disinherited*. Harding says that Hamer's witness reminds us that the ultimate issue is not to concern ourselves with being more moral than anyone else, "but becoming more free than we ever have been, free to engage our fullest powers in transformative tasks that await us."[39] Hamer did not think of her own freedom in the way many US Americans are prone to do, as a freedom from the encumbrance of others. Rather, she exercised her freedom for others. *what we should be doing*

Filling the Theological Void in Contemporary Public Discussions of Wealth Inequalities

Today, a theological void exists in the larger public discussion in the United States concerning how to respond to wealth inequal-

---

[38] Jazmine Walker, "Fannie Lou Hamer and Her Dream for Jobs and Freedom," *Rewire*, August 28, 2013.

[39] Vincent Harding, "Foreword," in Howard Thurman, *Jesus and the Disinherited* (Boston: Beacon, 1996; reprint of 1976 edition), 5.

ity and poverty. This void remains despite many efforts made by religious leaders and ecumenical and interfaith organizations to identify the root causes of poverty and underscore the flawed ideology of our current dominant forms of wealth creation. Pope Francis in his address before the US Congress in September 2015 called attention to the lives and work of Abraham Lincoln, Martin Luther King, Dorothy Day, and Thomas Merton as four US Americans who challenged systemic and structural injustices and inequalities. What they recognized and the pope emphasized was that "a future of freedom requires love of the common good and cooperation in a spirit of subsidiarity and solidarity."[40] The pope's speech appears all but drowned out by the caustic and hostile rhetoric of the 2016 US presidential campaign. Religious leaders like King, Day, and Merton clearly confronted definitions of freedom that fail to see individual freedom inextricably tied to community and love of others. Statements made by the World Council of Churches and World Communion of Reformed Churches in recent years identified the "intertwined crises" of poverty, wealth inequalities, and the exploitation of the environment, and affirmed their belief "that God has made a covenant with all of creation (Gen. 9:8–12). God has brought into being an earth community based on the vision of justice and peace. The covenant is a gift of grace that is not for sale in the marketplace (Is 55.1). It is an economy of grace for the household of all of creation."[41]

Faith Traditions Challenge Hyperindividualism and Market Idolatry

I intend to add to these rich responses by drawing upon the theological imagination of religious social activists and the wisdom of the world's great traditions of faith, and offer an alternative perspective that focuses on the problem of wealth.[42] People of

---

[40]Ryan Teague Beckwith, "Transcript: Read the Speech Pope Francis Gave to Congress," *Time*, September 24, 2015.

[41]Two of the most important statements have come from the World Council of Churches (WCC) Poverty, Wealth and Equality program and the World Communion of Reformed Churches (WCRC). See "Economy for Life, Peace and Justice for All" (which was endorsed by the WCC's 2006 General Assembly), oikoumene. org. See also WCRC, "The Accra Confession," wcrc.ch.

[42]Three examples of important theological responses to wealth inequalities and

faith are uniquely situated to draw upon sacred stories, traditions, rituals, and confessional statements of their communities in ways that challenge our society's hyperindividualism and idolatry of the market. An authentic concept of self-existing-in-relationship holds a central place in the great traditions of faith. The concept of the commons was introduced to me by colleagues in the ecumenical movement. Throughout this book I use the term *commons* to refer to the web of relationships that are the ground, source, and sustenance of all life. Theologically, the commons emanate from God and support an expansive vision of economy that includes the whole community of living organisms, not just human life.[43]

I am trained as a Christian theological ethicist, but I think outside of my own faith tradition because I believe that an authentic response to problems we are facing can only come through collaboration and movement-building. Theologian Joerg Rieger observes, "There is a long history of compartmentalization of religion, economics, and other aspects of life, but the pressures of (economic) downturn make us take another look at how everything belongs together."[44] Methodological and religious boundaries must be traversed in an effort to increase our collective theological and moral imagination.

Faith traditions and rituals emerge from a complex and more textured understanding of human beings and our limitations as we live in symbiotic relationship with a larger delicate web of life. The world's great religious traditions have much to teach us about being allies with those pressed into the most precarious positions in US society and around the world and inspire us—those with relative wealth—to see in new ways our own role in movements

the problem of poverty include William Cavanaugh, *Being Consumed: Economics and Christian Desire* (Grand Rapids: Eerdmans, 2008); Daniel Groody, *Globalization, Spirituality, and Justice* (Maryknoll, NY: Orbis, 2007); and Kathryn Tanner, *Economy of Grace* (Minneapolis: Fortress, 2005). Tanner's book is now twelve years old and emphasizes an otherworldly sense of divine economy. Cavanaugh's and Groody's work are both grounded in Roman Catholic tradition. None of these books frames the problem as the problem of wealth.

[43]I am indebted to Ulrich Duchrow and Franz Hinkelammert for introducing me to the term *the commons*, which I have defined here in a way to attend to the ecotheological conversation. See Duchrow and Hinkelammert, *Transcending Greedy Money* (New York: Palgrave Macmillan, 2012), 181.

[44]Joerg Rieger, *No Rising Tide: Theology, Economics, and the Future* (Minneapolis: Fortress, 2009), 48.

for change. Buddhism, Hinduism, Judaism, Christianity, Islam, and the spiritualities of indigenous peoples give the commons a central place, instill compassion, call us to imagine alternatives to consumerism, and inspire the creation of sustainable and solidarity economies. Moving from self-centeredness to other-centeredness, focusing on authentic community, and struggling from the trenches as or alongside vulnerable peoples and a planet placed in peril by human exploitation are central to the calls for love and justice. The only way to create change in the current US context of debates about wealth inequalities, poverty, and environmental destruction is to challenge and reconceive the old social and economic boundaries as well as those defining faith traditions and intellectual fault lines. Religious leaders and theologians must become comfortable navigating between different disciplines and speaking new languages as we communicate between the worlds of theology and economics, religion and science, commitment to a particular tradition and the pluralistic context in which we live, faith and secularism and more.

Sacred stories, ancient traditions, confessions of faith, and engaged spiritualities invite us to enter the debate over wealth inequality and poverty by focusing on the problem of wealth and challenging the belief that all things can be valued in money form. Buddhism, for example, emphasizes alternatives by focusing on "more being" as opposed to "more having."

Justice in the Hebrew Bible is relational. What is so unique about the legal codes of the Hebrew Bible is that in their context they emphasized the violation of people and the land as problematic precisely because they were part of God's creation, as opposed to considering the violation of people or land as the property of another human being. Social concepts of Trinity inspire Christians to ground and steady themselves and act in and out of the abundant overflowing love of God. Wealth and freedom in God understood as the Three-in-One are not defined in individual terms but by the nature of community and the free and equal exchange of love. Love in God's relational ecology is not overly sentimental or self-focused but tied to justice for the most vulnerable.

Concern for others is central to Muslim practice as well. Islam is today the only remaining faith tradition of the three that trace their origins to the story of Abraham, Sarah, and Hagar which maintains a prohibition of usury. Institutions of Islamic finance and banking make special provisions in their banks not to charge interest to those who need to borrow money. Native American theologies turn Euro-Western concepts of self and community upside down as they emerge from the relational reality of the Earth, our Mother. Cooperative economics create wealth through sharing of decision-making and ownership. This rich theo-social imagination can begin to focus our collective attention more clearly on a realistic picture of our place embedded in a broader web of life as well as our tremendous potential to create authentic community.

A survey of economic values conducted in 2013 by the Brookings Institution asked whether US residents believe that capitalism is still working. While most people surveyed thought that capitalism is working, differences in perception were significant regarding the fairness of our economic system. The majority agreed that "hard work and determination are no guarantee of success for most people."[45] Close to half of the respondents saw capitalism at odds with Christianity. What was most intriguing is that "religiously *unaffiliated* Americans are more likely than any other religious group to say that the gap between the rich and poor is America's most serious economic issue."[46] Religiously unaffiliated Americans are three times more likely than white evangelical Protestants and Roman Catholics to view the wealth divide as the most significant moral problem we are facing—two times more likely than white mainline Protestants and 5 percent more likely than black Protestants. Significant variations were also apparent when considering the income level, race, and ethnicity of the people who were surveyed. For example, black Protestant churches were much more likely than white Christian communities to view the wealth divide as the most significant problem the United States is facing as a nation. With the depth of wisdom offered by religious traditions, people of faith have a distinctive role to play—*if* we are willing to ask new questions, work together, and take this opportunity to create change.

Throughout this book I wrestle with a theology that can inspire

---

[45]E. J. Dionne, Daniel Cox, Juhem Navarro-Rivera, William A. Galston, and Robert P. Jones, "Economic Values Survey: Do Americans Believe Capitalism & Government Are Working?" Brookings Institution, July 18, 2013, www.brookings.edu.
[46]Ibid.

personal initiative and inform a new vision for political economy, and that is intended to contribute to the formation of faith communities with flexibility to see themselves as spaces in our society to give rise to creativity. My own approach to this debate is from a progressive Christian theological perspective, but the conversation developed here is, I hope, relevant for people representing a much wider variety of theological perspectives and faith traditions. I take a *progressive* approach by drawing significantly upon social-scientific research in examining dominant forms of wealth creation, incorporating ecumenical and interfaith perspectives, assuming that Christian faith requires public action, and emphasizing the systemic and structural causes of wealth inequalities and poverty.[47] Additionally, I draw significantly upon my own experience working in national and international ecumenical and interfaith movements to advocate for and envision a more just economy.

I argue that the way in which we create wealth matters not only for human well-being but for the well-being of God and the planet Earth, our home. Reframing the public debate over the wealth divide from a theological perspective invites an alternative social logic informed by a much richer picture of human beings and our limits and responsibilities as we live in interdependence within a much larger web of life. Beginning the debate with the problem of wealth invites people of relative privilege to ask what will motivate those who profit from the current systems and structures to transform them for the sake of the commons.

I believe that people of faith and the communities we serve are uniquely situated in US society to create the space for alternative economies to emerge and to inspire and envision much-needed attitudinal, systemic, and structural change.

Chapter Outline

The book is divided into four main sections to guide you, the reader, through a process of exploring and examining the problem of wealth. The first part, "The Problem Is Wealth, Not Poverty," focuses on naming and defining wealth, and introduces

---

[47]I have written more extensively about "progressive" faith in the Introduction of *To Do Justice: A Guide for Progressive Christians*, a chapter I coauthored with Rebecca Todd Peters (Louisville, KY: Westminster John Knox Press, 2008), xviii.

a theological reframing of the debates about the poverty, wealth inequalities, and overconsumption that place people and the planet in peril. Theological reflection enables us to discover and explore alternative ways of living and calls us to consider how the ways we create wealth matter to people, to the Earth, and to God. In this chapter I identified a key problem in the way we raise questions about poverty and wealth inequalities. Anthropological and sociological studies of poverty tend to study poverty, but too often fail to look upward socially at the problem. Drawing upon the insights of traditions of faith, the chapters that follow invite you to consider the radical reversal of the conversation that occurs when poverty, wealth inequalities, and environmental devastation begin from a theological perspective: The problem is wealth, not poverty.

Theologians and ethicists, particularly those involved in ecumenical and interfaith movements, have received a great deal of criticism from leaders both within and outside the churches for commenting on economic theory. Many economists, entrepreneurs, financiers, politicians, and church leaders argue that conversations about the economy should left up to the experts. Economics is relatively new as a stand-alone discipline in the US academy when compared to fields such as theology, history, and moral philosophy. However, economics is not new to Christian theology. Chapter 2, "The Centrality of Economics in Christian Theology," provides a brief outline of the way the Christian faith arose in the ancient world due to the call heard and felt by Jesus's early followers to embody a set of values that contrasted those held in greatest esteem by the elites of the Roman Empire.

Part Two, "Economism and the Ethic of Scarcity," calls into question the priority placed upon money and market-based logic in US society. When and why was the field of economics separated from other disciplines such as moral philosophy, theology, and history? Chapter 3, "When, Why, and How? The Boundary between Economics and Theology," answers questions related to when the field of economics became a stand-alone discipline in the US academy that is being given such a priority in public discourse. I argue that prioritizing business, market-based logic, and economics over against other fields in the academy and in public debate is draining our society's theological and moral imagination.

Chapter 4, "The Current Dominant Forms of Wealth Creation and the Ethic of Scarcity," examines the two dominant forms of wealth creation in the US and the larger global economy: social developmentalism and neoliberalism. Social developmentalism is the product of Keynesian economic theories and is a term most often applied to the relationship between wealthier, heavily industrialized and technologically advanced countries of the Global North to the low-income nations in the Global South. This chapter investigates the origins of social developmentalism in the United States and its impact on the Appalachian region. I pay the most attention to neoliberalism, a particular form of capitalism that became the engine driving economic policies in the late 1970s. Neoliberals think of freedom and the market as synonyms. Neoliberalism is a form of market faith, in which markets are trusted to determine more efficiently the value of goods, labor, and other resources and looked to, even relied upon, as means of social salvation. Both of the dominant approaches emerge from an individualistic understanding of self. Neoliberalism, sometimes called "turbo-capitalism," is incompatible with Christian ethics. Today, an ethic of scarcity dominates our public discourse and practice, in our society and within churches, that leaves us ill-equipped to challenge the unequal distribution of wealth in our nation and around the world and to offer creative visions for life lived in authentic relationship with God and one another as part of an interrelated, dynamic, and organic whole.

The title for the third part of this book, "Digging for Roots to Nourish an Ethic of Enough," is a reference to one of the ways that people living in Appalachia, a region near my home, survived when extractive industries introduced dependence upon wage labor. The residents cultivated earlier practices like digging for roots that could be used to make teas and tonics to cure diseases and ailments and eliminate toxins from the body. Chapters 5 and 6 turn the focus to images of God and community in Christian thought and other religious traditions that can cultivate a new understanding of self in relation to the commons. Theologians agree that the individualistic anthropological assumptions informing the dominant forms of wealth creation are deeply flawed. "Social Trinity, Love, and the Ethic of Enough," chapter 5, lifts up the concept of the Social Trinity, examines the abundance that could be offered by theologically informed concepts of human nature; defines *agape*, *hesed*, and *caritas*; and considers the implications of God as the overflowing ground of love for reenvisioning political economy.

Significant attention is given to the ideas of theologians such as Elizabeth Johnson, Catherine Mowry LaCugna, Jerry Pillay, and Vida Dutton Scudder, as well as the African concept of *Ubuntu*.

Chapter 6, "Extensive Roots: Ecocentric and Theocentric Visions of Economy from a Wider Variety of the World's Great Faith Traditions," suggests the need to expand the conversation among Christians to listen to and explore the rich and more textured understanding of human beings and our limitations as well as the vision of just and right relationships within the economy found in other religious traditions. This chapter underscores key concepts and principles—such as the Native American understanding of reciprocity and belonging represented by George Tinker's thought, Buddhist economics, Jewish Sabbath practice and the Jubilee, and Islamic banking—that help us deepen our understanding of a broader witness to mutuality and our life together.

The concluding section of the book is "Increasing the Theological and Moral Imagination of the US Middle Class," in which I discuss the growing social, economic, and spiritual resistance to market fundamentalism in the United States. Chapter 7, "Real People Embodying Different Values" provides a variety of stories, theories, and models that serve to illustrate what people are doing to hold a different set of fundamental social values at the center of their economic activities. All of these efforts begin with the understanding of self as radically interdependent and formed in community. These stories are of real people who play active roles in the Catholic Worker movement and a variety of different types of intentional communities, working to develop a local land economy and create successful businesses on the basis of cooperative economics.

The last chapter problematizes the problem of wealth for readers by honestly grappling with the fact that most, if not all, of the people reading this book are dependent for their own security upon the current system and dominant forms of wealth creation. How do people of relative wealth, particularly the middle class, navigate their role in the larger public debate about on poverty and wealth inequalities and find themselves within religious teachings about money and wealth? One way is to begin by cultivating our theological imagination and moral courage for authentic change. Chapter 8 draws upon a long tradition of storytelling among social reformers by offering creative contemporary "Parables for Sharing" and includes reflections on the story of Zacchaeus as a sort of representative of the middle class in the biblical text. These parables emerge from middle-class experience because it is almost totally missing in the stories of the biblical text. Moreover, drawing realistic comparisons between the economy of the ancient world and the complexities of our contemporary global economy is nearly impossible. I think this absence of middle-class experience in the biblical text is one of the reasons for a less than robust response from the middle class in contemporary movements for social change.

Ultimately, my intention is to provide a broadly ecumenical resource that is friendly to and informed by a wide variety of faith traditions. This book is a resource for information and personal reflection and can be used in a classroom setting. You can find prompts and questions for further reflection and discussion in the Additional Resources section. My hope is that the chapters that follow engage your imagination and call people of faith out of their own personal spaces, pews, pulpits, or classrooms to have the theological and moral courage to work together to directly confront the problem of wealth.

Chapter 2

The Centrality of Economics in Christian Theology

> Whenever you are reaping the harvest of your field and you leave some grain in the field, don't go back and get it. Let it go to the immigrants, the orphans, and the widows so that the Lord your God blesses you in all that you do. Similarly, when you beat the olives off your olive trees, don't go back over them twice. Let the leftovers go to the immigrants, the orphans, and the widows. Again, when you pick the grapes of your vineyard, don't pick them over twice. Let the leftovers go to the immigrants, the orphans, and the widows. Remember how you were a slave in Egypt. That's why I am commanding you to do this thing.
>
> *—Deuteronomy 24:17–22*

> Then he looked up at his disciples and said: "Blessed are you who are poor for yours is the kingdom of God. Blessed are you who are hungry now, for you will be filled. Blessed are you who weep now, for you will laugh."
>
> *—Luke 6:20–21*

Many conservative social commentators, economists, entrepreneurs, financiers, politicians, and even some religious leaders claim that conversations about the economy should left up to the so-called experts. Steven Forbes and Elizabeth Ames argue in their book *How Capitalism Can Save Us* that the problem with critiques of what they call "real-world economics" is the general lack of knowledge among politicians and average citizens about capitalism and how free markets actually work. They suggest that "the cultural roots of today's anger [with capitalism] go back thousands of years. In ancient times, people struggling to survive amid disease, famine, and other harsh conditions resented the relative wealth of 'money changers.' Christ believed rich people had less chance to go to heaven."[1] Forbes and Ames dismiss this Christian perspective as a remnant of the past and suggest that what we really need to know is more about how unfettered markets have the potential to save us.

Placing faith in markets also frequently means that successful business leaders are viewed as the most trusted "experts" to lead the United States toward social change. Conor Friedersdorf, a writer for *The Atlantic*, made an appeal during the 2016 race for the office of US president to his readers to ask, "What Do Donald Trump Voters Actually Want?" A letter returned to Friedersdorf by a thirty-nine-year-old communications executive for a hospital, who mentions his own conservative Christian identity, provides anecdotal evidence of a popular US trust of business acumen. The letter writer supports Trump's candidacy for president because he "leads an enormous, diversified organization that is worth billions . . . Leadership, by the way, is different from knowledge. When you lead a large organization you set vision, goals and expect results."[2]

Comments made by conservative talk-show host Glenn Beck provide more anecdotal evidence as he called into question Pope Francis's concern for people living in poverty. The pope is directing the attention of the churches to economic injustice, political corruption, and putting "the priority of life of all over the appropriation of goods by the few." Beck suggested that the pope simply must be ignorant of the benefits of capitalism and free-market economics. He said, "So tell me, is the Pope. . . . Is he a Communist? . . . So, I have asked the Pope's people if I could put together a team of people that could actually teach the Pope and find examples, left and right, and go visit the Pope and say, 'This

[1]Steven Forbes and Elizabeth Ames, *How Capitalism Will Save Us: Why Free People and Free Markets Are the Best Answer in Today's Economy* (New York: Crown Business, 2011; reprint of 2009 edition), 10.

[2]Conor Friedersdorf, "What Do Donald Trump Voters Actually Want?" *The Atlantic*, August 17, 2015.

is what Capitalism is.' "[3] Beck's views are extreme. Of course, the pope is beginning from a very different starting point with a more comprehensive understanding of human nature and that which ultimately determines value.

From a Christian theological perspective, debates about economics, the fair distribution of wealth, and freedom from living in bondage are the heart of Christian teachings. Economics, in Christian thought, is first and foremost about managing right relationships in God's household.[4] The Greek root of the word *economics* is *oikos*, which literally means household. Throughout the Gospel stories, Jesus rejects, abandons, and reforms the organization of the economy within the household as it was culturally defined in the Roman Empire by teaching and relating *oikos* to a larger commons. Jesus's understanding of *oikos* emerges directly in response to the needs of real people and rejects human constructs of appropriate kinship ties.

Postcolonial theorists have greatly aided my own understanding of *oikos*. Rohan Park observes that the paterfamilias (male head of the family) in Greco-Roman culture was given tremendous power within the household to organize resources to increase kinship ties and ensure wealth for a particular family line. The concept of paterfamilias compares to that of *Pater Patriae*, the role played by the Roman emperor as the Supreme Father of the Empire. Consistently, however, Jesus relates *oikos* to a community at large, thereby questioning and neutralizing the coalition between wealth and kinship and "imperial economic appropriation."[5]

Park cites two illustrations of Jesus's understanding of *oikos* as they appear in Luke's Gospel. Zacchaeus, whose name in Greek means "innocent" or "clean," distributes the resources he accumulated from his work of collecting taxes for the empire in quite an unorthodox manner. He promises to give half of his possessions

---

[3]Erica Ritz, "Glenn Beck Has Made a Unique Offer to Pope Francis," The Blaze, January 22, 2015, www.theblaze.com.

[4]Paul Samuelson, in what is now considered a classic textbook on economics, defines the science of economics as describing, analyzing, explaining, and "correlating the behavior of production, unemployment, prices," etc., and choosing what to do with scarce resources. See Samuelson, *Economics: An Introductory Analysis* (New York: McGraw Hill, 1948; reprinted 1955, 1958, 1961, 1964, 1967), 6.

[5]Rohan Park, "Revisiting the Parable of the Prodigal Son for Decolonization: Luke's Reconfiguration of Oikos in 15:11–32, *Biblical Interpretation* 17 (2009): 510.

to people in poverty, and if he finds he has defrauded anyone of anything, he will pay them back "four times as much" (see Luke 19:8). (I revisit the relevance of Zacchaeus's story particularly for the US middle class in fuller relief in chapter 8.) Park provides another illustration in the story of the prodigal son where the father of the family chooses to give his rowdy and rebellious son his inheritance when the dominant culture would have expected him to levy a harsh punishment against him (see Luke 15:11–32). In both stories the household economy is organized with the needs of a much larger community in mind so that everyone counts and is counted, rather than the socially accepted boundaries for the distribution of resources as defined by the dominant culture. Concern then for those who live in poverty or who are exploited by unjust social and economic systems is grounded in an under-standing of the very nature of God revealed in Jesus as one who redefines *oikos*. God's relationship with and involvement in the economy are not focused on God's action or agency upon our world, but emphasizes the radical nature of God's immanence and cooperative sharing of resources based upon needs of people and the planet.

For the purpose of this chapter, I focus on the development of Christian teachings on economics, poverty, and wealth because of the historical influence of the church in the West. A conversation about more contemporary Christian theological perspectives and the distinctive contributions made by a wider diversity of faith traditions appears in chapters 5 and 6.

There is an abundance of reflection within Christian thought on the problem of wealth and the circumstances of people living in poverty, greed, and economic injustice. I limit myself here to offer-ing only a brief outline that highlights the centrality of economics from the time of the early followers of Jesus to the Enlightenment. My intention is to elucidate the deep roots of Christian concern for economic injustice and authentic community that provide a different orientation to economy and wealth. Christian theological thought challenges the notion that markets and market-oriented thinking should govern every aspect of our lives. What follows is a brief outline that highlights the centrality of economic thought and tradition intended to underscore the relevance of Christian theological thought for contemporary debates about wealth inequalities and poverty. Christian traditions, rituals, and many institutional structures arose out of a deep sense of call to live by the norm of love and embody a different set of social values based upon reciprocity and mutuality.

Debt Codes and the Priority of the Teachings of the Prophets

Early Christian teachings, the shape of communities, and ritual practices emerged from a tradition of Jewish faith in the midst of a primarily agrarian society. The Israelites had long been familiar with God's call to resist the asphyxiating stranglehold grip of ancient empires. In periods of exodus and exile the ancient Israelites formed an identity around "covenantal relationship with God." This identity fundamentally opposed life under the rule of Pharaoh or any other emperors.

Consider the debt codes and the priority of the teachings of the prophets for the ancient Israelites and for the Christian communities that developed much later. Biblical scholar Walter Brueggemann argues that in the Deuteronomic tradition, economic justice prevails: "The economy is subordinated to and made to serve the infrastructure of the whole neighborhood. Obedience to [God] has to do with a countercultural practice of economic justice."[6] In his essay "Scriptural Strategies against Exclusionary Absolutism," Brueggemann comments specifically on Deuteronomy 15:1–18. The debt codes provide for the release of people in poverty from their debts every seven years so that they "may viably participate in the economy and in order that the community does not form a permanent underclass."[7] In Deuteronomy 15:11, Moses says that you must always release people in poverty from perpetual indebtedness because the "poor will be with you always." The

---

[6]Walter Brueggemann, *Disruptive Grace: Reflections on God, Scripture, and the Church*, comp. and with an Introduction by Carolyn Sharp (Minneapolis: Fortress, 2011), 320.

[7]Ibid., 319. "When you reap your harvest in the field you shall not go back to get it; it shall be left for the alien, the orphan, and the widow, so that the Lord your God may bless you in all your undertakings. When you beat your olive trees, do not strip what is left; it shall be for the alien, the orphan, and the widow. When you gather the grapes of your vineyard, do not glean what is left; it shall be for the alien, the orphan, and the widow. Remember that you were a slave in Egypt" (Deut. 24:19–22).

legal codes frame this saying also in relation to an earlier verse, "because if you do this"—provide for the release from debt— "there need be no poor people in the community" (see Deut. 15:4). This commandment "warns against tightfisted hard-heartedness"[8] toward people in poverty. What is so unique about the legal codes of the Hebrew Bible is that in their context they emphasized the violation of people and the land as problematic because they were part of God's creation, as opposed to considering the violation of people or land as the property of another human being. Ultimately, the whole creation is God's and intended to sustain all that lives therein. In Leviticus, the land itself is to have rest. In Deuteronomy, the land produces enough to care for the widow, the orphan, and the alien—in other words, the most vulnerable in the community.

One of the most well-known and best-loved concepts named for the churches by Brueggemann is that of "prophetic imagination." Brueggemann argues that "the most important aspect of [the prophets'] speech is their re-perception of the world as the arena of God's faithful governance."[9] In the prophets, God's word is not an absolute and everywhere the same. God's word is spoken to particular people, in particular contexts, with the promise to "impinge upon perception and awareness, to intrude upon public policy, and . . . to evoke faithful and transformed behavior."[10] The Holy One is conveyed as a God who grabs the greedy by the collar, gets into their faces, commands their attention, and disrupts economic schemes that place the resources of communities and the natural world at the mercy of individual self-interest.

The Priority of Economic Justice in Jesus's Teachings and for His Public Ministry

Jesus and his followers practice a faith relevant to the total social realm. They traversed well-established boundaries of race and ethnicity, gender, and social class. In the synoptic gospels, the prophetic tradition shapes Jesus's teachings. Jesus quotes Moses saying, "The poor will be with you always." Among Jewish followers of Jesus the phrase certainly would have been connected to its context in

---

[8]Ibid.
[9]Ibid., 95.
[10]Ibid., 96.

the Hebrew Bible of releasing the captives from debt. Jesus told thirty-one parables that are included in the synoptic Gospels of Mark, Matthew, and Luke; nineteen include direct references to social class, indebtedness, the misuse of wealth, worker pay, and the distribution of wealth. One of the most memorable is Jesus's saying, "It's easier for a camel to squeeze through the eye of a needle than for a rich person to enter God's kingdom" (Mark 10:25).

Less obvious references aren't easily understood with just a surface reading of the Gospel stories, as Jesus's story in the Gospel of Mark shows. In Mark, Jesus is quite public throughout his ministry about the fact that he has come to suffer. He seems to do the opposite of what the disciples expect of him at nearly every turn. Rather than choosing to keep his ministry within the bounds of the synagogue he goes out to public spaces that were under the authority and scrutiny of agents of the Roman Empire.

Near the end of the story yet before his trial and death, he goes to a garden called Gethsemane to pray. At first glance, it may seem to be a secluded and isolated space, but the term *Gethsemane* is a derivative of a Hebrew word meaning oil press. Oil was one of the most lucrative industries in the Roman Empire, a mainstay of the agricultural economy. The three main products in this region would have been wheat, wine, and oil. Oil was important for cooking and preserving food and could be used to grease the axles of wagons and chariots. Before cultivating olive trees in Italy the Romans relied heavily upon the olive oil produced in their colonies. It was one of the products in the area "strictly controlled by the government, which made it more difficult for peasants to find good prices."[11] When Jesus goes to pray he goes to the site where olives are grown and oil is pressed. To use language more familiar to our contemporary experience, he goes to the heart of industry—to the heart of the income of the Roman Empire. Jesus prays not in the synagogue but in a place of risk and in opposition to the way that the Romans held some people economically captive for the empire's benefit.

The context out of which the Gospel stories emerge bears significance for interpreting them. Historians estimate that at least

---

[11]Justo González, *Faith and Wealth: A History of Early Christian Ideas on the Origin, Significance, and Use of Money* (San Francisco: Harper and Row, 1990), 73.

90 percent of the residents of Rome lived in poverty,[12] which speaks to the perspective of the Gospel stories. They may have been recorded by members of the curial class, but they are told from the perspective of Rome's impoverished majority. Jesus, as he is remembered in the Gospel of Luke, inaugurates his ministry by reading from Isaiah: "For [the Lord] anointed me to proclaim good news to the poor" (Isa. 61:1). In the synoptic Gospels, Jesus's good news looks like transforming scarcity into abundance—challenging social boundaries that gave privilege to elites at the expense of others, feeding thousands with five loaves of bread and two fish, welcoming tax collectors back into community, and sharing out of one's limited means.

Paul, Himself a Colonized Apostle, Calls for the Redistribution of Wealth

Letters written by Paul or one of his followers are arguably the most influential in Christian theology, not only because their authorship predates the canonical Gospels, but also due to the number of letters included within the canon. Biblical scholars such as Pamela Eisenbaum, Paula Fredriksen, Mark Nanos, Krister Stendahl, and N. T. Wright have opened up new ways to understand Paul's writings in his ancient Jewish context.[13] Accentuating Paul's Jewishness invites contemporary Christians to reconsider the past emphasis placed by theologians and religious leaders on the importance of Paul's conversion on the road to Damascus that is included in Acts.

Paul lived as a Jew and died as a Jew in the Jewish diaspora. As a Jew he held minority status within one of the most power-

---

[12]Some historians estimate as many as 95 to 97 percent of the people in ancient Rome lived in poverty. I have chosen to draw upon the research of historian Peter Brown here. See Brown, *Through the Eye of a Needle: Wealth, the Fall of Rome, and the Making of Christianity in the West, 350–550 AD* (Princeton, NJ: Princeton University Press, 2012), 8.

[13]Examples of significant works include N. T. Wright, *Paul: In Fresh Perspective* (Minneapolis: Fortress, 2005); Pamela Eisenbaum, *Paul Was Not a Christian: The Original Message of a Misunderstood Apostle* (New York: Harper Collins, 2009); and Mark D. Nanos and Magnus Zellerholm, eds., *Paul within Judaism: Restoring the First-Century Context to the Apostle* (Minneapolis: Fortress, 2015).

ful empires of the ancient world. Paul's writings don't introduce a finely tuned systematic theology. Rather, what we read in his letters is the way he was working out his understanding of what it means to live as a faithful disciple of Jesus. The significance of the crucified body of the Jewish Jesus lies at the heart of Paul's theology. Paul emphasized throughout his writings the radical priority of God's grace encountered and practiced in community, and he introduced an alternative social logic grounded in his Jewish faith. Theological concepts of the mystical body of Christ, love, fairness and balance in the economy, power in weakness, and the sufficiency of God's grace are all prominent throughout his writings. These ideas were radically countercultural in Paul's time, as in our own.

In 2 Corinthians, written to the faith community gathered in Corinth, Paul offers a description of how God's grace is experienced and the nature of giving within the community of faith. He refers in the letter to collections of money taken up for churches in Jerusalem. Past interpretations of these chapters suggested that Paul used the generosity of communities of faith to make a case for his own apostolic authority. However, Paul's description of God's grace found in 2 Corinthians 8 and 9 can be considered a description of the nature of the community of faith's work within a larger household economy. The primary concern conveyed is one of equality.

Second Corinthians 8:9 and 8:13–15 are the verses that stand out: "For you know the generous act of our Lord Jesus Christ, that though he was rich, yet for your sakes he became poor, so that by his poverty you might become rich" (2 Cor. 8:9). The Greek term used in this context is *charis*, which translators render as grace, generous act, or sometimes blessing. The passage describes Christ's self-giving love—one of mutuality, reciprocity and sharing. Jesus's own example of living is a response to God's grace within the economic categories of wealth and poverty. Paul continues, "I do not mean that others should be eased and you burdened, but that as a matter of equality your abundance at the present time should supply their want, that there may be equality. As it is written, 'He who gathered much had nothing over, and he who gathered little had no lack' " (2 Cor. 8:13–15). In the context of this passage, becoming poor means recognizing, claiming, and taking one's place within a larger community and refusing to be diminished by or to diminish the value of others.

Early Christianity in the Context of Empire

Prior to the conversion of Constantine, Christian communities of faith shaped themselves and became influential largely because of what they offered in contrast to Imperial Rome. Church historian E. Glenn Hinson observes that Roman elites did have some charitable impulse. They built grand buildings and monuments, constructed aqueducts and developed systems of sanitation, sponsored religious and public festivals, supplied patronage for scholars and scholarships for needy students, invented innovative albeit primitive air-conditioning systems, supported gymnasia, built baths, paved streets and roads.[14] However, their impulse to build was not primarily out of concern for those living in poverty; Roman philanthropy had another goal in mind: displaying the grandeur of the empire.

Wealthy Romans who lived in the capital city enjoyed a good quality of life. They lived on the hills outside of Rome in richly appointed single-family homes called *domus*. The most prestigious neighborhoods had impressive views of the Tiber River. The homes of the wealthy were located far enough away from the heart of the city to enable them to distance themselves from the odors of city life.

On the other hand, Rome's teeming underclass lived in quite different circumstances. The impoverished majority lived at near subsistence level and inhabited *insulae*, ancient high-rise apartments akin to tenement dwellings. These tenements outnumbered single-family dwellings by a ratio of twenty-six to one. The neighborhoods in which people in poverty lived were "cramped, squalid, and dangerous." At best, *insulae* were "equipped with communal latrines and water-fountains. Because of overcrowding, poor sanitation, and generally poor nutrition, diseases were rampant among Rome's

---

[14]E. Glenn Hinson, "Human Rights in Early Christian Perspective," in *Resurrection and Responsibility: Essays on Theology, Scripture, and Ethics in Honor of Thorvald Lorenzen,* edited by Keith D. Dyer (Eugene, OR: Pickwick Publishing, 2009), 150.

urban masses whose life span was, consequently, very short."[15]

Wealth at that time was gained by "land turned by labor into food, which, in the case of the rich, was turned into sufficient money to be turned into privilege and power."[16] In the country, impoverished farmers worked land owned by the wealthy. Historian Peter Brown estimates that "60 percent of the wealth of the Roman empire was gathered at harvest time by a labor force that amounted to over 80 percent of the population."[17] Little of each harvest stayed with farmers. At harvest time, taxes would be levied. I attend in more detail to the way in which taxes were collected in chapter 8 as I explore Zacchaeus's story, but for now the brief sketch of the circumstances of poor farmers offers fresh insight into Jesus's parable about the Rich Fool.

> Then he told them a parable: "The land of a rich man produced abundantly. And he thought to himself, 'What should I do, for I have no place to store my crops?' Then he said, 'I will do this: I will pull down my barns and build larger ones, and there I will store all my grain and my goods. And I will say to my soul, Soul, you have ample goods laid up for many years; relax, eat, drink, be merry.' But God said to him, 'You fool!' This very night your life is being demanded of you. And the things you have prepared, whose will they be?' So it is with those who store up treasures for themselves but are not rich toward God." (Luke 12:16–21)

In the midst of widespread poverty, Roman elites didn't set their sights on developing any kind of comprehensive or systematic approach to help the lower classes and people who were impoverished. Hinson writes that in Roman society, the lower classes "were commonly characterized with opprobrious epithets such as *leves* (crooked), *iniquinati* (evil), *improbi* (immoral), and *scelerati* (wicked)—characterizations far removed from the Hebrew

---

[15]Linda Gigante, "Death and Disease in Ancient Rome," www.innominate-society.com.

[16]Brown, *Through the Eye of a Needle*, 3.

[17]Ibid., 11.

Bible and early Christian identification of them as 'the pious.' "[18] Moreover, the Roman elite depended upon the underclasses and slaves to feed their desire for grandeur and the empire's appetite for war. The Roman economy relied upon slave labor. As the empire expanded so did the slave population, because vanquished people were treated as the spoils of war. Very little mobility or means existed for lower classes to increase their status in Roman society. As a matter of official state policy, the Greeks and the Romans both dealt with poverty by "forced emigration, hiring out the poor as mercenary soldiers, or regulating births." Orphans of lower-class citizens did not know the protections and solicitude enjoyed by those in the moneyed estate. Orphanages and hospitals as we know them today did not exist at that time. Roman laws afforded parents the right to sell their children into slavery to pay off their own debts. "The motto of classical humanism was not 'give to the penniless' but give to those who are deserving."[19]

Those who were attracted to following Jesus in the first century were attracted largely because of how those gathered in the community of faith resisted and spoke out against the empire's callous policies and disregard for people living in poverty. The early followers of Jesus introduced an alternative social logic and economic reality. Their faith and understanding of their role within the economy arose from a very different set of values. The primitive Christian catechism contained teachings from the Hebrew Bible and the sayings of Jesus concerning the dangers of wealth and the obligation to share. The early followers' understanding was that in times when God's intervention in human history was apparent to them, God repudiated the rich and chose people in poverty as instruments of salvation.

It should not be surprising, then, that early Christians began to develop their own practices, and later institutions, for a sort of comprehensive program to address the circumstances of people living in poverty. Following Jesus's concerns, they spoke out about their reservations about wealth and the wealthy and called for the redistribution of wealth through almsgiving; some radically

---

[18]Hinson, "Human Rights in Early Christian Perspective," 151.
[19]Ibid.

renounced their own attachment to worldly goods and voluntarily chose to live in informal communities or committed themselves to monastic communities. Private property was not seen as an evil in itself, but good as long as it was also used for sharing.

Christian theological tradition has a long history that places Jesus in line with the prophets of the Hebrew Bible and emphasizes the importance of faithful people practicing their beliefs by placing alternative social values at the center of their economic activities. The distribution of goods within early Christian communities was based upon the ideals of reciprocity and sharing articulated in Acts 4:32–35:

> Now the whole group of those who believed were of one heart and soul, and no one claimed private ownership of any possessions, but everything they owned was held in common. With great power the apostles gave their testimony to the resurrection of the Lord Jesus, and great grace was upon them all. There was not a needy person among them, for as many as owned lands or houses sold them and brought the proceeds of what was sold. They laid it at the apostles' feet, and it was distributed to each *as any might have need.* (emphasis added)

My use of italics above is to emphasize Justo González's interpretation of this passage. Gonzalez explains, "The use of the imperfect tense also points to a major difference between the community described in these texts and the Hellenistic and other communes."[20] The principle that guides relinquishing of worldly goods is for the sake of people with needs, not for the sake of renunciation. This ideal of distributing resources according to the notion that anyone "might have need" set the context for discussions about managing and ordering right relationships in society and in the church, as Christianity gained authority within the Roman Empire, and in establishing monastic communities.

Peter Brown argues that as Christianity became the official religion of the Roman Empire the bishops held a great deal of authority

---

[20]González, *Faith and Wealth*, 82.

and had some power to negotiate with Constantine. As pastoral leaders, they directed their attention toward developing the idea of poverty in order to signal deficiency in the way people living in poverty were treated. The bishops criticized the addiction to luxury, emphasized simplicity and sharing, and named God's purpose in human solidarity.[21] For the bishops to emphasize that they had a problem with wealth and the callous disregard of the wealthy does not mean that they lacked concern for the problem of poverty. Gregory of Nyssa, John Chrysostom, and Augustine denounced poverty as truly dreadful, but the bishops refused to see poverty simply as one's lot in life or the work of God's providence and called for the sharing of wealth for the sake of a larger community.

John Chrysostom, archbishop of Constantinople, was known for his eloquent preaching. He was given the name Chrysostom (which means "the golden-mouthed") nearly one hundred and fifty years after his death.[22] In his first sermon on Lazarus and the rich man (Luke 16:19–21), Chrysostom proclaimed, "For we were not born, we do not live, in order to eat and drink; but we eat in order to live. . . . For as the rich man lived in such wickedness, practiced luxury every day, and dressed himself splendidly, he was preparing for himself a more grievous punishment, building himself a greater fire, and making his penalty inexorable and his retribution inaccessible to pardon."[23] He believed that people had the potential to become more humane.

Augustine is one of the most influential theologians from the early church. Justo González points out that Augustine has been so influential that churches have lost sight of his teachings on wealth and greed. González presents a more expansive view of Augustine's teachings in his book *Faith and Wealth: A History of Early Christian Ideas on the Origin, Significance, and Use of Money*. For Augustine, the "fundamental vice of humanity consists precisely in enjoying things and using God to obtain things."[24] Humans tend not to spend "money for God's sake, but worship

---

[21]Brown, *Through the Eye of the Needle*, 35-45.

[22]González, *Faith and Wealth*, 198.

[23]John Chrysostom, *On Wealth and Poverty*, trans. and with an Introduction by Catharine P. Roth (New York: St. Vladimir's Seminary Press, 1984), 28.

[24]González, *Faith and Wealth*, 216.

God for money's sake," which leads them to hold on to what they consider their own property, rather than using what they have to build up the community.[25] People in poverty need resources to sustain themselves. According to Augustine, the excess resources held by the wealthy belong to people living in poverty.

Economies of Sharing within Monastic Communities Emerge in the West

Institutionalized centers of formal education in the West first emerged from the fascination with learning found within unofficial as well as official monastic communities of the Roman Catholic Church. One example is a women's bible study and prayer group organized by the noble woman Marcella in her palace on the Aventine Hill in Rome late in the fourth century. Drawing upon their knowledge of the practices of Egyptian desert monks brought to Rome by Athanasius and Peter of Alexandria sometime between 373 and 378 CE, Marcella and the other women designed a distinctive Christian community. In a women-directed environment, they were free to be creative, educate themselves, model their own leadership abilities, influence the formulation of ancient ascetic practices, and engage in friendships with men that social restrictions would otherwise not have permitted. Jerome praised Marcella for her character and the alternative economy she created together with other women of the Aventine Circle: "I shall not describe her illustrious household, the splendor of her ancient lineage, and the long series of consuls and praetorian prefects who have been her ancestors. I shall praise nothing in her save that which is her own, the more noble in that, despising wealth and rank, by poverty and lowliness she has won higher nobility."[26]

The Rule of St. Benedict (sixth century CE) was one of the most influential documents in establishing the practices of monastic communities in the West. The purpose of Benedict's Rule was to create community that fosters love for "the good of all concerned." The rule included provisions that all basic needs of the larger

---

[25]Ibid.

[26]Jerome, Letter 127 in *Selected Letters of St. Jerome*, with an English translation by F. A Wright (Cambridge: Harvard University Press, 1963), 441.

community would be satisfied. When new clothing was received, old clothing would be donated to help people in poverty. Great care was to be taken in receiving people in poverty and pilgrims because, in them, Christ is received. Abbots were instructed to pour water over the hands of guests and, along with the entire community, to wash their feet. Monastic communities were intended to be "schools for Christ's service." The economy of the monastery symbolized early Christian ideals and values of humility, sharing, community, service, and equality.

Peter Valdo of Lyon is another key figure worth mentioning. The practice of voluntarily renouncing worldly goods is usually associated with Roman Catholic religious orders. Valdo was a rich merchant who lived in Lyon, France. After an encounter with a traveling musician, Valdo became convinced that he should sell everything he had and give his assets away to people living in poverty. He believed and began to preach that "No one can serve two masters, God and mammon" (Matt. 6:21). Others joined him, and soon the group came to be known as the Poor Men of Lyon, the Poor of God, or the Waldensians. Over time, their teachings and practices were held with suspicion, and they were expelled from Lyon. They settled in an area now known as the Waldensian valleys. The Waldensian Church is recognized as one of the earliest Reformed communities of faith.

From the thirteenth to the eighteenth centuries, economic thought in Western universities was treated as a specialized branch of moral theology. Thomas Aquinas, a theologian and philosopher in the Middle Ages, was influential in the tradition of Scholasticism and taught that natural law dictates that human beings should provide themselves with the material goods necessary to satisfy basic needs while rendering assistance to others. He argued for the appropriate ordering of natural desires toward virtues such as love, humility, and charity. The accumulation of wealth for its own sake should therefore be subordinated to human virtue. Aquinas offered language to distinguish between the virtue of self-interest and the vice of greed, which maintains relevance for Catholic social teaching and its emphasis on the economy serving human need.

John Calvin, one of the formative thinkers for Reformed Christians, is often remembered for the role his thought played in the development of the Protestant work ethic, which Max Weber argued contributed to the emergence of modern capitalism. However, what may be less well-known is Calvin's clear commitment to social welfare and the way God's abundance and generosity were reflected in Geneva's practices and Calvin's teachings on usury.

Calvin and other magisterial Reformers aimed to reclaim the traditions of the earliest Christian communities. Early Christian leaders almost universally condemned usury. They developed a more distinctively Christian concept that in "giving to the poor, one lends to God." Concerns about Gnosticism and the distinctiveness of Christian communities led to arguments among early Christian leaders that material things were not evil in themselves; rather, the inordinate love of and unchecked desire to accumulate things were evil. Private property was justifiable when used for sharing.

Friends often wrote to Calvin seeking his advice on matters related to theology, politics, economics, and church practice. One such letter was referenced in a national synod of Verteuil, which met in 1567 because of Calvin's comments on usury or, in the context of the letter, the charging of interest on borrowed money. Calvin's friend was apparently asking whether charging interest should be permissible at all. In response to his friend's question, Calvin recognized the danger of usury as he wrote, "If we permit [usury], then some, under this guise, would be content to act with unbridled license, unable to abide any limits."[27] However, Calvin argued that there was no clear scriptural ban on usury. Rather, Christians should always "proceed with caution" when charging interest on money loaned to others and that interest should be carefully restrained. The guidelines for usury were clear in Calvin's mind. He urged that those who could afford to loan money to others should "lend to those from whom no hope of repayment is possible," as opposed to focusing only on considering loans where money will be kept "safe."[28] Calvin articulated seven exceptions that must be considered when charging interest on borrowed money:

---

[27]John Calvin, *Calvin's Ecclesiastical Advice*, trans. Mary Beaty and Benjamin Farley, Foreword by John H. Leith (Louisville, KY: Westminster/John Knox Press, 1991), 139.

[28]Ibid., 140.

1. Interest should never be charged to people living in poverty.
2. Those who are able to lend money should not be so preoccupied with increasing their own wealth that they neglect their obligation to people living in poverty.
3. All lending should consider Jesus's own teachings about equity and the Golden Rule.
4. Borrowers "should always make at least as much, if not more, than the amount borrowed."[29]
5. Lawful practices related to lending should not be determined by common practice but the principles should be derived from scripture.
6. One should never just consider what is best for the individual, but must keep in mind "the common good."[30]
7. Interest should never exceed what the laws of the country allow.

In addition, Calvin noted his disapproval of anyone engaging in usury as his or her occupation.

Historian Jeannine Olson observes that much of the social welfare in Geneva early on centered on the general hospital that began in 1535 in a former convent of St. Clare. Deacons served the hospital and were charged with caring for people in poverty. Calvin looked back to the early church to define the role of deacons, and he found a place for women within the diaconate as the early Christian communities held a place for some "mature widows for prayer and visitation of the sick."

The hospital's budget was charged to care for people in poverty. It provided a home as well as bread for the hungry that was cooked in the hospital's ovens. Calvin maintained an interest in the hospital and later recognized the need for people in poverty to have a craft enabling them to sustain their own lives and livelihood, so the silk industry was brought to the hospital to help people there develop a skill. When needs overwhelmed the hospital because of refugees pouring into the city from France, Italy, and Germany, Geneva found funds to care for those refugees. In the sixteenth century, poor relief was also designated for local residents. The most common way for cities to deal with people coming from outside their

---

[29]Ibid., 142.
[30]Ibid.

own territory was by expulsion; Geneva, under Calvin's leadership, had a larger imagination for sharing.[31]

John Locke: No Individual Has a Private Right to Property That Excludes Other Humankind

As an author whose work influenced the drafters of the US Constitution, British political philosopher John Locke concerned himself with challenging the divine right of royalty. He was one of the most well-known proponents of private property in the Enlightenment era and maintained a view consistent with the ancient and medieval church. God the Creator gave human beings the world "in common." Moreover, God endowed human beings with the reason and understanding necessary to "make use of it to the best advantage of life and convenience."[32]

Theologian Kathryn Tanner observes that, according to Locke, "property is fundamentally inalienable in a way that it is not to capitalism."[33] Property cannot be understood as a commodity in the sole possession of a private owner. Rather, "Exclusive property rights are simply the way that this common property right is individuated to be actually enjoyed by particular people."[34] In Locke's words, "The earth, and all that is therein, is given to men for the support and comfort of their being. And tho' all the fruits it naturally produces, and beasts it feeds, belong to mankind in common, as they are produced by the spontaneous hand of nature; and nobody has originally a private dominion exclusive of the rest of mankind . . ."[35] Further, he argued that though the Earth was held in common, everyone "has property of his own person."[36]

In his *Second Treatise on Government*, Locke asserts that legitimate government derives authority from the consent of the governed. Legitimate government had a moral obligation to pro-

---

[31]Jeannine Olson, "Calvin and Social-Ethical Issues," in *The Cambridge Companion to John Calvin*, ed. Donald K. McKim (Cambridge: Cambridge University Press, 2004), 163–69.

[32]John Locke, *Second Treatise on Civil Government*, ed. C. B. Macpherson (Indianapolis: Hackett, 1980), 18.

[33]Kathryn Tanner, *Economy of Grace* (Minneapolis: Fortress, 2005), 41.

[34]Ibid., 40.

[35]Locke, *Second Treatise on Civil Government*, 18–19.

[36]Ibid.

tect the natural right of citizens to life, liberty, and the pursuit of happiness. An aspect of that protection of natural rights is ensuring that all have access to the resources of the created world in order to benefit from their own labor and to provide for their own basic sustenance. Tanner points out that a right to the inalienably exclusive individual ownership of property and person associated with capitalism is quite different from Locke's arguments. In Locke's perspective, the land and "one's person and capacities [were] held in tenancy from God."[37] Therefore, ownership of land and one's labors are in essence inalienable both from God and from oneself. Locke's ideas provide at least one philosophical perspective that can help to challenge, among other things, contemporary perspectives regarding privatizing the resources of the commons, debt slavery, and government inefficiency.

Many other examples could be offered, but my intention in this chapter has been to retrieve and summarize key connections between Christian theology and debates about poverty, wealth inequalities, economics, property rights, and the fair distribution of wealth. The deep roots in Christian theology that contemporary theologians, ethicists, and religious leaders voice regarding wealth inequalities and economic policies provide a strong basis to confront the claim that we should leave this conversation up to the experts. Christian traditions, rituals, and many of its institutional structures arose out of a deep sense of call to live by the norm of love and embody a different set of social values based upon reciprocity and mutuality. In the past, within the Western academy at least, religious thought has also been crucial for economics. When, why, and how then has such an impermeable boundary been erected between theology and economics? I turn to this question in the next chapter.

---

[37] Tanner, *Economy of Grace*, 42.

PART II

ECONOMISM AND THE ETHIC
OF SCARCITY

CHAPTER 3

When, Why, and How?

The Boundary between Economics and Theology

> Economics have become as completely freed from the trammels of "natural theology," as has geology from the restraints of revealed religion.
>
> —*Francis Walker*[1]

Economism is a term that theologians and ethicists use to describe the assumption or viewpoint that economics as a highly specialized field, market-based logic, and money itself are of utmost and decisive importance in determining the route to human flourishing in our contemporary age. Robert H. Nelson, an economic historian, observes that economists today are viewed as the "modern priests of economic progress" who hold the keys to the kind of wisdom necessary to bring about a new "heaven on earth."[2] Nelson's observation rings true for the unequivocal trust often placed in corporate business leadership as well.

In 2009 I spoke at the Pinnacle Theological Center in Phoenix,

---

[1]Francis Walker, "Recent Progress of Political Economy in the US," Opening Address, American Economic Association, Third Annual Meeting (1888), 253.

[2]Robert H. Nelson, "What Is 'Economic Theology'?" *Princeton Seminary Bulletin* 25, no. 1 (2004): 63.

Arizona, as part of a series of lectures on the Social Creed for the Twenty-first Century. I served on the Presbyterian Church (U.S.A.)'s Resolution Team that drafted the creed as well as collaborated with others to write educational materials to promote it. After my lecture one of the members of the congregation that sponsored the event and the owner of a local family business objected to some of my comments saying, "You make business a foil!" What I understood him to mean was that I used economics as a discipline and the trust in corporate business leadership styles only in ways that contrasted with the best of Christian theological thought on economic justice and disregarded the contribution that markets and family businesses make to local communities. Out of a sense of pastoral concern for their congregations' members, pastors and priests have also expressed to me their reservations about making claims that appear on the surface to be an outright condemnation of economists and business leaders. Let me be clear as I introduce this chapter that I am well aware that some business leaders and economists recognize clearly that mathematics and markets are not comprehensive enough to be the sole determinants of value. Business leaders who come to mind include Charles Grawemeyer, Aaron Feuerstein, Warren Buffett, and Kim Jordan, and economists like Rogate Mshana, Julie Nelson, Athena Peralta, Thomas Piketty, Robert Reich, Amartya Sen, E. F. Schumacher, and Herman Daly.

But economics in the Western academy is more often taught today as a stand-alone discipline that focuses on "mathematical specification and statistical quantification of economic contexts."[3] Carlos Larrea, an expert in ecological economics, argues that in current mainstream economic thought, the economy is described and viewed "as a closed social system, ignoring or minimizing the relationship between society and nature."[4] An International Student Initiative for Pluralism in Economics (ISIPE) was created in 2014 to address the narrow focus on math and statistics and overrepresentation of neoclassical economics as well as the lack

---

[3]This is a quotation of Professor Erik Lundberg of the Nobel Committee used by Theodore Roszak's introduction to E.F. Schumacher, *Small Is Beautiful: Economics as If People Mattered* (New York: Harper and Row, 1973), 2.

[4]See Carlos Larrea, "Earth Jurisprudence, Biodiversity Conservation, and Unburnable Fossil Fuels" (2016), which can be found on the United Nations Harmony with Nature website.

of attention given to economic history and other social sciences in the curriculum developed by departments of economics and business schools. ISIPE conducted a study of economics curriculum taught at universities in France, Chile, Israel, Portugal, Spain, Denmark, Mexico, Turkey, Argentina, Italy, Germany, and Uruguay. They gathered most of their data from 2014–2015 and 2015–2016. ISIPE found that mathematics, statistics, microeconomics, macroeconomics, and management represent on average nearly 60 percent of the curriculum, with the majority of other courses focusing on professional issues, banking, money, and international economic issues. On average, only 3.9 percent of the curriculum focuses on the study of economics in historical perspective.[5] ISIPE did not study any US schools, but a casual Internet search of the economic curriculum at the top US institutions results in similar findings. What is so revealing about ISIPE's research is the lack of attention given to economic theories that *do attend* to a normative vision aimed toward using knowledge gained to benefit individuals, society, and the planet itself. Many liberal arts colleges and universities in the United States continue to offer the economics major within the social sciences instead of within a business school, but, as economists David Colander and Kimmarie McGoldrick point out, "economics today neglects to foster certain liberal education outcomes, on which it could, and once did focus." After the 1960s, they suggest that undergraduate and graduate programs in economics became much more about "technical mathematics and statistical training."[6]

Economism, as an "ism," subordinates nonmonetary values such as community, love, justice, mercy, equality, and fairness to the values of efficiency, perpetual growth, wealth, prosperity, and progress. An insightful observation made by philosopher Michael Sandel in his book *What Money Can't Buy: The Moral Limits of Markets* is that markets and market values have expanded "into spheres of life where they don't belong . . . The reach of markets, and market-oriented thinking into aspects of life traditionally governed by nonmarket norms is one of the most significant

---

[5]This data was presented by Arthur Jatteau at the Second General Assembly of ISIPE in Paris, France on March 25, 2016.

[6]David Colander and Kimmarie McGoldrick, "The Economics Major and Liberal Education," *Liberal Education* (Spring 2009): 27.

developments of our time."[7] When money, efficiency, and market values are lifted above entangled rationality and relationship, there is a failure to see the larger web of relationship that reflects the real circumstances of our lives.

For centuries in the Western university, economic thought was distilled within a larger intellectual matrix and intertwined with other disciplines such as theology, history, politics, and moral philosophy, thereby nurturing a more holistic understanding of self in community. The term *economics* did not become commonplace until about 1900. Before then, the language used to describe the study was *political economy*—a term that conveys the connections between economics, law, politics, and other social institutions. When, how, and why did economics become such a hyperspecialized field in the Western academy?

This chapter highlights the intellectual developments that laid the foundation for the priority placed upon market-based logic and the valuing of things in money terms in the United States. The discussion introduced here is more historical in nature than in other chapters. My intention in carefully laying the groundwork is to deepen our collective understanding of how, when, and why the boundary between economics and theology was erected in the Western academy and to invite you to consider the impact of prioritizing the values of efficiency, perpetual growth, wealth, prosperity, and progress above nonmarket values such as community, love, justice, mercy, equality, and fairness. Prioritizing business, market-based logic, and economics over against other fields in the academy and in public debate is draining our society's theological and moral imagination.

Erecting the Boundary between Theology and Economics in the Western Academy

Christian theology played a role in economic debates in the Western academy even as a distinct boundary was erected between theology and economics in the nineteenth and early twentieth centuries. In many ways, the boundary was created partly due to

---

[7]Michael Sandel, *What Money Can't Buy: The Moral Limits of Markets* (New York: Farrar, Straus, and Giroux, 2012), 7.

debates and disagreements about the nature of God and the role of the church in society. Many of the leading economists at this time were also clergy.

A. M. C. Waterman, Professor Emeritus of Economics at the University of Manitoba, argues that the origin of political economy as a distinct field of inquiry from Christian theology can be marked in Great Britain with the publication of Robert Malthus's *Essay on the Principle of Population* in 1798. Malthus was a clergyperson in the Church of England, serving from 1792 to 1794 as pastor of a church near the home where he was raised. After publication of his *Essay on the Principle of Population*, he was asked to fill the first position established in history and political economy at Haileybury, a college founded by the East India Company to educate staff before they went overseas. Malthus taught at Haileybury for twenty-eight years. The context of the East India Company for Malthus's work is worthy of some attention.

The East India Company was formed in 1600 to allow Britain a means to exploit the spice trade in East and Southeast Asia and India. From the eighteenth to the mid-nineteenth centuries, the company gained a strong political influence and acted as an agent of British imperialism. While Malthus was at Haileybury, he developed pamphlets on the Corn Laws, a tract on rent, and completed a major work titled *The Principles of Political Economy* (1820).

The ideas Malthus introduced in his *Essay on the Principle of Population* constructed the intellectual scaffolding for the methodological orthodoxy of political economy and the discipline now known as "economics." Malthus began his essay with a critique of those who focused on "a happier state of society" without awareness of the obstacles to progress. He argued that population grew at a geometric progression unless it was checked by the food supply. Malthus's argument contrasted with that of Adam Smith, the man widely cited as the "father of capitalism" and pioneer of political economy. Waterman suggests that Smith's *The Wealth of Nations* can be read as congruent with the theological assumptions of Anglican orthodoxy. In the context of that time, the development of the wealth of nations was seen as consistent with, and possibly originating from, the Christian religion. Smith asserted, "Every species of animals naturally multiplies in proposition to the means of their subsistence, and no species can ever multiply beyond it."[8] In contrast, for Malthus, as the population grows it doubles and redoubles, meaning that resources will become increasingly scarce. The world then has the potential to shrink in size so much that food and subsistence fall below what is necessary to sustain life. Malthus wrote, "This natural inequality of the two powers of population and of production in the earth, and that great law of our nature which must constantly keep their effects equal, form the great difficulty that to me appears insurmountable in the way to the perfectibility of society."[9] From a philosophical perspective, Malthus placed human beings in conflict and competition with each other and with nature; he identified the natural world as an object subordinated to human need rather than an essential part of an entangled web of life.

His work had significant political implications. Malthus's principle of population was used to revise English poor laws so that destitution was "considered a state of laziness and unemployment a state to be made as uncomfortable as possible."[10] Malthusian theories also bolstered the arguments against the trade unions on the basis that they could not improve the welfare of workers. Proponents arguing along this line suggested that an increase in wages would only cause workers to reproduce until there would be barely enough subsistence for all.

Malthus's book was an instant bestseller and generated a great deal of debate. Theologians and social reformers felt a sense of moral outrage as a result of Malthus's arguments and published a series of pamphlets and articles that cast him as a heretic and accused him of "hardness of heart." Popular authors and literary critics such as Samuel Taylor Coleridge, Robert Southey, William Wordsworth, William Hazlitt, Thomas Carlyle, Arnold Toynbee, and John Ruskin denounced Malthusian theory as callous and disregarding of the value God placed upon human beings.

At the same time—Malthus along with other economists, including James Mill, David Ricardo, Robert Torrens, and Edward West—shifted away from the study of wealth to the "new science

---

[8]Adam Smith, *The Wealth of Nations* (Blacksburg, VA: Thrifty Books, 2009), 60.
[9]Robert Malthus, *An Essay on the Principle of Population* (London: J. Johnson, 1798), 5, www.esp.org.
[10]Paul Samuelson, *Economics: An Introductory Analysis* (New York: McGraw Hill, 1948; reprinted 1955, 1958, 1961, 1964, 1967), 31.

of scarcity."[11] All of these factors contributed to the shift in public perception of "political economy" as "an intellectual enterprise altogether distinct from Christian theology." Malthus opened up a fault line previously unknown between economic thought and Christian theology in the Western academy. By 1832 a "reputable journal could remind its readers that the writings of Malthus and Ricardo had 'tended to lead the public away from the true path of inquiry' and to make of political economy 'a hideous chain of paradoxes at apparent war with religion and humanity.' "[12]

The boundary between political economy and Christian theology was solidified by Richard Whately, a fellow of Oriel College, principal of St. Alban's Hall, and an influential figure at Oxford University. Whately argued that political economy and theology should be distinct but noncompeting fields of inquiry. "Scripture is not the text by which the conclusions of Science are to be tried," he wrote.[13] Further, Whately insisted that political economy as a field should be value neutral. Whately's work paved the way for the arguments of influential economists such as John Neville Keynes and Lionel Robbins.

John Neville Keynes is less well known than his son John Maynard Keynes, but his writings give insight into the debates about political economy in his time. One of his most important books is *The Scope and Method of Political Economy*, published in 1891. In that book, Keynes entered into the debate among economists of his time who sought to reconcile methodological approaches to economics that normatively described political economy as theoretical, abstract, and deductive as opposed to ethical, realistic, and inductive. Keynes drew this conclusion:

> Political economy is . . . a science, not an art or a department of ethical inquiry. It is described as standing neutral between social schemes. It furnishes information as to the probable consequences of given lines of actions, but does not itself pass moral judgments, or pronounce what ought or ought not to be. At the same time the greatest value is

---

[11]A. M. C. Waterman, *Political Economy and Christian Theology since the Enlightenment* (New York: Palgrave, 2004), 118.

[12]Ibid., 119.

[13]As quoted in ibid., 122.

attached to the practical applications of economic science; and it is agreed that the economist ought himself to turn his attention to them—not, however, in his character as a pure economist, but rather as a social philosopher who, because he is an economist, is in possession of necessary theoretical knowledge.[14]

Standing as intellectual heirs of British economists, Francis Wayland of Brown University, William Graham Sumner of Yale, David A. Wells of Lawrence Academy, and Simon Newcomb of Johns Hopkins were all leading academics in the United States and had a profound influence on the study and shape of economic debates. Wayland authored a textbook in economics that argued for a secularized version of the stereotypical Protestant work ethic for an expanding commercial society.[15] Sumner advocated for an extreme laissez-faire economics and opposed any government measures that would interrupt trade. Wells was known for his advocacy for low tariffs.[16] Newcomb was primarily a mathematician and astronomer, but his writings on economics won him a place at the table among leading economists of his time. Newcomb argued that economic science in his time formed its own body of doctrine and advocated for economics to become a distinct positive science.[17] Around the same time of these debates, the first business school emerged at a university when the Wharton School of Business was founded at the University of Pennsylvania in 1881.

Resistance to Methodological Orthodoxy in Economics within the US Academy

The US academy also offered significant resistance to the growing methodological orthodoxy in economics. Theologians, social activists, and progressive economists in the late nineteenth

---

[14] John Neville Keynes, *The Scope and Method of Political Economy* (London: MacMillan and Company, 1891), 13.

[15] Wayland's textbook, *The Elements of Political Economy*, was first published in 1837.

[16] See these and other publications by David A. Wells: *A Primer of Tariff Reform* (1884), *Practical Economics* (1885), and *The Theory and Practice of Taxation* (1900).

[17] See Newcomb, *Principles of Political Economy* (1885).

and early twentieth centuries reflected back on the long history of Christian commentary on the problem of wealth and the importance of sharing of resources. Their dissatisfaction with the outcomes of political economy, particularly for wage laborers and people living in poverty, led them to critique unrestrained competition and poverty caused by rapid industrialization and the unchecked growth of capitalism in their time. They argued for religious people to stand in solidarity with people in poverty and workers. Several important voices in the United States should be considered, all of them theologians who focused their attentions on a broader public debate over the problem of wealth and the impact of industrialism on the average worker.

John Ryan on Distributive Justice and the Living Wage

Roman Catholic moral theologian John Ryan shaped a tradition of Catholic social ethics in the United States in the first half of the twentieth century. He departed from the traditional approach to Catholic moral theology by insisting on incorporating studies in economics and society into his dissertation to apply the teachings of the church to the circumstances of the working class. Ryan developed his critique of the US economic system on the basis of a tradition of Catholic social teaching evident in the papal encyclicals of Pope Leo XIII and Pius XI. He centered his work on the understanding of dignity and the right of all individuals to all things that are essential to the reasonable development of the human personality. This understanding of human dignity had enormous implications for his view of economic rights. For Ryan, concepts of individual freedom were not defined regarding competing interests in markets, but liberty served as means to a right and reasonable self-development.

Ryan's doctoral dissertation was later published in 1906 as a book titled *A Living Wage*. *Rerum novarum* was foundational for the arguments Ryan developed, as Leo XIII argued, "To defraud any one of wages that are his due is a great crime which cries to the avenging anger of Heaven. . . . The rich must religiously refrain from cutting down the workmen's earnings, whether by force, by fraud, or by usurious dealing. . . ." In *A Living Wage*, Ryan advocated for fair pay, the redistribution of wealth, and industrial reorganization by determining the effects of any system on the welfare of human beings and the communities in which they lived.

Ryan devoted himself to movements for social reform for more than forty years. When compared to progressives like the Social Gospelers, he offered an alternative perspective to debates regarding economic justice and social reform that was rooted in natural law. Richard Gaillardetz, a professor of systematic theology, says, "Natural law theory's contention that there existed absolute human rights provided for Ryan the basis for a consideration of *human* welfare, a combination of both *social* and *individual* welfare."[18] Later works included *Distributive Justice*, published in 1916, which advanced an understanding of private property in line with Aquinas's thought.[19]

The influence of Ryan's work was felt beyond academic circles in local communities. For example, Ryan inspired and collaborated with Patrick Henry Callahan, president of the Louisville Varnish Company, to implement the social teachings of the Catholic Church in his business by creating a profit-sharing plan. The plan specified that all workers would be paid union wages. Then, a valuation was placed on the business as a whole, "without any 'watering of capital,'" and profit of 6 percent was set as a charge against that valuation. All remaining profits after these two charges were equally divided between the owner and the workers.[20]

Walter Rauschenbusch, Richard Ely, and Social Gospel Resistance to Economism

Another example is found in the writings of Walter Rauschenbusch, a Baptist pastor and church historian who is widely recognized as a leading voice among Protestant Social Gospelers in the twentieth century. Rauschenbusch placed Jesus in line with the prophets. In *Christianity and the Social Crisis* (1907) Rauschenbusch accents the prophets' "indifference or hostility to ritual religion" and their turn to "the full power of the religious impulse

---

[18]Richard R. Gaillardetz, "John A. Ryan: An Early Revisionist?" *Journal of Religious Ethics* 18, no. 2 (1990): 110.

[19]See Charles E. Curran, *Catholic Social Teaching, 1991–Present* (Washington, DC: Georgetown University Press, 2002), 178.

[20]"An Experiment in Profit Sharing That Worked," *Christian Century*, January 30, 1946, 132–33.

into the sluice of ethical conduct. Jesus was a succession of the prophets in this regard."[21] The purpose of Jesus's announcement of the kingdom of God is to create a "true society" that embodies love, service, and equality. Rauschenbusch has been fairly and sometimes harshly criticized for being overly optimistic and for failing to understand the reality of the social circumstances of women and people of color in his time. These criticisms, however, should not take away from his observations about Jesus as a political reformer in line with the prophets.

Richard Ely, an economist and Social Gospeler, was also a leading voice in critiques of the economic system. He challenged the conviction held by contemporaries such as Sumner and Newcomb that economics should be considered a distinct and positive science. Ely had experienced poverty firsthand when his father was let go from a railroad job. He was educated at Columbia University in New York City and then did his graduate work in Heidelberg, Germany. In Germany, he studied with Karl Knies, who was well known for disliking classical economics. Like his teacher, Ely "mastered the historical, statistical approach to economic analysis," whereas classical British economists refused "to look at actual economic conditions."[22] Ely's first job was in New York City, where he allowed himself to see the homeless people living on the street and to feel the distress of the destitution he saw there.

At the heart of Ely's economic arguments lay his understanding of social solidarity. He wrote, "The oneness of human interests . . . signifies the dependence of many upon man, both in good things and in evil things. Social solidarity means that our true welfare is not an individual matter purely, but likewise a social affair, our weal is a common weal; we thrive only in a commonwealth; our exaltation is the exaltation of our fellows, their elevation is our enlargement."[23] These statements reflect a broader sentiment held by prominent Social Gospel leaders. Ely's notions of solidarity and

---

[21]Walter Rauschenbusch, *Christianity and the Social Crisis*, with an Introduction by Douglas F. Ottati, Library of Theological Ethics (Louisville, KY: Westminster/John Knox Press, 1991), 71.

[22]Bradley W. Bateman and Ethan B. Kapstein, "Retrospectives between God and the Market: The Religious Roots of the American Economic Association," *Journal of Economic Perspectives* 13, no. 4 (Autumn 1999): 252.

[23]As quoted by Eugene Lowe in "Richard T. Ely: Herald of a Positive State," *Union Seminary Quarterly Review* 42 (June 1988): 22.

commonwealth were influenced by new discoveries in the social sciences, Christian teachings, socialist visions of democracy, and the writings of progressive theologians such as Richard Rothe and F. D. Maurice.

Ely became a founding member of the American Economic Association (AEA), which William Barber, a professor of economics, suggests should be seen as his way of fighting "the influence of 'the Sumner, Newcomb crowd.' "[24] The purpose of the AEA was to bring a particular view of Christian ethics into the profession of economics. When the AEA was founded, debates about political economy were primarily framed as a controversy between those Ely called the "free traders" and others he described as "protectionists." Ely observed that "'a crust' had been formed over economics." A group of older men had "almost a monopoly" and "exercised a good deal of harshness." The AEA formed due to a belief that a new economics was needed to break through that crust and inspire innovative approaches. In the speech Ely gave during the AEA's organizational meeting, he said, "We hold the doctrine of laissez-faire is unsafe in politics and unsound in morals; suggest an inadequate explanation of the relations between a state and its citizens." Ely advocated for social ethics to be part of any debates over political economy. Founding principles established for the American Economic Association included:

1. Regarding the state as an agency whose positive assistance is indispensable to human progress
2. Acknowledging that political economy as a science is still in an early stage of its development
3. Acknowledging that the conflict between labor and capital has brought a vast number of social problems that require attending to by the united efforts of the church, the state, and science
4. Asserting that the study of the industrial and commercial policy of governments should be nonpartisan.[25]

---

[24]William J. Barber, "Should the American Economic Association Have Toasted Simon Newcomb at Its 100th Birthday Party?" *Journal of Economic Perspectives* 1, no. 1 (Summer 1987): 179.

[25]*Publications of the American Economic Association: Volume I. 1887*, 6-7.

Economic associations were founded in other countries, including Great Britain, South Africa, and Japan, soon after the founding of the American Economic Association.

The AEA was not as successful as Ely had hoped. So many laissez-faire economists "held positions of power in every major university in the country" that many young members did not want to antagonize them. Younger members of the AEA asked Ely that the principles not be made personally binding. In December 1888, just three years after the AEA was founded, Francis Walker, the president of the Massachusetts Institute of Technology, gave the opening address for the meeting on the theme of "Recent Progress of Political Economy in the US." Walker held that he had no "quarrel with natural theology," but asserted the "right of political economy to be entirely independent of it." His observations are worth quoting at length as they illustrate the solidification of the boundary between economics and theology in the United States:

> The temper of self-assertion, proper to the teachers of any subject, has been re-enforced by the "spirit of the age," to the point of finally freeing political economy from this subjection to an alien authority. Not only is it fully recognized that "right divine" has not more to do with economics than with politics; that men should inquire what is best for them in matters of industry equally as in matters of government, without any presumption from arrangements supposed to have been made for them; but the subserviency of temper, which, for longer or shorter times, always survives the breaking bands of authority, has wholly disappeared. Economics have become as completely freed from the trammels of "natural theology," as has geology from the restraints of "revealed religion."[26]

For Walker, the usefulness of the first stage of the organization had passed, and economics as a discipline made steady progress toward freeing itself from limitations imposed by religious belief. Seven years after the AEA was founded, Ely felt that he had to avoid the annual meeting of the organization because so many

---

[26]Walker, "Recent Progress of Political Economy in the US," 252–53.

laissez-faire economists had joined. He later returned to become president of the organization in 1900–1901.

During his career, Ely and other Social Gospel economists suffered political attacks as violence related to strikes cast doubt in the public eye as to the effectiveness of labor organizing. Some of Ely's writings were also dealt with harshly. While he was teaching at Johns Hopkins, Newcomb, one of Ely's colleagues at the school, stated in a review of Ely's book *The Labor Movement in America* that "a man who held such views was not fit to hold a position in an American university."[27] The economics department at the University of Wisconsin hired him as chair in 1892, where Ely pursued his interests in labor and land economics.

The primary goal that I outlined for this chapter was to pinpoint when, how, and why the boundary between economics and theology was solidified in the Western academy. By the turn of the twentieth century, the place of economics as a separate and distinct subject from moral philosophy, theology, and history had been secured within colleges and universities. The boundary is even clearer today, with the strong influence of corporations on US universities.[28] The rich history of Christian thought, commentary, and tradition that focuses on economic justice, releasing people and the land from perpetual bondage, fair worker pay, and the just distribution of wealth stands as a challenge to legitimacy and priority placed upon economics, money, and market-based logic in the academy and within US society. In addition, marketplaces are inherently relational. Human beings make economic decisions within a larger social context, for good or ill. An unbalanced focus on economics in terms of mathematical specification and statistical quantification fails to attend to the realities of marketplaces themselves.

In the next chapter I turn to the moral worldviews and impact of the two dominant forms of wealth creation in the United States and around the globe: social developmentalism and neoliberalism.

---

[27]Ely, 146.

[28]A number of studies have been done on corporate influence on higher education. See, for example, Jennifer Washburn, *University Inc.: The Corporate Corruption of Higher Education* (New York: Basic Books, 2005), and Sheila Slaughter and Larry Leslie, *Academic Capitalism: Politics, Policies, and the Entrepreneurial University* (Baltimore, MD: Johns Hopkins University Press, 1997).

These approaches to wealth creation assume an individualistic understanding of self and hold in common the idea that self-interest plays an essential role in human motivation. I argue that approaches to wealth creation that begin from an individualistic standpoint, focus on unlimited economic growth, and view nonhuman nature merely as a resource instrumental in fulfilling human needs delude us into thinking that such ways of living will lead to authentic community.

Chapter 4

The Current Dominant Forms of Wealth Creation and the Ethic of Scarcity

Economics is a method, but the object is to change the soul.
—*Margaret Thatcher*[1]

Almost everything in US society today can be monetized, even things once considered sacred. Philosopher Michael Sandel has written, "Over the past three decades, markets—and market values—have come to govern our lives as never before."[2] Sandel points out that it is standard industry practice for money to buy things like hefty life insurance policies that promise a return to corporations on their investments (employees) when they die. Money can buy prison cell upgrades for inmates with the financial means to afford private cells in local jails and cheaper and easier access for infertile couples in the heavily industrialized countries of the Global North to the bodies of surrogate mothers in the Global South. Markets, Sandel rightly observes, can "crowd out morals."

Consider also a more personal example of the way in which markets crowd out morals: the experience of my maternal grand-mother, Flossie Burks. Momo, as I affectionately called her, was a seamstress. She grew up without access to many of the advantages

---

[1] As quoted by Philip Mirowski, "The Political Movement That Dared Not Speak Its Own Name: The Neoliberal Thought Collective under Erasure," Institute for New Economic Thinking, Working Paper 23 (August 2014): 22.

[2] Michael J. Sandel, *What Money Can't Buy: The Moral Limits of Markets* (New York: Farrar, Straus and Giroux, 2012), 5.

that could be afforded by my middle-class life. Her formal education ended with the sixth grade, and yet her natural talent enabled her to become highly skilled at making and mending garments. We think she married at a young age, although we have no wedding pictures to prove it. Her husband, whom I never met, was a bright man, but unable to apply his gifts because of his addiction to booze and possibly an undiagnosed depression. In her youth, Momo was so talented with a needle that she could hand stitch the hem of a dress with the precision of a sewing machine. Momo made my wedding dress when she was eighty-seven years old. The pattern required her hands, at that time contorted by arthritis, to cover over a dozen tiny buttons with slipper satin.

For many years, Momo had worked at Carlye Dress Corporation in St. Louis, Missouri. Carlye holds a place in fashion history as one of the great junior dress houses of the 1940s. The garments that my grandmother made were highly valued by the market, but the labor she put into them was not. Historical studies record the average wage of a female factory worker in 1938, the year that Carlye opened in St. Louis, was $31.21 for a week's work; male workers earned about $55.00. In addition to working for incredibly low wages, my grandmother ended up being a single mother of three. When she died, her pension was a meager $83.00 a month. There was no consideration of the amount of money she needed to live a decent life or the skill put into the dresses she made. After she retired and was unable to pick up small sewing jobs to bring in extra money, Momo moved into Section 8 housing and my parents helped to supplement her income. The last few years of her life she lived in my parents' home.

Sandel argues that, at least on the surface, it appears in our society as if we have allowed and become comfortable with the idea of "the market" determining the value of things like quality of life, death, birth, and human freedom without "any deliberate choice. It is almost as if it came upon us."[3] He is of course all too aware that markets and market-oriented thinking enjoy unrivaled prestige because of the moral worldviews, understanding of human nature, and deliberate choices that inform the dominant approaches to wealth creation in the United States.

---

[3]Ibid.

The research included in this chapter began with my work as a consultant for a series of hearings and forums held between 2007 and 2014 that were sponsored by the Poverty, Wealth, and Ecology (PWE) project of the World Council of Churches. The first PWE hearing and forum in which I participated took place in 2010 in Budapest, Hungary. PWE emerged as a continuation of the A.G.A.P.E. (Alternative Globalization for People and the Earth) process. The WCC clearly states that economic globalization has created new forms of injustice and inequality. PWE is an effort to "bring churches and ecumenical partners from North, South, East, and West together to reflect and act together on finding new and creative ways to use global wealth to eradicate poverty."[4] Goals of the PWE project include determining the extent to which the current dominant methods and structure of wealth creation in the United States and around the world are responsible for poverty and wealth inequality, establishing a "wealth line" and "greed line" to offer guidance for people of faith alongside a poverty line, and exploring the spiritual and ethical implications of wealth creation for people and the planet. PWE hearings and forums made clear that neither the social development nor neoliberal approach to wealth creation provide a rich enough and well-textured understanding—of human beings and the common space and theater of God's grace that people and the whole planet share—to create a more just economy and help us realize an authentic vision of community. These hearings and forums also provided an opportunity to reflect on alternative economic theories, such as ecological economics and concepts of solidarity economies. A basic fundamental assumption made by ecological economics is that "human economy is embedded in and part of natural ecology—that is (among other things), the dynamics of the physical world—energy, matter, entropy, evolution, etc.—have been neglected by standard economics,"[5] and, I assert, by the dominant approaches to wealth creation today. We neglect our essential relatedness to nature at our own peril.

In this chapter I explore the two dominant approaches to

---

[4]World Council of Churches, "Poverty, Wealth, and Ecology: Impact of Economic Globalization," www.oikoumene.org.

[5]Peter Brown and Peter Timmerman, eds., *Ecological Economics for the Anthropocene: An Emerging Paradigm* (New York: Columbia University Press, 2015).

wealth creation in the United States and around the world: social developmentalism and neoliberalism (see Table 4.1).[6] There are two main goals to keep in mind for this chapter. First, I want to give you the tools necessary to define clearly and consider the consequences of social developmentalism and neoliberalism. Both social developmentalism and neoliberalism assume an individualistic understanding of self. Social developmentalism does not support the idea that human beings act out of self-interest alone or that markets are morally neutral, but there is ample evidence from projects in the United States and abroad, particularly in the Global South, that this theory of wealth creation assumes the cultural superiority of developed and technologically advanced urban communities. Introducing development projects too often means introducing a psychological rift between people and the land as well as private ownership and control of properties with an abundance of natural resources. The model originated in the US context in the Tennessee Valley Authority (TVA) projects in Appalachia where land was developed in the 1930s. TVA became a model for the world. The original intent of the project was to harness natural resources to modernize the region, but the consequence was to make people dependent upon an economy driven by the interests of outside investors. The main point that I make in highlighting this history is not that all economic development projects are problematic in nature, but to emphasize that development needs to begin from an understanding of self as radically interdependent with neighbor and nature and be driven by the distinctive needs and concerns of particular communities. Most importantly, I argue that neoliberalism, the theory and form of wealth creation driving our economy today, is incompatible with Christian ethics as it assumes an understanding of human beings as atomistic individuals who act out of self-interest alone and the maximization of profits at the expense of neighbor and nature. The impact of neoliberalism is staggering. Neoliberalism falsely leads us to believe that individualism and the pursuit of human self-interest at the expense of a larger common good have the potential to create authentic and flourishing communities.

---

[6]I am indebted to Rebecca Todd Peters for her careful analysis of neoliberalism and social development theory in *In Search of the Good Life: The Ethics of Globalization* (New York: Continuum, 2004).

Table 4.1 Characteristics of the Two Dominant Theories
of Wealth Creation

	Neoliberalism	Social Developmentalism
Defined	A theory of political economy that proposes that human well-being can be advanced by liberating individual entrepreneurial freedoms and skills within an institutional framework characterized by strong private property rights, free markets, and free trade.	An economic theory that emphasizes the responsibility of government for protecting those who are most vulnerable in society and addressing true scarcity through efforts to promote equitable economic growth and development.
Essential Understanding of Human Nature	*Homo economicus*. Human beings are consumers who act on the basis of their own self-interest to maximize wealth.	Human beings are motivated by self-interest but have a moral obligation and responsibility to care for their neighbors.
Humanity's Ultimate Purpose	Prosperity	Progress
Nonhuman Nature's Ultimate Purpose	Nonhuman nature is passive matter to be monetized according to human need and used for the purpose of unlimited economic expansion and growth.	Nonhuman nature is a resource to be tamed to provide for human needs. Nature should have limited protections primarily to ensure human access to this source for unlimited economic expansion and growth.
View of Moral Questions in Relation to the Economy	The economy is passive and does not pass moral judgments.	Two assumptions are at play in this approach. Human beings have a moral obligation to help others, and the market provides the best economic means to satisfy basic needs.
Political Supporters	Big business (multinational and transnational corporations).	Social democracy parties in Europe and the Democratic Party in the United States.
Beginnings	The Mont Pèlerin Society. Gained significant traction in the 1980s Reagan/Thatcher era.	Pioneered by John Maynard Keynes.

View of Role of Government	Government should stay "small" and only provide services that the market cannot provide for itself. Regulatory behavior of government is an interference with the "natural behavior" of the market.	Government is responsible for protecting those who are most vulnerable in society; government initiatives, including spending, should have the goal of stimulating the economy; and regulations should support workers' rights and provide safety nets.

The second goal of this chapter is to raise a far more disruptive question. When there is abundant evidence that proves the limitations of both of the dominant forms of wealth creation and the centuries-long investment in economic justice among people of faith, why do people living in the United States, a country with a majority Christian population, continue to fail to demand better economic alternatives? I think that most people are aware of wealth inequalities, poverty, and climate change caused by production and overconsumption in the United States, but don't as clearly understand how they are connected to the way we create wealth. My efforts in this chapter are to simplify the explanation enough to equip readers with the tools necessary to identify the problems caused by the current dominant forms of wealth creation and to begin to imagine and work for alternatives.

Social Developmentalism: The US Story in Appalachia

Social developmentalism is a term that is most frequently applied to the relationship between the wealthier industrialized countries of the Global North and the low-income countries of the Global South. According to this economic theory, governments have the responsibility to assist the most vulnerable in society in promoting their capabilities and providing opportunities. Government spending should have the goal of stimulating the economy and inspiring progress through technological advance and modernization, and regulations should be put in place that support workers' rights and provide for valuable social safety nets. Within the United States, the economic theory of social developmentalism emerged first in projects related to Franklin Delano Roosevelt's New Deal. The Tennessee Valley Authority (TVA), one of the earliest projects of the New Deal, is of particular significance when considering growing wealth inequalities in our contemporary world and similarities between impoverished communities in the United States and the experience of people living in poverty in other nations. The TVA was touted for modernizing the US Southeast and became the model in the mid-twentieth century for US foreign development projects in countries such as China, Colombia, Iran, and Vietnam.

British economist John Maynard Keynes was an early pioneer in development economics. FDR never claimed to be a follower of Keynes, but his New Deal policies very closely resembled Keynesian economics. John Maynard Keynes, the son of John Neville Keynes, lived through an era in which British industry expanded while the country experienced a great deal of social, political, and economic turmoil. He witnessed two major world wars as well as periods of prolonged economic depression and widespread unemployment. The US economy plummeted as a result of the stock market crash of 1929. Economic depression in the United States sent shock waves throughout the global economy. Britain was already struggling to pay off debts after World War I. In the wake of the US stock market crash, the value of British exports was cut in half and unemployment doubled. By 1933, one-fourth of the British workforce was unemployed. In this context, Keynes was unconvinced by the idea that some invisible hand of fate alone guided the economy. He argued that, because of the negative effect of private-sector decisions on the economy, the government in times of depression had a responsibility to restart the economy. During economic depression, if the unemployed were put back to work, even with borrowed money, then the economy would improve. He believed that investments that would create jobs must come first to stimulate the economy. These arguments had a profound effect on how governments at that time considered prosperity and progress and continued to play a role in shaping assumptions about and attitudes toward regions in the United States and other countries that are impoverished, have lesser access to technology, and are thus considered economically undeveloped.

The TVA and "Modernizing" Appalachia

Keynesian economics enabled the United States to begin to recover from the Great Depression of the 1930s. Projects such as the Tennessee Valley Authority, the Civilian Conservation Corps, and the Works Progress Administration were all informed by Keynes's arguments. When the TVA was introduced as part of the "First New Deal" in 1933, the project sought to modernize the Appalachian region of the United States. *Appalachia* refers both to the diversity of cultures within and the geographical area surrounding a mountain range that stretches across a fifteen-hundred-mile region of North America—all the way from the Gapsé Peninsula of Québec, Canada, to the US state of Alabama. Central to Southern Appalachia, including the mountain ridges of Tennessee, Kentucky, Virginia, and West Virginia, has always been a land of contrasts, where people live in the breathtaking beauty of mountain hills and valleys and yet know some of the worst material deprivation in the nation. Popular media has often characterized the region as socially and culturally backward and referred to the people there as living in a state of feudalism. You may remember twentieth-century stereotypes of hillbillies as poor whites, as depicted in Al Capp's cartoon *L'il Abner*, legendary stories of family feuds between the Hatfields and the McCoys, and simple-minded, down-home characters like the Clampetts in the TV sitcom *The Beverly Hillbillies*. These stereotypes never accounted for the rich diversity of cultures always found within the region.

There is also an abundance of wealth in natural resources in the Appalachian mountains—iron, coal, limestone, shale, gold, silver, copper, lead, and marble. Large-scale coal mining began in Appalachia in the late nineteenth and early twentieth centuries. Industrial speculators and robber barons such as J. P. Morgan bought up land and mineral rights in Appalachia to ensure access to coal for their industries. Companies were planted in the area to manage mining towns. These companies brought with them wage-paying jobs and dramatically altered the way of life of people who were already living in the mountains. Before the robber barons, people in the mountains worked the land to produce chestnuts and ginseng that were sold in US cities or exported to other countries. The introduction of the coal mining industry in Appalachia represented a shift in the economy and introduced a psychological and cultural rift between people and the land. The coal mining industry transformed the land from a common resource to a privately possessed commodity that excluded mountain people from ownership. People living in the mountains had previously sustained themselves by operating small farms according to the cycles of the seasons. Practices, disciplines, policies, and the understanding of property ownership associated with the mining industries were imposed on people living in the mountains. Tennessee Ernie Ford's song "Sixteen Tons" expresses well the impact of these psychological, cultural, and economic shifts:

> You load sixteen tons, what do you get?
> Another day older and deeper in debt
> Saint Peter don't you call me 'cause I can't go
> I owe my soul to the company store.

As coal mining grew and outside investors began to see it as the way to define the region's economy, people living in Appalachia became increasingly dependent upon industries to sustain their families. Companies consistently resisted workers' efforts to receive higher wages. When miners would strike in the early twentieth century, the coal companies would hire recent immigrants from European countries such as Hungary, Russia, and Italy to work in the mines and used violence to break the strikes and block workers from forming a union.

Mining engineers and developers largely saw mountain people as socially backward, and as a result, they also became the objects of charitable missionary efforts. Christian denominations established a variety of missions to address what was perceived to be the cultural backwardness and need for education in the region, including schools and colleges. Faith communities in this way gave their blessing to economic development efforts in the region.

By the 1930s, the plan to modernize the region was to harness energy locked in the Tennessee River by building dams for public use and increasing technology to provide more efficient access to these resources. The TVA brought dams and new forms of technology to Appalachia to control flooding, improve navigation of the Tennessee River, harvest electricity for a variety of purposes, and assist in industrial development. In addition to these projects, educational and agricultural programs were introduced as part of a larger program intended to modernize Appalachia. David Lilienthal, the TVA's first director, argued that the uniqueness of the project lay in the philosophy that development of the region would be both grassroots and democratic. The moral right and authority of the TVA were sanctioned by a larger national agenda to provide energy to urban communities with an ever-increasing appetite for electricity and a charitable goal of providing electricity for people living in poverty in the region.

The TVA became a model for development in the United States and the means for the United States to extend its democracy by exporting this type of economic development to so-called underdeveloped nations around the world. Historian David Ekbladh observes that throughout the late 1930s and 1940s, foundations bent on modernizing Chinese society "sent a number of Chinese engineers and agriculturalists to Tennessee to witness the accomplishments of the New Deal effort."[7] In 1941, Lilienthal broadened his interests more toward international development. Lilienthal articulated his views on the importance of the organization in a book titled *Democracy on the March*, in which he wrote that TVA was "an effective response to the world in the throes of decolonialization" (see Figure 4.1). The problem was that the projects were frequently not adapted to their contexts, didn't hire workers from the regions they sought to develop, and thus often benefited investors more.

Keynesian development economics furnished for many politicians and economists in the 1930s and 1940s an alternative to Marxist theory by providing a way to escape from the horrors of unemployment and economic depression without violent revolution. During the Cold War, US politicians emphasized the stark contrast between the nation's development programs of "technological dynamism" to communist development programs of "political dynamism." The TVA came to be viewed as the fulfillment of the promise of economic reform of the 1930s, which made Henry A. Wallace, vice president of the United States, call for the founding of two institutions to confront the task of reconstruction: "an international bank and an international TVA."[8] At the famous Bretton Woods conference in 1944, Keynes and Harry Dexter White, a US Department of Treasury official, were instrumental in laying the intellectual foundations for a post war global

---

[7]David Ekbladh, "'Mr. TVA': Grass-Roots Development, David Lilienthal, and the Rise and Fall of the Tennessee Valley Authority as a Symbol for US Overseas Development, 1933–1973," *Diplomatic History* 26, no. 3 (Summer 2002): 339–40.

[8]As quoted in ibid., 347.

Figure 4.1. Global Reach of the Tennessee Valley Authority

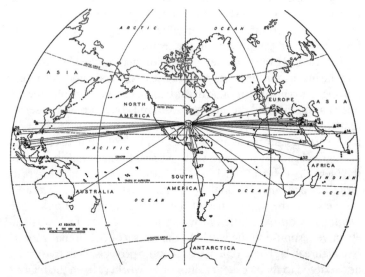

Source: The Historical Photographs Collection of the National Archives at Atlanta in Morrow, Georgia. Photograph No. K-3386, "World Map" (April 1962), Records of the Tennessee Valley Authority, Record Group 142.

economy and an international bank. Keynes was later elected a vice president of the World Bank and Fund. Individual countries adopted Keynesian policies within the framework of the World Bank and International Monetary Fund. Programs and projects of the World Bank, IMF, and TVA cemented the position of the United States, Britain, and other highly industrialized countries as the leading policymakers for the larger global economy.

Projects such as the TVA informed US aspirations to fill in the gaps in what were considered a lack of competencies in other countries or regions within the United States and to provide the means to deliver technical assistance. President Harry Truman unveiled his Point Four program in his inaugural address of 1949. He introduced a "bold new program" to help peoples of the developing world. In 1955 Lilienthal became one of the founders of the Development and Resources (D&R) consultant group, which advised Colombia, Puerto Rico, Iran, and South Vietnam on a number of modernization projects.

Critical challenges have been brought to the social development approach to wealth creation within the United States and in other countries. Like many other areas dependent upon extractive industries, Appalachia in many ways remains held under the spell of the "resource curse." Richard Hasler, a South African anthropologist, argues that "the case of coal mining in Appalachia is . . . an example of the tragedy of privatization" and the result of a mentality rooted in "frontierism," where the natural world is seen solely as a source for unlimited expansion and in need of being tamed.[9] Religious social activists have likened Appalachia to an "internal colony" and suggest that the region "reveals relationships between the powerful and the powerless" similar to those in two-thirds-world countries.

It is worth commenting more here on the issue of power.[10] Obviously, we need to use natural resources and sustainable development achieved with community cooperation and collaboration, and shared ownership is beneficial. However, the problem in Appalachia and in the Global South is that the local people have little or no power to get any benefit from or to preserve the land. What happens all too often is that local elites and the national government align with powerful corporations. The resource curse is largely related to the powerlessness of local people in the face of corporate power and corruption. In some sense, social developmentalism is corporate power combined with corrupt corporate and political elites (in the Global North and South) working together. Government studies show that by the 1970s, "Absentee owners, primarily coal, timber, and petroleum companies [held] title to nearly half the surface area in 80 counties of the impoverished Appalachian Mountain region."[11]

The economy of Appalachia is similar to countries that rely heavily on mineral wealth in that it became overly dependent upon forestry, farming, and extractive industries, which resulted in an

---

[9]Richard Hasler, "The Tragedy of Privatization: Moving Mountains in Appalachia, A Southern African Critique," *Journal of Appalachian Studies* 11, no. 1/2 (Spring/Fall 2005): 95–103.

[10]I am indebted here to the Rev. Dr. Edith Rasell for observations she made related to power dynamics when reading a draft of this chapter.

[11]Ben A. Franklin, "Appalachian Regional Study Finds Absentee Ownership of 43% of Land," *New York Times*, April 5, 1981.

atypically high poverty rate. According to the 2007–2011 report of the Appalachian Regional Commission, the poverty rate in the United States was 14.3 percent compared to 16.1 percent in the Appalachian region of Alabama, Kentucky, Tennessee, Virginia, and West Virginia; Appalachian Kentucky has the most impoverished conditions, with 24.8 percent of people living in poverty. The situation is so dire in Appalachian Kentucky because coal represents 13.7 percent of total employment—and when calculating the economic impact including indirect, induced, and total economic impacts represents nearly one-third of the total share of employment.

Coal's contribution to the Kentucky economy is hotly debated, and the state is one of two dozen that opposed a Clean Power Plan by the Environmental Protection Agency and lags behind in alternative forms of energy. Many people are strong advocates for the coal industry because they believe that it provides jobs and energy for communities in the state. However, even though Kentucky is the nation's third-largest producer of coal, the power plants in the region "use only a fraction of the coal they once did from the state's struggling eastern coalfield."[12] Kentucky is burning more coal than it did in 1983, and yet more than half of the state's mining jobs have disappeared. These facts raise serious questions about whether Appalachia's dependence upon the coal industry continues to benefit the people living in the region.

Social developmentalism has largely been discredited in the eyes of people living in the Global South who have become the objects of US-style economic development. In other contexts, modernization has become synonymous with "[US] Americanization." Liberation theologian Gustavo Gutiérrez argued in what is now a classic theological text, *A Theology of Liberation*, that, "For some, the origin of the term development is, in a sense, negative. They consider it to have appeared in opposition to the term underdevelopment, which expressed the situation—and anguish—of poor countries compared with that of rich countries."[13] Postcolonial theorists take offense at the "universalizing discourse" of

---

[12]Curtis Tate, "Kentucky Is Buying Other States' Coal Instead of Its Own," *McClatchy DC*, January 8, 2016.

[13]Gustavo Gutiérrez, *A Theology of Liberation* (Maryknoll, NY: Orbis Books, 1990; reprint of the 1973 edition), 14.

the West assuming that Western countries alone have the answer to the problems of economic development. Moreover, wealthy industrialized countries are often presumed to have great social and cultural superiority. There is no clear definition of what a fully "developed" region or country is, but to advance economically implies becoming more like urban areas in the United States or other highly industrialized nations in the Global North.

Appalachia has become one of the areas in the United States appropriated by European and northeastern US companies for economic development in order to access timber, labor, and natural resources for energy. The coal industry shifted in the 1970s its methods of extraction by combining traditional methods with a new approach: mountaintop removal mining. Mountaintop removal entails clearing the forested peaks of all timbers and violently blasting the tops off mountains to extract "the new black gold." Inhabitants of the region live with the sounds and fallout of the process on a daily basis. Those who benefit most from the extracted coal live far away, mainly in urban areas, for coal has been—and continues to be—one of the main resources used to generate electricity in the United States. The coal industry claims that mountaintop mining is more efficient and more cost-effective than traditional methods and that it reshapes the mountain terrain into a more "useful" environment for other forms of industry. What the coal industry fails to own up to is how the process destroys forest beds, turns animals into refugees, takes away a natural system of water purification, removes trees that offset the pollution that clouds the sky over urban areas, and threatens the livelihood and homes of the people who belong to the mountain landscape. To understand we need to turn our attention to the second dominant approach to wealth creation—neoliberalism.

The Neoliberal Vision

The current public discussion of wealth and the economy in the United States is dominated by the anthropological assumptions and economic theories that inform the neoliberal approach to wealth creation. Market values have come to play more of a role in social life in the last forty years because of a political-economic project known as *neoliberalism* or sometimes called *turbo-capitalism.*[14] The term *neoliberalism* is not as frequently used by economists in the United States as it is by Christian ethicists, theologians, and religious leaders seeking to identify the root cause of surging inequalities. Some historians, anthropologists, leaders of financial institutions, and religious leaders argue against naming and defining neoliberalism because they think it is too diffuse to serve as a serious analytic category. On this point, I disagree and think it is important to name clearly and define neoliberalism's contours. A growing consensus among Christian ethicists, theologians, and many religious leaders in ecumenical and interfaith movements is that neoliberalism is the driving factor in increasing wealth inequalities and patterns of consumption leading to ecological destruction.

Philip Mirowski, an economic historian and philosopher, argues that neoliberalism is a political economic project dating back to 1947 with the founding of the Mont Pèlerin Society, a partisan "thought collective," that first met in Vevey, Switzerland. Neoliberalism is a general philosophy of the market and a political-economic project. Mirowski says that the Chicago School was established in the postwar era to serve as a complement to the Mont Pèlerin Society and "was dedicated to the reconciliation of the nascent neoliberal idea with a rather simplistic form of neoclassical economics."[15] Neoliberalism was intended as a direct response to the idea of the state as a "night watchman . . . that would set the boundaries for the natural growth of the market, like a shepherd tending his flock."[16] Both Frederich Hayek and Milton Friedman were among the founding members of the Mont Pèlerin Society and used the term "neoliberalism" in print. There is disagreement among economic historians about whether neoliberalism is rooted in neoclassical economics. Some, such as David Harvey in *A Brief History of Neoliberalism*, say neoliberalism is rooted in neoclassical economics. Mirowski argues that neoliberals are resistant to "heavy dependence on mathematics, and have a conflicted relationship to neoclassical economics."[17]

---

[14]Lawrence Grossberg, *Caught in the Crossfire: Kids, Politics, and America's Future* (Boulder, CO: Paradigm, 2005), 112.
[15]Mirowski, "Political Movement That Dared Not Speak Its Own Name," 9.
[16]Ibid., 12.
[17]Ibid.

For neoliberals, freedom and the market are synonymous terms. Mirowski writes, "The market no longer gave you what you wanted; you had to capitulate to what the Market wanted. All areas of life could be better configured if they were more market like."[18] As a political project, neoliberalism "removed the foundation of liberty from natural rights tradition."[19] Proponents of neoliberal capitalism argue that markets are "more efficient at providing services than governments."[20] Neoliberalism is informed by the belief that human beings are atomistic individuals possessing the absolute freedom to act rationally for their benefit. Within this framework of thought, "the free market is the most rational and democratic system of choice [and therefore] every domain of human life should be open to the forces of the marketplace."[21] Neoliberal capitalism reduces the value of nearly everything to money form.

Social ethicist Rebecca Todd Peters in her book *In Search of the Good Life* marks the beginning of the shift toward neoliberal economic public policies with the leadership of British prime minister Margaret Thatcher and US president Ronald Reagan. Neoliberal capitalism has dramatically accelerated the growth of wealth inequality in the United States and worldwide. For the last forty years, neoliberalism has been the primary ideological fuel for changes in economic policies, the shaping of public perceptions and ideas, the reshaping of social and political institutions, the commodification of our culture, and the "spiritualization" of the free-market economy. US economic and public policies have favored deregulation, market efficiency, privatization of goods and services, dismantling of social programs, opening of economies across national borders, and incentives, such as tax breaks, under the guise that these policies encourage the wealthy owners of industries to increase employment. The impact of policies driven by these goals is well documented.[22]

---

[18]Ibid.

[19]Ibid.

[20]Peters, *In Search of the Good Life*, 41.

[21]Grossberg, *Caught in the Crossfire*, 112.

[22]There is no doubt that turbo-capitalism creates wealth. By 2000, fifty-one of the world's largest one hundred economies were corporations, many of them based in the United States. The sales of the top two hundred corporations equaled 27.5 percent of the world's economic activity, but these corporations employed

The Impact of Neoliberalism

Economists measure wealth in two ways, income and net worth as the total value of assets minus total debt. The survey of statistics that follows examines trends in income and wealth in the United States over the last forty years. A higher income allows people to save in order to accumulate and expand wealth. These trends are well-documented by organizations such as the Pew Research Center and the Economic Policy Institute.

When I have spoken in classes or churches on the problem of wealth, I often ask members of the congregation how they think the United States compares to other countries in terms of family income inequality. One of the most common answers is that the United States is similar to Europe. Actually, in comparison with other countries, the United States now ranks forty-fourth in terms of the distribution of family income.[23] Countries with comparable levels of inequality in the distribution of family income are not those most people expect, including Uruguay, Peru, Cameroon, Guyana, and Iran.

Over the last forty years, the lowest-paid US workers experienced a reduction in income and wage stagnation, whereas the highest-paid workers experienced a dramatic increase in income. In his groundbreaking *Capital in the Twenty-First Century*, French economist Thomas Piketty observes, "U.S. inequality in 2010 is quantitatively as extreme as in old Europe in the first decade of the twentieth century, but the structure of that inequality is rather clearly different."[24] A report released by the Economic Policy Institute shows that between 1979 and 2007 average family income grew overall in the U.S. by 36.9 percent. On the surface, that growth appears to be good. But, the lion's share of that growth, 53.9 percent, went to the top 1 percent. Average income among the top 1 percent tripled during that time, a 200.5 percent

---

less than 1 percent of the world's workforce. See John Cavanaugh and Sarah Anderson, "Top 200: The Rise of Corporate Global Power," Institute for Policy Studies, December 4, 2000.

[23] The CIA World Factbook, www.cia.gov.

[24] As quoted by Paul Krugman, "Why We're in a New Gilded Age," *New York Review of Books*, May 8, 2014.

increase whereas for the bottom 99 percent the increase was only 18.9 percent.[25] What is the income level needed to be among the 1 percent? You would have needed to make at least $389,436 annually. The average family in the top 1% had an income in 2013 of $1,153,293 compared to the average income of the 99 percent at $45,567.

The impact of the Great Recession (December 2007–June 2009) was not felt equally by people of all income levels. Statistics show the top 1 percent recovering with an income growth of 38.9 percent between 2009 and 2012. In contrast, the bottom 99 percent actually experienced a decline in their incomes of –0.4 percent. Overall, between 1979 and 2012 the income level of the top 1 percent increased 180.9 percent. The increase for the bottom 99 percent was a mere 2.6 percent.[26]

Paul Krugman attributes the shift to the rise of "super salaries." Compare executive pay to earlier eras. Robert Reich observes, "During the 1950s and '60s, CEOs of major American companies took home about 25 to 30 times the wages of the typical worker. . . . By 2007, just before the Great Recession, CEO pay packages had ballooned to about 350 times what the typical worker earned."[27] To underscore this point he cites that in 2005 "the CEO of Wal-Mart—by then the largest US company—took home 900 times the average worker."[28] CNN reported that average CEO pay was $15.2 million in 2013—296 times the average worker's. Another EPI study showed that between 1978 and 2011, CEO compensation increased 725 percent.[29] Politicians in the United States, unlike lawmakers in other industrialized countries, have completely avoided a serious public discussion about reasonable and tolerable wage differentials. With the election of Donald Trump as US president, this conversation is unlikely to happen anytime in the near future.

---

[25]Mark Price, Estelle Sommeiller, and Dan Essrow, "Lopsided Income Growth in the United States," Economic Policy Institute, www.epi.org.

[26]Ibid.

[27]Richard Wilkinson and Kate Pickett, *The Spirit Level: Why Greater Equality Makes Societies Stronger*, with a Foreword by Robert Reich (New York: Bloomsbury, 2010), x.

[28]Ibid.

[29]Lawrence Mishel, "CEO Pay 231 Times Greater Than the Average Worker," Economic Snapshot: Poverty and Inequality, Economic Policy Institute, May 3, 2012.

According to the Organisation for Economic Co-operation and Development (OECD), the United States has the highest number of workers in low-wage jobs of all the OECD members. Low-wage workers don't fare very well in the United States in comparison to those working in other countries either. In the United States, "Low-wage workers earned just 46.7 percent of that of the median worker—far beneath the OECD average of 59.9 percent in 2012."[30] One in four of all US jobholders are employed in low-wage jobs. Forty percent of US single parents are in low-wage employment, an exceptionally high percentage compared to other groups of workers in the nation. About 80 percent of those single parents working in low-wage jobs are mothers. A larger proportion of women and people of color are paid low wages, poverty-level wages, or minimum wage. African Americans and Hispanics are overrepresented among persons working in low-wage jobs. A far higher percentage of people of color are unemployed when compared to whites.[31]

In December 2015 the Pew Research Center released a report of its analysis of middle-class income data they gathered from the US Census Bureau and the Federal Reserve Board of Governors. They define the term "middle income" in the report as "adults whose annual household income is two-thirds to double the national median, about $42,000 to $126,000 annually in 2014 dollars for a household of three."[32] The middle-class is shrinking and losing ground (see Figure 4.2).

A key factor in this shift that should be named relates to the stagnation of middle-class incomes while the cost of college education has increased in recent decades. In August 2016, *Consumer Reports* published an article titled "Lives on Hold," which tells the stories of traditional-age college students who are overly burdened by college debt. They report that "just about everyone involved in the student loan industry makes money off of the

---

[30]Lawrence Mishel, "The United States Leads in Low-Wage Work and the Lowest Wages for Low-Wage Workers," Working Economics Blog, Economic Policy Institute, September 4, 2014.

[31]According to a Pew Forum report, the "black unemployment rate is consistently twice that of whites." For more information, see www.pewforum.org.

[32]Pew Research Center, "The American Middle Class Is Losing Ground," Pew Social Trends, December 9, 2015.

Figure 4.2. Middle Class Income on the Decline

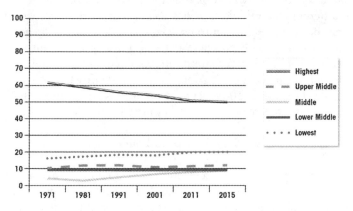

The chart above is based upon 2014 data gathered by the Pew Research Center of a three-person household in each income tier. Tiers are defined as follows: lowest ($31,000 or less), lower middle ($31,000 to $42,000), middle income ($42,000 to $126,000), upper middle ($126,000 to $188,000), and highest (more than $188,000).

students—and the best kind for banks and debt collectors."[33] These circumstances were created by the states' disinvestment in education accompanied by decisions made a generation ago for the federal government to open its student loan bank to for-profit corporations. *Consumer Reports* estimates that there are "about 42 million Americans bearing $1.3 trillion in debt that's altering lives, relationships, and even retirement."[34] About one-fourth of borrowers are in arrears and "an estimated 7.6 million in default."[35] What is even more distressing is the fact that "contractors are expected to make more than $2 billion in commissions from the federal government" in 2016.[36]

This shrinking of the middle class represents a significant change in US identity. The Pew Research Center reports, "After more than four decades of serving as the nation's economic majority, the American middle class is now matched in number by those in the economic tiers above and below it."[37] Alice Evans, Robert Evans,

[33]"Student Debt: Lives on Hold," *Consumer Reports*, August 2016, 29.
[34]Ibid., 30.
[35]Ibid., 33.
[36]Ibid.
[37]Pew Research Center, "American Middle Class Is Losing Ground."

and Bean Kennedy made the powerful observation in their book *Pedagogy for the Non-Poor* that the perception of a huge and undifferentiated middle class has meant that, in the First World, it has been "more difficult to use 'class' as a descriptive category" than in other contexts where extreme poverty is ubiquitous.[38] But that is changing. A Gallup poll conducted in 2015 revealed that only 51 percent of US Americans now identify themselves as middle class, down 10 percent since 2008. Nearly half of all US Americans (48 percent) now say they are working or lower class.[39]

Wealth's Upward Surge

Another way to measure economic inequalities is overall net worth, which includes all assets and real estate holdings minus debt. The shift in wealth that has occurred in the United States since the 1960s is well-documented. According to data from 2010, the estimated net worth of the richest 1 percent of US citizens is 288 times the average or median household's; the top 1 percent own about 50 percent of all wealth.[40] Wealth is even more concentrated than income. The top 1 percent in terms of income take home "just" 20.1 percent.[41] Set in the larger global context, the richest 10 percent own 85 percent of global wealth, with the top 1 percent accounting for 46 percent of global assets. The bottom half of the world's population possesses barely 1 percent of total global wealth.[42]

Significant differences in reductions in wealth resulted from the Great Recession beginning in 2007. In his Foreword to *The Spirit Level: Why Greater Equality Makes Societies Stronger,*

---

[38]Alice Frazer Evans, Robert A. Evans, and William Bean Kennedy, *Pedagogies for the Non-Poor* (Maryknoll, NY: Orbis Books, 1994), 4.

[39]Frank Newport, "Fewer Americans Identify as Middle Class in Recent Years," Gallup, April 28, 2015.

[40]For a fuller summary of data gathered by the Economic Policy Institute, see Elizabeth Hinson-Hasty, "'As Any Might Have Need': Envisioning Communities of Shared Partnership," World Council of Churches, North American Forum and Hearings on Poverty, Wealth, and Ecology, Calgary, Canada, November 2011, www.kairoscanada.org.

[41]See www.epi.org.

[42]Richard Kersley and Michael O'Sullivan, "Global Wealth Reaches New All-Time High," Credit Suisse Research Institute, September 10, 2013, www. credit-suisse.com.

public policy expert Robert Reich wrote, "The Great Recession of 2008–2009 destroyed the value of [people's] homes, undermined their savings, and too often left them without jobs."[43] Sylvia Allegretto, a research economist for the Economic Policy Institute, observes, "From 2007 to 2009, average annualized household declines in wealth were 16% for the richest fifth of Americans and 25% for the remaining four-fifths."[44] A study conducted by the Pew Research Center concluded that "Hispanic families accounted for the largest single decline in wealth of any ethnic and racial group. . . . The median wealth of Hispanic households fell by 66% from 2005 to 2009."[45] In contrast, "The median wealth of whites fell by 16% over the same period." The drop in wealth for African Americans was 53%. Asian Americans experienced a similar decline as their household wealth plummeted by 54%. The median net worth of Hispanic households in 2009 was $6,325. In the same year, black households had a net worth of $5,677 and white households had a median net worth of $113,149. The Pew Research Center further emphasized in their report that median white wealth is 18 to 20 times that of Hispanic and black households.

Shift in Wealth Exacerbated by Tax Cuts for the Wealthiest

The shift in wealth in the United States that has occurred in the last forty years has been exacerbated by huge cuts in the top marginal tax rates for individuals (top rate reduced from 70% to 28%) and on capital gains (top rate reduced from 49% to 20%) that began in the 1980s.[46] Social ethicist Gary Dorrien observes that "these measures had a very large effect on the kind of society the U.S. became, fueling a huge surge in inequality."[47] Similar tax cuts were envisioned and enacted during George H. W. Bush's

---

[43]Wilkinson and Pickett, *Spirit Level*, ix.

[44]Sylvia Allegretto, "The State of Working America's Wealth, 2011," Economic Policy Institute, Briefing Paper #292, www.epi.org.

[45]Rakesh Kochhar, Richard Fry, and Paul Taylor, "Wealth Gaps Rise to Record Highs between Whites, Blacks, Hispanics," Pew Research Center, July 26, 2011.

[46]Gary Dorrien, "Lessons from the Social Gospel: Financial Collapse," *Christian Century*, December 30, 2008, 30.

[47]Ibid.

presidency. Tax breaks ensuring that the rich stay rich include capital gains where long-term capital gains are taxed at a rate of 23.8 percent for the highest-income filers, well below the 39.6 percent maximum for ordinary wages.[48] In 2010 the US Congress extended these tax cuts, while the affordability of reauthorizing unemployment benefits at a cost of $33 billion was hotly debated. Tax breaks for the wealthiest citizens compelled Warren Buffett, an investor who measures his wealth in the billions, to write an op-ed piece for the *New York Times* calling for Washington to "Stop Coddling the Super-Rich." Buffett observes that "while most Americans struggle to make ends meet, we mega-rich continue to get our extraordinary tax breaks."[49] A year before, Buffett joined forces with Bill Gates to take "The Giving Pledge" and called upon the world's wealthiest to give away half of their fortunes. The Tax Policy Center estimates that between 2004 to 2012, "the average tax cut that people making over $1 million received exceeded $110,000" a year.[50]

The Wealthier Have an Increased Ability to Consume

Consumption patterns are directly tied to individual income and wealth and the prosperity of particular nations. It is estimated that people living in North America and western Europe account for "60 percent of private consumption spending"[51] worldwide, but make up only about 12 percent of the world's population. US residents make up 5 percent of the world's population, but account for almost one-fourth of the world's fossil fuel consumption and one-third of the world's paper consumption. In addition, US residents use 27 percent of the aluminum and 19 percent of the copper supply. Since 1970 US food consumption has increased by 16 percent. US restaurants are well-known for supersized portions.

---

[48]See "How Are Capital Gains Taxed?" Tax Policy Center Briefing Book, www. taxpolicycenter.org.

[49]Warren Buffett, "Stop Coddling the Super-Rich," *New York Times*, August 14, 2011.

[50]Chye-Ching Huang and Nathaniel Frentz, "Bush Tax Cuts Have Provided Extremely Large Benefits to Wealthiest Americans over Last Nine Years," Center on Budget and Policy Priorities, July 30, 2012.

[51]Worldwatch Institute, "The State of Consumption Today," www.worldwatch. org.

Less well-known among US residents is that 42 percent of US greenhouse emissions result from the production, consumption, and disposal of food. US affluence also means that the nation has the largest water footprint.[52] The average US family uses approximately 300 gallons of water per day whereas the average family in Africa uses closer to 5 gallons of water per day.[53] According to Dave Tilford of the Sierra Club, "A child born in the U.S. will create thirteen times as much ecological damage over the course of his or her lifetime than a child born in Brazil."[54] In contrast, the regions of South Asia and sub-Saharan Africa are home to one-third of the world's people yet account "for only 3.2 percent of private consumption spending."[55]

Studies have proven that wealth and the ability to consume do not necessarily lead to greater happiness, once income reaches a basic threshold. Richard Wilkinson and Kate Pickett investigate the impact of social hierarchies and privileging one social group over another in their book *The Spirit Level*. They show that societies with greater levels of income equality and that reduce social hierarchies have higher life expectancies, lower obesity rates, less drug abuse and mental illness, and better job performance. Moreover, decreasing wealth inequalities makes societies more generous. The authors argue that "the evidence strongly suggests that narrowing income differences within rich countries will make them more responsive to the needs of poorer countries."[56]

The Market as the Ground of All Being

There are many reasons to be alarmed by the impact of neoliberalism and to respond with a sense of moral indignation at the growing divide in income and wealth in the United States and around the globe. Peace should be the reason placed first on the list. Max Fisher, a former editor for the *Atlantic Monthly*, says

[52]See Christina Peppard, *Just Water: Theology, Ethics, and the Global Water Crisis* (Maryknoll, NY: Orbis Books, 2014), 22.

[53]See US Environmental Protection Agency, "Water Use Today," www3.epa.gov, and statistics available on Water.org.

[54]"Use It and Lose It: The Outsize Effect of U.S. Consumption on the Environment," *Scientific American*, September 14, 2012.

[55]Worldwatch Institute, "State of Consumption Today."

[56]Wilkinson and Pickett, *Spirit Level*, 235.

the level of income inequality in the United States is "on par with some of the world's most troubled countries and perpetual conflict zones of Latin America and Sub-Saharan Africa."[57]

Another significant cause for concern is the privilege that money *can* buy. According to Wilkinson and Pickett, the problems for wealthy countries like the United States are not "caused by the society not being rich enough (or even by being too rich) but by the scale of material differences between each society being too big. What matters is where we stand in relation to others in our own society."[58] Social hierarchies create social anxieties and the fragmentation of communities, which in turn lead to problems such as unequal educational opportunities and reduced performance levels for all, not just in lower-income families, and health disparities and reduced life expectancy for all, not just people living in poverty. Moreover, inequality damages individuals and communities on all levels of the social hierarchy, from the richest to the poorest. In societies where values are centered on the individual acquisition of material possessions, fame, and social status, people place themselves at greater risk of depression, anxiety and personality disorders, and substance abuse. Communities engender lower levels of generosity and trust as well as weaker connections.[59]

Another cause for concern is theological. A distinctive feature of neoliberalism and the economy that it has shaped in the United States is that the market itself is understood to transcend human control, tied to a conservative sense of religious faith and morality, and expresses the will of the divine. Lawrence Grossberg, a professor at the University of North Carolina at Chapel Hill, observes that neoliberal economic doctrine is informed by its own "metaphysics" or understanding of that which is the ground of all being. Grossberg cites arguments made by George Gilder, one of the architects of Ronald Reagan's supply-side economics and a Senior Fellow of the Discovery Institute. Gilder claims that capitalism is a moral good and argues that the most productive element of the economy "is 'the metaphysical component . . . hu-

---

[57]Max Fisher, "Map: US Ranks Near Bottom on Income Inequality," *Atlantic Monthly*, September 19, 2011.
[58]Wilkinson and Pickett, *Spirit Level*, 25.
[59]Ibid., 69–70.

man creativity in conditions of freedom."[60] According to Gilder, altruism is the capitalists' ultimate goal. What capitalists aim to do is to foster opportunity, particularly for the underclasses. "Wages and salaries are philanthropy, trickled down from above."[61] Gilder has been quoted as saying that entrepreneurs more than any other people "embody and fulfill the sweet and mysterious consolations of the Sermon on the Mount."

It is quite striking to hear in Gilder's statements the way in which capitalism is associated with altruism and charity and equated with Christian ideals, even the Sermon on the Mount, a central text in Christian social ethics. There is no recognition in Gilder's conflation of capitalism with Christianity of the value of workers and the fact that even those dependent upon wages to sustain their livelihoods are in themselves creative beings and contribute their own imagination and labors to production. Grossberg observes that neoliberalism has created an economy in which the moral and economic status of workers is no longer seen as significant or valued.

Gilder is not the only one to equate capitalism with Christian ideals and apply theological concepts to businesses, industry, and the free market (see Figure 4.3). An early example is found in *The Man That Nobody Knows* written by advertising executive Bruce Barton and published in 1925. Barton depicted Jesus as the "founder of modern business." More recently, Laurie Beth Jones, author of *Jesus CEO*, a book first published in the mid-1990s during an economic boom, applied what she called Jesus's divine leadership style to corporate management in an effort to turn the tide of leadership problems she identified in US corporations. Among those problems she sought to address, she aimed to help "homeless" employees within the corporation find ways for their own leadership and intelligence to be "tapped" and "utilized" for the common corporate good. Jones observed that Jesus was a master at working with his "board" of twelve disciples. Jesus exemplified—incarnated—the true model for contemporary corporate motivational leadership.

---

[60]Grossberg, *Caught in the Crossfire*, 116.
[61]Ibid.

Figure 4.3. The Cathedral of Commerce

This display stands prominently in the foyer of HSBC in Hong Kong's city center. Photo by Elizabeth Hinson-Hasty.

Kenneth Lay, former CEO of Enron, made some equally note-worthy comparisons between Christianity and capitalism when he compared his understanding of the free market with freedom known in God and found in Christ. Lay confessed, "I believe in God and I believe in free markets. Certainly Jesus attempted to take care for the people around him, attempted to make their lives better, [but] he was also a freedom lover. The freer the country in terms of its market and political system, the higher the standard of living."[62] Steven Forbes attributed salvific force to the market in the wake of the Great Recession of 2008 as he claimed, "Free market capitalism will save us—if we let it."[63]

Neoliberalism becomes in this worldview not only a vision for

---

[62]Kenneth Lay, "The Son of a Baptist Minister," *San Diego Union Tribune*, February 2, 2001.

[63]Steven Forbes, "How Capitalism Will Save Us," *Forbes*, October 23, 2008.

the nation's economy, corporations, organizations, and institutions, but also an eschatological vision for the new earth. Time is fulfilled through the creation of wealth, unlimited growth, and technological progress. Families persistently in poverty or people who are deemed inefficient because of disabilities or caregiving responsibilities are often identified as anomalies with personal moral failings. Sometimes poverty is even associated with moral failure or sin. Robert Rector and Rachel Sheffield, two researchers for the Heritage Foundation, suggest that "among families with children, the collapse of marriage and erosion of the work ethic are the principal long-term causes of poverty."[64]

The Power of Naming

When I began serving as a research consultant for the World Council of Churches' PWE project, a number of religious organizations and churches asked me to give lectures and other presentations on my research. After one of the presentations, a participant and friend forthrightly challenged me: "Elizabeth, Neoliberalism doesn't preach!" I think he meant that people in the pews of churches often don't have ears to hear the diagnosis that the root cause of poverty and environmental destruction is the way we create wealth or eyes to see the strong bond between neoliberal capitalism and some interpretations of US Christian faith.

On one level, the explanation is too complex and overwhelming, which leads people to feel a sense of paralysis when considering how to respond. It is vitally important to remember that arguing to begin the discussion by taking the position that the problem is *the way we create wealth and for whom we create it* does not mean that one isn't concerned about the circumstances and problems that people living in poverty face. Rather, it situates the conversation in the experience of people who are poor, who have the least privilege, and whose voices often remain unheard in current debates. There are deep theological reasons to clearly name the root cause of the problem as the problem of wealth. In the Hebrew Bible, the act of naming brings with it the power to fully know,

---

[64]Robert Rector and Rachel Sheffield, "Understanding Poverty in the United States: Surprising Facts about America's Poor," Heritage Foundation, September 13, 2011, www.heritage.org.

understand, and control. Only one being cannot be named and therefore fully understood by human beings: God alone.

Recall the story of Sarah and Hagar. Hagar, a slave, brings the ultimate challenge to the economy of the patriarchal household. Sarah held the privilege and the power within the confines of the patriarchal family structure as the wife of Abraham, a wealthy herdsman; she was also barren. At the time, Sarah's barrenness was both a self-esteem issue and an economic one. If Sarah had no son, then who would be Abraham's rightful heir? Who would inherit his fortune? What if something happened to Abraham? Who would secure Sarah's future? In what likely would have been an acceptable way according to the dominant logic of her time, Sarah took the situation into her own hands and uses her slave, Hagar, as a form of insurance to secure her family's well-being.

Biblical scholar Phyllis Trible analyzes and interprets the story of Sarah and Hagar in *Texts of Terror*. Hagar's reality as it is told in the story is the ultimate contrast to that of Sarah's. Hagar has the least social clout and privilege. Sarah is the wife of a wealthy herdsman, so therefore powerful and with a lot of social clout. Hagar is young; Sarah is old. Most important, Hagar is fertile; Sarah is barren. Hagar's resources of power, privilege, and fertility are undermined at every turn in the story. Hagar, the one without privilege, has the potential at least early on in the story to build her power and her authority in a patriarchal economy by giving birth to a son. Remember that after Hagar becomes pregnant, Sarah mistreats her. Hagar flees. In the scene announcing the birth of Hagar's son, an angel of the Holy One appears to her and asks where she is going. The angel tells Hagar to name her son Ishmael, which in Hebrew means "God hears." An intriguing aspect to this part of the story is that Hagar calls the name of God. It isn't her son and the continuation of the family line that bring Hagar freedom. Hagar dares to name the deity and by doing so she brings the ultimate challenge to the economy of the patriarchal household. She cries out, "You are the God who sees me. . . . I have now seen the One who sees me." Hagar doesn't allow herself to be used merely as an instrument of creating wealth for someone else, but she names God's disruptive presence in the midst of challenging the patriarchal economy. Naming the root cause of poverty, wealth inequalities, and ecological destruction calls us out in faith to challenge the abysmal outcomes of our current political economy, particularly for those who are most vulnerable and least valued by markets.

On another level, clearly naming the root cause of poverty and wealth inequalities will be frightening for many US Christians because it calls into question how we in the United States have defined and understood our identities as citizens and people of faith. Social developmentalism, neoliberalism, and the moral philosophies informing these approaches to wealth creation falsely lead us to believe that individualism and the pursuit of human self-interest for the sake of unlimited growth, progress, and prosperity will enable authentic community to flourish. Christianity in the United States has a tendency to become so absorbed into market society that at times there appears to be no distinction between Christian logic and market-based logic. How many Christians do you know who identify material wealth with God's blessing?

The prosperity gospel evidences just how deeply entrenched capitalist ideology is in the United States. You may be familiar with the preaching of televangelist Joel Osteen, senior pastor of Lakewood Baptist Church, the largest megachurch in the United States, with a membership of forty-five thousand people. Numerous videos of Osteen's sermons are available online. Central to his preaching is the association of God's blessing with monetary wealth, physical well-being, and good fortune. In an interview by Mark Lamont Hill with Joel and Victoria Osteen for HuffPost Live, he resisted the idea that he was a "prosperity minister" because "prosperity to me is being blessed so you can be a blessing." Historian Daisy Machado asserts that a critical connection must be made between the prosperity gospel evident in Osteen's preaching and the "exceptionalism" of the early English settlers who believed that their mission was to create a " 'city on a hill,' a nation chosen to be divinely blessed so it could be a blessing to other nations."[65] When Osteen was asked whether God wants people to be rich he said, "I don't think God has any problem with us being blessed."[66] The association of God's blessing with material wealth undergirds capitalism as we know it and obscures the ability of many Christians in the United States to see their relatedness

---

[65]Daisy L. Machado, "Capitalism, Immigration, and the Prosperity Gospel," *Anglican Theological Review* 92, no. 4 (Fall 2010): 724.

[66]Mark Lamont Hill, interview with Joel and Victoria Osteen, HuffPost Live, June 2, 2014.

to a larger global community as well as fully comprehend biblical notions of love and justice. In the Hebrew Bible, blessing is not associated with financial wealth, but with the commons, covenant, and life in community. Theologian M. Douglas Meeks writes, "The more the market logic threatens to become the church's way of organizing its life, the more the economy of the church is defined by the prevailing economy of our society and the more market rules determine what we mean by justice."[67]

The term *conversion* comes from a Latin root *conversio*, which literally means "to turn around." In the Christian scriptures, conversion (in Greek, *metanoia*) is an act of "turning away from dead works" and toward new visions of community. To turn around not only this debate but the practices that lead to the destruction of other people and the planet means taking a turn toward the commons—the common space and theater of God's grace that people and the whole planet share. The commons is the very basis of life and theologically emanates from God.

Cultivating consciousness of the commons is not an easy task. The odds are stacked against us. One of the ways that people living in Appalachian Kentucky used to provide for their own livelihoods was by digging for roots—sassafras, ginseng, wild yam, yellow root, golden seal, blood root. Folk remedies include roots as key ingredients for teas and tonics to treat fevers, cancer, asthma, alcohol addiction, and so on by aiding the body in eliminating harmful toxins. Searching for the best roots takes a great deal of time, energy, intuition, and expertise about the abundance of life that teems beneath the tree canopy shading the forest bed. In the next two chapters, I invite you to go digging for roots within a variety of religious traditions for images of God and community that can help cultivate a new consciousness of the relationship of the self to the commons and nurture and sustain visions for alternative forms of political economy. Theological reflection has the potential to offer an extensive root system to support and nourish social and moral imagination when it challenges people of faith to imitate God's resistance to oppressive economic systems and structures, to transcend self-interest, and to see themselves lively in interdependence as part of the commons.

---

[67]M. Douglas Meeks, *God the Economist: The Doctrine of God and Political Economy* (Minneapolis: Fortress, 1989), 37.

Part III

DIGGING FOR ROOTS
TO NOURISH AN ETHIC
OF ENOUGH

CHAPTER 5

Social Trinity, Love, and the Ethic of Enough

Christianity means the release of love into human life.
It can never be satisfied till love governs institutions and
governments as it governs persons.
                                        —*Vida Dutton Scudder*[1]

The Trinity is a uniquely Christian symbol that inspires followers of Jesus to ground and steady themselves, and act in and out
of the abundant overflowing love of God. Wealth and freedom in
the Three-in-One are not defined relative to money or financial
prosperity and growth, but by the nature of community and the
free and equal exchange of love. As a feminist theological ethicist I
look to the *Social Trinity* as a key concept to enable US Christians
to transform our society's individualistic anthropological assumptions, to challenge false theologies that center on individual salvation in an otherworldly context, and to create the consciousness
and call to resist the market idolatry of our culture. As a metaphor
for God, the Social Trinity conveys God's inherently relational
nature. God's own relational ecology is a useful metaphor and
norm for human relationships that resist hyperindividualism and
hypercompetition.

I am not the first theologian to suggest the potential for the
Social Trinity concept to deepen our understanding of the essence
of relatedness in God and to enable Christians to reenvision the

---

[1]Vida Dutton Scudder, "Christianity: Conservative or Revolutionary?" *The
World Tomorrow* 7 (August 1924): 244.

shape of social, economic, and political systems and structures. The hierarchical nature of the immanent doctrine of the Trinity remained uncontested for much of its history in the Western Christian church, but in the twentieth century, theologians began to explore intentionally the implications of a Social Trinity as a concept that directly confronts social hierarchies and wealth inequalities. I was first drawn to a social concept of Trinity by Vida Dutton Scudder, a leader of the twentieth-century Social Gospel movement in the Episcopal Church.

Scudder was not academically trained as a theologian. She taught as an English professor at Wellesley College and played a key role in shaping the curriculum there as the school transitioned from a "female seminary" toward an institution that would educate women to be agents of social change. Creating authentic community was Scudder's passion through her work within the church, the academy, and her society. Scudder was active in and led many organizations praying and working for economic justice, including the Society of Companions of the Holy Cross and the College Settlements Association. Scudder thought that one would never be misguided by reflecting upon and considering the profound social significance of doctrines used for centuries to guard and preserve the image of Jesus. Christian thought, she argued, struggled to express in the doctrine of the Trinity the "superb perception that love was eternal, and belonged in its origin, not to the contingent, the transitory, but to the essence of Infinite being."[2]

Praying the Trinity opened Christians up to the devotion and personality of Jesus, whose actions always pointed beyond self-interest. Jesus embodied love as he confronted the inequalities of wealth that provided the scaffolding to uphold the Roman Empire. For Scudder, a Social Trinity inspired collaboration, cooperation, and love and became the metaphor and model for a society based on equality and love. The Social Trinity provided the basis for her social ethic, commitments to democratic socialism, and her emphasis on class consciousness. In turn, she believed that movements toward class consciousness raised awareness of a deeper sacramental unity of the common life. The concept of the Three-in-

---

[2]Vida Dutton Scudder, *Socialism and Character* (Boston: Houghton Mifflin, 1912), 352.

One symbolized God's abiding in "fellowship; not in self-seeking, but in a giving of self to the uttermost; not in personality shut in upon itself, but in an equal interchange of love attaining the highest unity which only differentiation can produce."[3] She argued for the founding of a cooperative commonwealth that would embody the best principles of democracy and divine society.

Significant work on the Social Trinity has been done more recently by an ecumenically diverse group of thinkers including Leonardo Boff, Elizabeth Johnson, Nico Koopman, Catherine Mowry LaCugna, Sallie McFague, M. Douglas Meeks, Jürgen Moltmann, Jerry Pillay, Letty Russell, Miroslav Volf, and Patricia Wilson-Kastner.[4] The Trinity for these theologians is the social thought of God. Brazilian liberationist theologian Leonardo Boff asserts that "as long as the present social inequalities remain, faith in the Trinity will mean criticism of all injustices and a source of inspiration for basic changes."[5] The Social Trinity situates God's "economy" of salvation within time and shapes an understanding of self-in-community that disrupts the logic informing the dominant approaches to wealth creation in US society and around the world.

In the Trinity, the good of and for individual persons is never at odds with the good of and for the whole. God's very nature resists being reduced to quantification, and wealth is never measured by unlimited growth for one at the expense of a larger community. God's freedom is not defined in terms of individual choice, but always social and discovered in love. According to divine logic, One plus One plus One equals One alone, never three. God un-

---

[3]Ibid.

[4]Significant works include Letty Russell, *The Future of Partnership* (Philadelphia: Westminster, 1979); Patricia Wilson-Kastner, *Faith, Feminism, and the Christ* (Philadelphia: Fortress, 1983); Sallie McFague, *Models of God* (Philadelphia: Fortress, 1987); Leonardo Boff, *Holy Trinity, Perfect Community* (Maryknoll, NY: Orbis, 2000), which is an English translation of *Santíssima Trindade é a melhor communidade* (1988); Catherine Mowry LaCugna, *God for Us: The Trinity and Christian Life* (San Francisco: HarperSanFrancisco, 1991; reprint of 1973 edition); Jürgen Moltmann, *The Trinity and the Kingdom* (Minneapolis: Fortress, 1993); M. Douglas Meeks, *Trinity, Community, and Power: Mapping Trajectories in Wesleyan Theology* (Nashville: Abingdon, 2000); and Elizabeth Johnson, *Quest for the Living God: Mapping Frontiers in the Theology of God* (New York: Continuum, 2007).

[5]Leonardo Boff, *Trinity and Society* (Eugene, OR: Wipf & Stock, 1988), 13.

derstood as three interrelated, interdependent, yet distinct persons is a uniquely Christian description of God's challenge to the fragmentation of communities created by the dominant forms of wealth creation defining the market in our contemporary world. God doesn't just desire or envision communities of sharing; God's very essence is sharing in partnership. To be drawn to God is to be drawn into and transformed by love for others.

The concept of the Social Trinity serves as a means for retrieving a vision of a just economy as revealed in the scriptures, the life of Jesus, and many of the traditions and rituals of Christian communities. In this chapter, I invite you to think about the Trinity as a metaphor for God worthy of human imitation and an image of God's "oikosystem." The Three-in-One confronts us with the reality that our existence as human beings is continuous with nature. As beings created in the image of God, we become conscious of God's interdependence with the community of living organisms working together within an abundant web of life. The Social Trinity calls us to live together in love, disrupts our conscience regarding the outcomes of the current shape of political economy for people and the planet, and invites us to reimagine just economic policies and social relationships.

For some theologians, ethicists, and religious leaders, love appears at first to be an overly sentimental concept incapable of informing proposals for just economic systems and policies. Scudder made the observation early in the twentieth century that "religion contemplates civilization as it were from behind the scenes. . . . This world is seen from the point of view, no longer of time but of eternity."[6] Eternity, Scudder thought, was "a corollary from the perception of a quality in mortal deeds that lifts them out of the category of time."[7] She had in mind deeds that transcended self-interest for the sake of the commons. Love, in the context of a larger Christian theological conversation about the problem of wealth, is a radically countercultural norm and must be carefully defined in terms of *hesed*, *caritas*, and *agape*. Love is intimately and inextricably linked to justice in the biblical story. Human loves in the biblical narrative are intertwined with and transformed by

---

[6]Scudder, *Socialism and Character*, 106.
[7]Ibid.

God's fierce, loyal, and disruptive love. What is missing in our field of vision regarding the current dominant forms of wealth creation is the love that is strong enough to counter our tendency to reduce the commons—God's oikosystem—merely to a resource for the fulfillment of privatized human ends.

Firmly Situating the Economy of God's Salvation in Time

Catherine Mowry LaCugna argues in *God for Us: The Trinity and Christian Life* that one of the great theological and political mistakes in Western history was for the Christian church to affirm and adopt a doctrine of the Trinity that essentially became a description of hierarchically ordered relations in God's inner life. I won't rehearse all of LaCugna's detailed historical study of the debates that led up to the adoption of an immanent Trinity, but I do want to highlight her observation that the doctrine of the Trinity of the Western church created a gap between *theologia* (the mystery of God) and *oikonomia* (God's providence, dispensation, and ordering). We have to look to the Council of Nicea (325 CE) called together by Emperor Constantine after his conversion to the Christian faith to understand the way in which the doctrine of the Trinity ultimately came to be understood as a concept focused on an intradivine discussion that created a divide between God's economy of salvation in eternity, that which is to come, and in time, the here and now. Constantine hoped that the council would define the authoritative understanding of the Trinity for those who served a church that was under the emperor's authority in alliance with the Roman Empire.

Fourth-century debates about Christology and Trinity were largely spurred in response to the theology of Arius. Arius believed that the biblical narrative revealed Jesus to be a lesser god. He argued, "We say and believe, and have taught, and do teach, that the Son is not unbegotten, nor in any way part of the unbegotten. . . . We are persecuted, because we say that the Son has a beginning, but that God is without beginning."[8] Theologians from the Greek East and the Latin West found Arius's position intolerable

---

[8]William C. Placher, *Readings in the History of Christian Theology*, Volume 1, *From Its Beginnings to the Eve of the Reformation* (Louisville, KY: Westminster/ John Knox Press, 1988), 52.

because, in their understanding, it jeopardized salvation in Christ, a salvation that they understood to be in eternity. The Council of Nicea arrived at the conclusion that Jesus is *homoousios*, "of the same substance," with God. Their conclusions continue to be ensconced in the doctrine of the Nicene Creed, the most ecumenical Christian creed affirmed by Roman Catholic, Orthodox, and Protestant churches. You will likely be familiar with the description of Jesus's relationship with God in the Trinitarian formula defined in the Nicene Creed: "I believe in . . . one Lord Jesus Christ, the only-begotten Son of God, begotten of the Father before all worlds; God of God, Light of Light, very God of very God; begotten, not made, being of one substance with the Father, by whom all things were made. . . ." The Council of Nicea by no means fully settled debates about the meaning and nature of the Trinity or the Western churches' understanding of Christ. One hundred and twenty-six years after the Council of Nicea, Constantine's successor Emperor Marcian brought together a new council at Chalcedon (451), which rendered what came to be known as the Chalcedonian definition of Christ or the two natures' theory of Jesus—as fully human and fully divine.

Conclusions drawn at the Council of Nicea and expressed in the words of the Nicene Creed became a distinctive trajectory in Christian thought that LaCugna argued became overly focused on the Trinity as an intradivine discussion. Accentuating otherworldly salvation served to uphold the privilege and power of the wealthy in an empire where the vast majority of people lived in poverty. LaCugna observed that, over time, many clichés surrounded "the doctrine of the Trinity, for example, Thomas Aquinas has a static idea of God; that Anselm thought he could prove the doctrine of the Trinity; that Latin theology on the whole is ultrarationalistic; that Orthodox theology on the whole is philosophically naïve; that the doctrine of the Trinity is itself a mystery."[9] The doctrine of the Trinity, she suggested, became irrelevant to our common life. Contemporary Christians in the Global North still today continue to confess the concept in theory, but we neglect the profound practical implications of Trinitarian thought for our daily lives.

LaCugna argues that soteriology and theology, *oikonomia*

---

[9]LaCugna, *God for Us: The Trinity and Christian Life*, 11.

and *theologia*, belong together as "two aspects of the one self-communication of God. God comes to us through Jesus Christ in the power and presence of the Holy Spirit, which suggests that God exists in differentiated personhood."[10] She finds firm footing in a revolutionary claim made by the Cappadocians and asserts that "person, not substance, is the ultimate ontological category."[11] In her words, "To say that person rather than substance is the cause and origin of everything that exists means that the ultimate sower of all reality is not a 'by-itself' or an 'in-itself' but a person, a toward-another."[12]

Theologian Elizabeth Johnson argues along similar lines. For the last one thousand years in the West, Johnson asserts that an authentic interpretation of the doctrine of the Trinity "has been neglected, literalized, treated like a curiosity, or analyzed with conceptual acrobatics entirely inappropriate to its meaning."[13] The Social Trinity is a symbol of what the community of faith takes to be the highest good—love in fellowship and not in self-seeking. Johnson retrieves an earlier understanding of the original Greek term *hypostasis* used in the Nicene Creed. She says that, in the original Greek, *hypostasis* did not "connote 'person' as we mean it today, a social being with a distinct center of consciousness and freedom, but something in philosophy to a distinct manner of subsistence."[14] The first task to retrieve the meaning of the symbol is by reclaiming "the groundedness of the Trinity in the experience of salvation coming from God in Jesus through the power of the Spirit."[15] Trinitarian language points to a God known and experienced in the fullness of mutuality and relationship. The key to our contemporary understanding must be found in Jesus's preaching about the reign of God. In Luke's Gospel, Jesus says, "The Spirit of the Lord is upon me, because the Lord has anointed me. He has sent me to preach good news to the poor, to proclaim release to the prisoners and recovery of sight to the

---

[10]Ibid., 13.

[11]Ibid., 14.

[12]Ibid.

[13]Elizabeth Johnson, "Trinity: To Let the Symbol Sing Again," *Theology Today* 54, no. 3 (October 1997): 301.

[14]Ibid., 304.

[15]Ibid., 303.

blind, to liberate the oppressed, and to proclaim the year of the
Lord's favor" (4:18–19). God's reign to which Jesus refers in this
passage is not one of competitive, dominating power, but rather
a noncoercive reign of love, mutuality, and inclusion. The earliest
followers of Jesus experienced God as "beyond them, with them,
and within them."[16] In this way, the Social Trinity draws people
of faith into a holy mystery and experience of God's salvation in
the midst of our time.

While there are no direct references to the Trinity in the Christian scriptures, the biblical narrative suggests an awareness of
God's nature in community. Contemporary biblical scholarship is
recovering a strong biblical grounding for a symbol of God that
conveys social and ecological solidarity. One example is found in
the work of David Horrell, Cheryl Hunt, and Christopher Southgate as they interpret Paul's writings from an ecotheological perspective. Horrell, Hunt, and Southgate suggest that "every creature,
human and other, is on the way to salvation; every creature has a
part, actual or proleptic, in the community of Christ's redemptive
purpose."[17] The great hymn in Colossians reflects Paul's deep sense
of *koinonia* and understanding of God's nature in community:

> The Son is the image of the invisible God,
>   the one who is first over all creation,
> Because all things were created by him:
>   both in the heavens and on the earth,
>   the things that are visible and the things that are
>   invisible.
> Whether they are thrones or powers,
>   or rulers or authorities,
>   all things were created through him and for him, . . .
> Because all the fullness of God was pleased to live in him,
>   and he reconciled all things to himself in him,
>   Whether things on *earth* or in the heavens.
>   (Col. 1:15–17, 19–20, emphasis added)

[16]Ibid.

[17]David Horrell, Cheryl Hunt, and Christopher Southgate, *Greening Paul:
Rereading Paul in a Time of Ecological Crisis* (Waco, TX: Baylor University Press,
2010), 210.

Emphasizing the importance of the mutually beneficial relationship of the three persons has invited some criticism. Social Trinitarians avoid the charge of modalism or tritheism by describing the unity of persons within the Trinity as *perichoresis*, a Greek word meaning "rotation." Orthodox theologian John Zizioulas draws upon the writings of early church thinkers and suggests that the substance of God "*possesses almost by definition a relational character.*"[18] Feminist theologians such as LaCugna reclaim *perichoresis* and its language of mutuality as a model that human beings can imitate. God's relationship with the world is not focused on God's action or agency upon people and the planet, but emphasizes the radical nature of God's immanence and the mutually beneficial sharing of resources within and for the sustenance of the whole. The statue of the Buddha Christ that you see below welcomes visitors to a Franciscan Ashram located in Karukutty, Kerala, that I have visited on two occasions. Buddha Christ comfortably rests on a lotus flower within and among the Trinitarian symbol. The statue here offers an excellent visual representation of God's oikosystem.

Figure 5.1. The Buddha Christ

This Buddha Christ statue comfortably sits on three rings symbolizing the Trinity and welcomes visitors to Assisi Shanthi Kendra (Assisi Peace Center) in Karukutty, Kerala, India. Photo by Leslie Scanlon. Used with permission.

---

[18]John Zizioulas, *Being as Communion: Studies in Personhood and the Church* (Crestwood, NY: St. Vladimir's Seminary Press, 2002), 84.

Most of my observations about the Social Trinity up to this point have been highly abstract. Let me offer an example that illustrates where I have seen this idea of the ultimate sower of all reality as "a toward-another" embodied in the lives of ordinary people. From 2002 to 2004 I taught at St. Andrews Presbyterian College, a small college located in the town of Laurinburg, North Carolina. Laurinburg is about an hour and a half from the Atlantic coast and was once the site of many textile factories and a more vibrant community. The town has been hit hard by outsourcing and closures of small factories, like so many other rural towns in the southeastern United States. One of the reasons St. Andrews was founded in Laurinburg is that the terrain is flat. In 1958, when St. Andrews was founded, the vision for the school was to create a fully inclusive community and an accessible institution where people with disabilities and able-bodied students could learn to work together and earn a college degree.

Disability has always been both a cause and consequence of poverty. A recent study done by the Center for Economic and Policy Research found that people with disabilities frequently confront job loss, reduced earnings, barriers to education, lack of access to adequate health insurance, and economic deprivation. There is little surprise then in their discovery that "the income poverty rate for persons with disabilities is two to three times the rate for persons without disabilities."[19] St. Andrews was ahead of its time when it established an institution and a curriculum with the mission of educating able-bodied students alongside students with disabilities. The college was not only breaking down social barriers, but it was also addressing inequalities in wealth by envisioning a new life together in a community where people shared care and concern, came together as equals, and worked together to ensure their livelihoods.

One of the classes that I taught there on spirituality included a retreat held at a nearby small Presbyterian camp called Camp Monroe. The camp had several ropes courses to challenge retreatants to face obstacles and work together. Ropes courses, if you have never seen one or challenged yourself to take one on, are

---

[19]Shawn Fremstad, "Half in Ten: Why Taking Disability into Account Is Essential to Reducing Income Poverty and Expanding Economic Inclusion," Center for Economic and Policy Research, September 2009, 1, cepr.net.

often built in wooded areas of camps and can be constructed either high in the trees or low to the ground. Central to the underlying philosophy is pushing people to move out of their comfort zones and building resilience as they immerse themselves in nature and confront a variety of human-made obstacles. Both able-bodied and "wheelies" (the term students at St. Andrews affectionately used for themselves or their peers with physical disabilities) participated in the ropes courses on the retreat that semester.

The students began the challenge by determining that they would work together to complete both the high and low ropes courses. As you might expect, there were many times that the able-bodied students assisted their peers with physical disabilities as they traversed low and high ropes challenges or helped push chairs to get them across obstacles. Near the end of the course, however, just as everyone was getting tired, one of the students named Willie wheeled his chair up to an obstacle and invited two or three able-bodied students to pile on. His friend, Kevin, did the same. Willie and Kevin wheeled the able-bodied students through the remaining segment of the challenge course. All of the students were surprised by how they responded to the context of their new surroundings. When the students faced the challenges, they entered into a sort of dance; learning how to work together, collaborating to find a way through. Everyone was involved, and as a result, a household of equal partners emerged. Everyone was valued according to what they contributed as anyone might have needed help on that day. The Social Trinity as a metaphor for God and model for daily life suggests a way of ordering social, economic, and political systems and structures in forms appropriate to what LaCugna calls "the mystery of persons in communion." She writes, the "reign of God (in three persons) is the rule of the new household (oikos) providentially intended by God to become the dwelling place of all creatures."[20]

From *Oikonomia* to Oikosystem

LaCugna's theological propositions resonate with the best aspects of the ancient Greek understanding of *oikonomia*. In chapter

---

[20]LaCugna, *God for Us.*, 16.

2 I discussed the concept of *oikos* as the etymological root of the English words economy, ecology, and ecumenism. It is worth revisiting that discussion at this point to expand our understanding of the Greek notion of *oikonomia* that Christian theologians have drawn upon to refer to events within God's economy of salvation.

Oikonomia is composed of two Greek words: *oikos*, meaning household, and *nemein*, meaning management and dispensation. The term first appeared in a poem by Phocilides in the sixth century BCE and was used specifically in reference to the work of women. *Oikonomos*, in the context of Phocilides's poem, is usually translated as "steward," suggesting that all members of the household must be active participants in managing resources in order for the household to be sustained. People in the ancient Greek-speaking world believed that abundance was an attribute of nature. There would have been no assumption of the possibility of scarcity that informs neoclassical economics and the idea of economics as allocating scarce resources. Good stewards within the household economized resources rationally when their actions were taken toward a praiseworthy end. Political scientist Dotan Leshem points out that "the ancient philosophers had a distinct view of what constituted such an end—specifically, acting as a philosopher or as an active participant in the life of the city-state."[21] Nature had great potential to satisfy much more than everyone's needs, if and when economized rationally.

Considering one's moral and ethical role in a household economy is an ancient idea worth reclaiming. However, certain assumptions are embedded within the ancient Greek ordering of the household that should have been jettisoned long ago. Ancient Greek concepts of *oikonomia* assumed the authority of well-to-do, land-owning male citizens and included the uncritical acceptance of slavery. Women and slaves were seen as less than fully human. Much of the presumed surplus of the ancient Greek "ethical" economy was "generated by slave labor and the denial of citizen rights to women."[22]

There is ample evidence within the biblical narrative of the ways in which early followers of Jesus challenged the patriarchal

---

[21]Dotan Leshem, "Retrospectives: What Did the Ancient Greeks Mean by Oikonomia?" *Journal of Economic Perspectives* 30, no. 1 (Winter 2016): 226.
[22]Ibid., 235.

ordering of economy in the ancient Greco-Roman household. Rational ordering and management of the household among early followers of Jesus emerged from the experience and reality of the impoverished majority, which meant developing a sort of comprehensive program to redistribute wealth because anyone might at some point have needs. For example, one of my favorite stories about Jesus is found in the Gospel of Mark, in which he defends a woman using expensive perfume to anoint him as he visits the house of Simon the leper in Bethany. We don't know much about the woman from the story. I speculate that the woman did not have great financial means. There are some other people (also unnamed in the story), but who I suggest hold greater social and economic clout. They scoff at her behavior. "Why waste this perfume? It could have been sold for more than a year's pay. The money could have been given to poor people" (Mark 14:4–5). Perfume—in this case, a fragrance made from expensive nard—would have been considered appropriate only for the wealthy. Jesus confronts the dominant social assumptions about those who should have access to the best resources within the household. Jesus asks, "Why do you make trouble for her? She has done a good thing for me. You always have the poor with you; and whenever you want, you can do something good for them. But you won't always have me. She has done what she could. She has anointed my body ahead of time for burial. I tell you the truth that, wherever in the whole world the good news is announced, what she's done will also be told in memory of her" (Mark 14:8–9). He alludes to people in poverty as those who anticipate resurrection in God's economy of salvation.

Our twenty-first-century economy still bears a few similarities to that of the ancient Greek-speaking world where the gospel was first preached and the doctrine of the Trinity defined. But there are also crucial differences that cannot be overlooked. Christian theologians have long been aware of the importance of the biblical witness to provide insight from the experience of people living in poverty and the impact of wealth inequalities on social realities. Today, however, we are becoming increasingly aware of the tremendous importance of expanding our definition of members of the household. Michael Hogue, professor of theology at Meadville Lombard Theological School, asserts that the "radical extension of human power significantly differentiates the 'moral space' of this time from other historical periods. We have crossed a moral threshold from the inevitable fact of limited human incursion into nature to the possibility of nature's present and future total alteration."[23] People in the ancient world could not have envisioned the tremendous power of human technologies to use natural resources to fulfill our own needs and desires. God's household is composed of a much larger web of life. Human persons are wreaking such havoc on nonhuman nature that the costs of our actions are yet to be fully calculated.

We have to find new ways, including new language and terminology, to help us understand what it means for human and nonhuman nature to be created in the image of God and the essential relatedness of all God's household. Therefore, I want to suggest an alternative way of describing the significance of the Social Trinity as an image of God's oikosystem. Theologians have used the term *economic* to emphasize God's activity in the "economy of salvation," the building of the kingdom of God or reign of God on earth. Recent discussions of social concepts of the Trinity continue to use the term *economic* in reference to God's life and work in the here and now, in contrast to the immanent concept of the Trinity. There is a problem that must be faced with use of this term, particularly in the US context. The impact of economism upon the shaping of the dominant US understanding of self and view of community cannot be underestimated. In contrast, the Social Trinity describes the sacramental unity of the whole creation.

The One-in-Three doesn't exist somehow separate from and above the tangled web of life but is a metaphor for the life-giving force that pervades the whole cosmos. The creation and the community of living organisms working together for the abundance and sustenance of the whole is not separate from God's reality, but integrally and intimately related to it. Human self-interest and the interests and well-being of the commons are intertwined. Oikosystem as a way of thinking about God's action within God's household calls us to be conscious of the contingency of our existence and our life together in the fullness of God's love. Drawing upon Sallie McFague's words, "All life grew from one cell into millions

---

[23]Michael Hogue, *The Tangled Bank: Toward an Ecotheological Ethics of Responsible Participation* (Eugene, OR: Pickwick, 2008), xxi.

of species, into the rich, diverse, and infinitely interesting forms we know—from mushrooms and mice to wheat and giant cedars, from fungi and frogs to chimpanzees and human beings. We are all related: we all came from the same beginning."[24] We are part of a whole community of living organisms and collaborators with God for the mutual benefit and flourishing of the commons. To express one's faith in God's vivifying force of love means that some human beings do not have the right to create wealth for themselves at the expense of the commons or to consume more of the world's abundant resources simply because of their financial ability to do so.

Why the Trinity Is Love

An enduring dimension of reflection on the Trinity is the understanding that God is love. Late in the first century of our common era, John of Patmos expressed the belief of the Johannine community that *agape* love is the very essence of the divine. "Dear friends, let's love each other, because love is from God, and everyone who loves is born from God and knows God" (1 John 4:7). If human beings are made in the image of God, then we are to embody God's love within the oikosystem.

Mystics and sages throughout the centuries have recognized the way we embody and share in God's loving nature. Julian of Norwich, a medieval woman mystic and the first woman to compose a book in English, wrote about her profound intuitive experience of God. She described the Trinity as God's nature and a model for human relationships:

> And I saw no difference between God and our substance, but, as it were, all God; and still my understanding that our substance is in God, that is to say that God is God, and our substance is a creature in God. For the almighty truth of the Trinity is our Father, for he made us and keeps us in him. And the deep wisdom of the Trinity is our Mother, in whom we are enclosed. And the high goodness of the Trinity is our Lord, and in him we are enclosed and he is in us.[25]

---

[24]Sallie McFague, *A New Climate for Theology: God, World, and Global Warming* (Minneapolis: Fortress, 2008), 207–8.

[25]Julian of Norwich, *Showings*, in *The Classics of Western Spirituality* (New

By sharing in God's nature we are expressions of the depth, breadth, and vivifying force and love of the commons.

There are many different ways to define love. Theologian Daniel Day Williams argued in his book *The Spirit and Forms of Love* that the biblical story itself is a story of God's love moving in the midst of human loves. Biblical stories never leave human loves independent from the love of God. Human loves and their involvements, including parent, child and sibling, relationships, sexual intimacy, friendship, love of neighbor, love of self, love of wealth, love of one's enemies, and love of property and land are shaped by or fail to respond to the Holy One who is Ultimate Love. Consequently, every human love shapes not only our life together with each other, but also our life together with God.

Authentic love transforms human relationships throughout the biblical stories and is discovered and displayed in the reordering of the priorities of the patriarchal household. The stories of Ruth and Mary at the wedding of Cana offer a powerful witness to the way in which human love, God's love, and questions of wealth and poverty are intertwined. Ruth is described in the story as a Moabite, a label that stigmatizes her in ancient Israel. Deuteronomy 23 excludes Ammonites and Moabites from the Lord's assembly: "Not even the tenth generation of such people can belong to the LORD's assembly." Moabites were associated with sexual promiscuity. Postcolonial theorist and biblical scholar Peter H. W. Lau says that the first step that Ruth takes in transforming her social identity in her host culture is to challenge the stigma surrounding Moabites and embodying lovingkindness—in Hebrew, *hesed*.

Lovingkindness in the context of Ruth's story is not an abstract principle. Ruth and Naomi were in the most vulnerable position in their ancient society after the death of their husbands. Biblical scholar Johanna van Wijk-Bos writes that "deprivation of sustenance, lack of security, and loss of life define the context of these women."[26] Ruth resolves their vulnerability by forging an "unorthodox" alliance with the most "unlikely partner," her mother-in-law Naomi. Moreover, van Wijk-Bos argues that Ruth

---

York: Paulist Press, 1978), 285.

[26]Johanna W. H. van Wijk-Bos, "Out of the Shadows: Genesis 38; Judges 4:17–22; Ruth 3," *Semeia* 42 (1988): 64.

takes a risk in that there is "ostensibly no advantage for Ruth in her initial alliance to Naomi."[27] She "willingly joins weakness to weakness, death to death."[28]

Ruth no longer had the identity established for her by the relationship with her husband after his death. She was an undocumented migrant, if you will. Integral to preserving Israelite identity was the prohibition of intermarriage so that the dominant ethnic group could maintain wealth, power, and privilege. Ruth, however, claims a more open application of what Lau describes as the "moral logic underlying the law" found in passages such as the Jubilee (Lev. 25:8–55). Ruth transforms the identity defined for her by her ancient society as she crosses cultural boundaries and barriers to bind herself to her mother-in-law in love. In many ways, she is the least likely character that you would want to be the representative of God's lovingkindness—she's a woman, a foreigner, a migrant, a daughter-in-law, and a widow.

Naomi urges Ruth to return to Moab. But in a pledge similar to a marriage contract, Ruth responds by saying, "Don't urge me to leave you or to turn back from you. Where you go, I go; your people will be my people; where you lodge, I lodge" (Ruth 1:16–17). Van Wijk-Bos says that "the entire story and its developments must be viewed in terms of Ruth's statement to Naomi in 1:16–17." The object of Ruth's love is her mother-in-law. She transcends ancient social boundaries to ensure the survival and flourishing of two women. Later in the story, Ruth "plans an essential alliance with Boaz" to ensure their survival.[29] The story and the language within the text itself resist the patriarchal ordering of the household economy and the grounding of Israelite identity in ethnocentric religious practices. *Hesed* ensures the survival of these two women and invites us to think about a new way of being and living in community.

In the Gospel of John, God's nature is in relationship. The story of the wedding at Cana and the transformation of water into wine symbolizes the future abundance that Christ embodies and the real possibility that God's vision for the world, for abundance for all, is realized as Jesus, his mother, and the disciples act together in

---

[27]Ibid., 58.
[28]Ibid.
[29]Ibid., 64.

miraculous ways that meet very real needs. Jesus's mother calls her son's attention to imminent disaster as she notices that the wine is running out at a wedding feast. Running out of wine was no small embarrassment for families in ancient Galilee. Common people drank little wine and ate even less meat. Cheese, bread, and olive oil most often satisfied their hunger; water quenched their thirst. Wine was reserved for truly festive occasions such as weddings. Failing to pull off a wedding in style would have been regretful, even shameful. Family and friends would have noted the host's failure. Mary persuades Jesus to invite all of the wedding guests to participate in making a miracle happen, and the guests at the wedding change an empty table into a table that has enough. The table is a symbol of God's vision for abundance here and now.

As the rituals, disciplines, and institutions of the Christian church developed over time, many people who wanted to devote their lives to expressing God's love through prayer and communal living were drawn into monastic life. They believed that the best chance they had in their context to imitate the life of Jesus with the greatest authenticity was to embody a perfect love by giving of themselves to a community that did not practice the pursuit of wealth within the Roman Empire. Historian Roberta Bondi suggests that the term *perfect* as it was used in early monastic settings bears a distinctive meaning and gives us a sense of what love meant when it met with Hellenistic culture. *Perfect* was used in a pagan sense to reflect the belief held by Aristotle and Plato that there was only one perfect being—God. Human beings were made in the image of God and yet not in a perfect way. However, human beings can move toward God by freeing themselves from the enslaving quality of appetites and emotions. The growth of *agape* love then was thought to be discovered in a continuous movement toward God. Being drawn to God meant being drawn into the depth, fullness, and dance of God's love in relationship.

What might that love look like in the world in which we live? One of the classes that I teach on a regular basis at Bellarmine University is called Theology from the Margins. The class draws upon the educational philosophy of Paulo Freire and emphasizes conscientization and social change. Increasingly I am finding the need to shift some of my teaching strategies from assuming that students in the classroom come from middle-class backgrounds because of the high cost of college education and student indebtedness. There are many more students living in poverty in my classroom today despite their middle-class veneer than when I began teaching fourteen years ago.

Recent research conducted by the Pew Center supports my assumptions. Pew reported in its study "America's Shrinking Middle Class" that "from 2000 to 2014 the share of adults living in middle-income households fell in 203 of the 229 U.S. metropolitan areas"[30] and suggested that the middle class soon will no longer be a majority in the United States. Cidnei, a student who took the class in spring 2016, made the astute observation that the margins have now moved to the center of discourse in the classroom when considering issues of economic justice. Cidnei was well aware of the financial precariousness of most people's lives, as 40 percent of US residents have no retirement savings; lack of savings means that most people in the United States are one tragedy away from living in poverty.

In light of this social reality, the goals for the class include conscientization concerning the systemic and structural causes of poverty, reflecting upon and writing theologies out of the experience of vulnerability and poverty, and something that I call love training. *Love training* involves a variety of immersion experiences that create cognitive dissonance across faith traditions and enable students to learn to build relationships across boundaries of social class.

For about six years, I have worked with Crossroads, a local ministry sponsored by St. Williams Catholic Church, which plans retreats in low-income areas in Louisville. One of the immersion experiences requires taking students to eat at the Open Hand Kitchen, a ministry of the St. Vincent de Paul Society. All that is required of the students is to eat there. The only thing that they are *not* allowed to do is to serve the meal. For some students the experience is quite a challenge because they have been engaged in so many service activities by the time they are juniors or seniors at Bellarmine. What happens at the Open Hand is learning how to cross invisible yet tangible boundaries of social class and to build relationships with people who, at least at first, appear on the exterior to be different.

---

[30]Pew Research Center, "America's Shrinking Middle Class: A Close Look at Changes within Metropolitan Areas," May 11, 2016, www.pewsocialtrends.org.

The Open Hand Kitchen offers a unique environment for the meal because the cafeteria buffet line is set up in an old church sanctuary. After going through the line and picking up your food tray, when you turn toward the tables where seating is provided for the meal, you face the chancel area of the old sanctuary. The chancel area is still adorned with images of saints, and a plastic folding table surrounded by six chairs sits in the place of the altar. One cannot avoid thinking of Jesus's greatest feast of love.

A young man named Cole was another one of the students who took my Theology from the Margins course in the spring of 2016. He eagerly signed up for the immersion experience at the Open Hand Kitchen and, because of his excellent social skills, was easily able to engage in conversation with people sitting at his table. He met a couple whom I will call Sally and Anirudh. Sally and Anirudh had recently moved to Louisville from eastern Kentucky, which was also Cole's home. Early on in the conversation Cole realized that they came from the same county. The reason the couple decided to move to Louisville was to get away from some "toxic people" in their lives. Neither of them had much money. They just had enough to pay for gas to drive to the city and planned to stay with Sally's brother until they got back on their feet. What was most surprising to Cole was that Sally's brother turned them away when they arrived at his doorstep because Anirudh was from India. Sally's brother didn't want to help a couple of what he called "mixed blood." By the time Sally and Anirudh reached her brother's doorstep, their savings were depleted by the move, so they didn't have anywhere else to go. They were both picking up odd jobs for minimum wage, and neither of them could get enough hours to qualify for full-time benefits. So they regularly eat at the Open Hand Kitchen.

Cole reflected on his experience sitting at the table with Sally and Anirudh in his final project for the class. He wrote, "I had an epiphany. . . . This may sound strange and hard to understand, but it has greatly impacted my outlook on those waiting in soup lines, standing on street corners asking for change, and sleeping in their vans night after night." Cole allowed himself to encounter "the full humanity of those [he] was speaking to" and to face up to the fact that almost anyone could be in that situation if they were turned away or cast out by their family. He felt a sense of righteous indignation at the fact that someone would claim a sense of moral superiority by turning away his sister just because of who she loved. While sitting at the table of the Open Hand Kitchen, Cole "realized the importance of showing love for people in poverty, not pity." Cole transformed his way of thinking. What happened through love training was that he was able to begin moving away from a long-held belief that providing charity for people in poverty addressed the problem of poverty to face up to the idea that real love faces up to the problems created by the current dominant forms of wealth creation and demands just economic policies. What Sally and Anirudh need most are family-sustaining wages and affordable housing.

Devoting Ourselves to the Social Trinity Will Have Profound Practical Implications for Life Together in Our Contemporary Economy

Allowing ourselves to be transformed by the alternative social logic of the Three-in-One and One-in-Three directly challenges US notions of hyperindividualism and hypercapitalism. To confess that God is not self-centered, egotistical, self-interested, and self-sufficient in Godself means that God does not just hope for community; God lives and thrives in the fullness of relationship. Theologian M. Douglas Meeks points out, "Many proponents of the market system would say that *liberty* is its most essential component."[31] Neoliberalism is an extreme example of the notion that owning and possessing oneself means "having no claims laid upon oneself by others."[32] The Social Trinity challenges this concept of liberty and individual freedom. Recovering the radical roots of Trinitarian doctrine has profound conceptual and practical implications for the way followers of Jesus can live out their faith as a challenge to the current dominant forms of wealth creation.

In the West, property and possessions have been key determinants of individual rights and an individual's net worth. When thinking about property, possessions, and stewardship of the planet, if we are acting as we are created in God's image, then our ownership is not grounded in self-possession but in self-giving.

---

[31]M. Douglas Meeks, "The Social Trinity and Property," in *God's Life in Trinity*, ed. Miroslav Volf and Michael Welker (Minneapolis: Fortress, 2006), 17.
[32]Ibid.

Meeks suggests that "Christian anthropology stresses a universally recognized inclusive property right in what it takes to be human. . . . All human beings have a property in or claim on what is appropriate to life against death and what he or she needs to fulfill his or her humanity (*imago Dei*, God's likeness or God's image) by serving God and neighbor."[33]

I want to stress that giving of self is not interpreted here as self-effacement and self-deprecation. White women and people of color have too often been forced to stand at intersections created for them by property-owning, privileged men. Self-giving and humility are concepts that can be mistakenly used to force people to claim identities that fail to recognize the complexity of their multistoried experiences as they are informed by social constructions of race, gender, faith, and national culture. The giving of self can be accented in ways that divinize whiteness and claim the superiority of Western cultures, and that have fueled the historical processes of colonization and conquest.[34] God's love described in Trinitarian terms is never coercive or used for the sake of preserving the power and privilege of one person at the expense of another. God's love in the Trinity is always a person toward-another. Each person in the Trinity willingly gives to others without diminishing their own person and is fully known in the contribution made to the whole. God freely limits Godself in love so as not to limit others. God's nature of love in mutuality moves us to see ourselves not only as part of a social community but interdependent with the commons.

Darwin began to describe poetically the interdependence of the ecosystem in *On the Origin of Species*. "It is interesting," Darwin wrote, "to contemplate a tangled bank, clothed with many plants of many kinds, with birds singing on the bushes, with various insects flitting about, and with worms crawling through the damp earth, and to reflect that these elaborately constructed forms, so different from each other, are dependent upon each other in so

---

[33]Ibid., 18.

[34]Quentin Kinnison offers a wonderful exploration of how the Social Trinity breaks down constructed tools of division in the US Southwest in his article "The Social Trinity and the Southwest: Toward a Local Theology in the Borderlands," *Perspectives in Religious Studies: Journal of the National Association of Baptist Professors of Religion* 35, no. 3 (Fall 2008): 261–81.

complex a manner."[35] The flourishing of the commons and survival of the planet depend on human beings of relative wealth in the United States and other technologically advanced and highly industrialized countries authentically grappling with the complex consequences of our current dominant approaches to wealth creation and patterns of overconsumption. There is no doubt today that *our actions impact God's oikosystem*, some aspects of the system experiencing greater deprivation than others.

In large measure, the United States and other countries in the Global North bear the burden of responsibility for the impact of our carbon emissions on the rest of the world. Dr. Jesse Mugambi, a professor of philosophy and religious studies at the University of Nairobi in Kenya, stressed this point in a presentation he gave on ecological debt at the Global Forum on Poverty, Wealth, and Ecology in 2014. Kenya, where Mugambi is from, literally means "the mountain of whiteness" because of the snow-capped peak of Kirinyaga (Kerenyaga), the tallest mountain in the country. The peak of the mountain is not so white anymore. Mugambi explained that countries within the tropics have summer twice and winter twice, which means that Kenya experiences the hot summer winds two times a year and therefore twice the impact of carbon emissions. Gothenburg University in Sweden conducted a study of pollution in Kenya's capital of Nairobi and released its findings in 2015. The study revealed that "the amount of cancer-causing elements in the air within the city [of Nairobi] is 10 times higher than the threshold recommended by the World Health Organisation."[36] An article published in the *Guardian* attributed the pollution problem to the high number of old cars driven in Africa's cities and smoke from "roadside rubbish fires, diesel generators and indoor cooking stoves."[37] One of the reasons the problem is so bad is that so many cars are "shipped in secondhand from Japan and Europe with their catalytic converters and air filters dismantled."[38]

Mugambi argues that pollutants can be tracked to an additional cause: the overproduction and overconsumption of highly

---

[35]As quoted in Hogue, *Tangled Bank*, xiii.

[36]John Vidal, "'There is No Escape': Nairobi's Air Pollution Sparks Africa Health Warning," *The Guardian*, July 10, 2016.

[37]Ibid.

[38]Ibid.

industrialized countries.[39] Scientists have tracked many of the pollutants that blow through countries that lie on the equator and found that they could not have originated in African nations. He called attention to a conflict map of Africa. Outsiders often assume that conflicts in Africa are primarily tribal differences. This may be true in some instances, but Mugambi observed that conflicts frequently result from disputes over natural resources, particularly water, that are increasingly limited because of higher temperatures resulting from climate change.

About 1 billion people (roughly 14 percent of the world's population) live on the continent of Africa. However, the people of Africa generate only about 3 percent of the world's carbon emissions. Recall that US residents make up a little less than 5 percent of the world's population but are responsible for almost one-fifth of all carbon dioxide emissions worldwide. The US contribution to global carbon dioxide emissions is second only to China's. Grappling with and challenging the current dominant forms of wealth creation require more than looking deep within ourselves and the shape of our society; addressing wealth creation requires learning how to practice an ethic of enough. US Americans of relative wealth must be transformed by others whose lifestyles are in far greater harmony with the commons.

Social Trinity as Ubuntu: "I Am Because We Are. We Are Because I Am."

South African Reformed theologian Allan Boesak prophetically proclaims that hope is born as people of faith identify with those most wounded and vulnerable as a result of the current dominant forms of wealth creation. In his book *Dare We Speak of Hope?* Boesak makes profound connections between the story of people in South Africa and the US story; the connections can help in our exploration of the implications of the Social Trinity for political economy and underscore the importance of theological imagination for creating systemic change.

South Africa and the United States are countries with long histories of slavery and social and economic segregation, includ-

---

[39]See Jesse N. K. Mugambi, ed., *Christian Faith and the Current Ecological Crisis* (Geneva: WCC Publications, 2013).

ing policies and systems of apartheid, Jim Crow, and mass incarceration. Within the South African context, policies of racial and economic apartheid were very much a theological problem, and churches as a result had to be leaders in creating authentic change. The Dutch Reformed Church in South Africa shaped powerful norms, values, and ideas of community. At the beginning of the white occupation, the distinction of primary importance was made "between Christian and heathen, baptized and unbaptized."[40] For the first two hundred years of white occupation, people of color were regarded as full members of the faith community after they were baptized and there was common worship. The perception of white superiority gained fuller force early in the eighteenth century as entrepreneurs decided to use West African and Malaysian slaves rather than white immigrants to meet labor needs. Whites, even within the church, began to identify falsely manual work with nonwhites. The Dutch Reformed Church increasingly insisted upon white superiority and policies of segregation.

Many pastors and parishioners argued for similar degrading attitudes and discriminatory policies of racial and economic apartheid, particularly in the southeastern United States, defending slavery and Jim Crow with flawed appeals to the Bible. Attitudes of racial superiority are still deeply embedded in US society as evidenced by the nation's system of mass incarceration, in which one in three black men will be imprisoned in his lifetime. Boesak rightfully observes that both countries have very progressive constitutions but poor track records in fully overcoming social, economic, and political injustices, and an obscene gap between rich and poor continues to grow. Where does Boesak find hope? He calls people of faith to live in hope by reimagining their understanding of God in terms of the Social Trinity. Boesak draws upon the writings of South African feminist theologian Juliana Claassens, who describes God as "Mourner, Mother, and Midwife." She asserts that metaphors conveying the sense of God's vital life-giving and liberating work resist the violence associated with warrior imagery used in the Hebrew Bible and throughout the Christian tradition, and give hope for the remaking of con-

---

[40]Susan Rennie Ritner, "The Dutch Reformed Church and Apartheid," *Journal of Contemporary History* 2, no. 4 (October 1967): 18.

temporary social relationships.[41] Claassens's Social Trinity is a metaphor for God emerging from the experience of those most wounded by the history of apartheid.

Jerry Pillay, professor of theology at the University of Praetoria in South Africa and president of the World Communion of Reformed Churches, explores the resonances of the Social Trinity with the African notion of *Ubuntu* as it relates to John Calvin's theology. He suggests that that the organizing principle of Calvin's theology is "ecodomy,"[42] not sovereignty, as Reformed theologians have argued in the past. In Greek, *ecodomy* means to build and refers to building life in its fullness. For Calvin, our wisdom is deemed the only "true and solid wisdom" as it connects knowledge of God to the whole community. Calvin drew upon the writings of the early church fathers as he described the three persons as "Beginning of Action and Source," "Wisdom, Counsel, Arrangement in Action," and "Energy and Efficacy of Action." The very essence of divine activity is action.

Ubuntu is not easily translated into English, but the term expresses a theology or philosophy of life among Africans that no one should be left behind. Suzanne Membe-Matale, general secretary of the Council of Churches of Zambia, writes, "Ubuntu has been defined as a transformative spirit that connects us to others and motivates us to serve the common good. It inspires us to stand firmly against marginalization and discrimination. It seeks the redemptions of the whole earth, resists life-destroying values, and inspires us to discover innovative alternatives that promote life in all its forms."[43] Other translations of Ubuntu include, "I am because we are. We are because I am," "collective personhood," or "collective morality." Ubuntu is "an ancient African worldview based on the primary values of intense humanness, caring, sharing, respect, compassion and associated values, ensuring a happy and

---

[41]See L. Juliana Claassen, *Mourner, Mother, Midwife: Reimagining God's Delivering Presence in the Old Testament* (Louisville, KY: Westminster John Knox Press, 2012).

[42]Jerry Pillay, "An Exploration of the Idea of Ecodomy in Calvin's View of God and the World: Its Implications for the Churches in South Africa Today," *Verbum et Ecclesia* 36, no. 3 (2015): 1.

[43]Suzanne Membe-Matale, "*Ubuntu* Theology," *Ecumenical Review* 67, no. 2 (July 2015): 274.

quality community life in the spirit of family."[44] Within poor communities in South Africa, Ubuntu is the fundamental principle that informs informal social arrangements that provide social safety nets. People pool resources together to provide for others who live in poverty. The concept continues to play a critical role for the South African state by providing an African basis for "democratic values, social justice, and fundamental human rights."[45]

The Social Trinity resonates with Ubuntu as a model for group solidarity and collective personhood. I find myself wondering at this point in history which US communities live according to the philosophy that no one should be left behind. Where will we find our own store of resources for concepts of collective personhood and collective morality? Boesak's comparison of the US and South African contexts provides us with some direction to look toward solidarity protest movements as at least one prominent source for that inspiration.

Sola Caritate *and Personal Initiative*

From a Reformed perspective, I am in agreement with the theologians who in recent years have called for a new *sola* to be added to the principles of movements advocating for economic justice—*sola caritate*. In the sixteenth century, the magisterial reformers introduced solas, which were Latin phrases intended to summarize the central theological principles of the Protestant Reformation and enable people of faith to see the critical role they would play in creating not only a new form of church but a new life together in community. Reformers directed their attention toward religious leadership in the Roman Catholic Church, which held both religious and political authority. The solas represented a challenge to the demands made for obedience to their authority and the uncritical acceptance of the church's teachings. Two of the principles of the sixteenth-century Reformation are very well known: *sola scriptura* (scripture alone) and *sola fide* (faith alone). But there were more; at least five Latin phrases were introduced in

---

[44]Clarence I. Tshoose, "The Emerging Role of the Constitutional Value of Ubuntu for Informal Social Security in South Africa," *African Journal of Legal Studies* 3, no. 1 (November 2009): 13.

[45]Ibid., 16.

the Reformer's writings, including *solus Christus* (through Christ alone), *sola gratia* (by grace alone), and *soli Deo gloria* (glory to God alone). What appears missing from the list composed by sixteenth-century Reformers is the call to take personal initiative to embody love in the midst of community.

Christian religious social activists and reformers, particularly those who are Reformed, have new allies in the twenty-first century. A wide variety of Christian churches are eager to face the problem of wealth head-on and to share an alternative social logic emerging from Christian theology, ritual, and tradition. Pope Francis is a new ally for Reformed thinkers, particularly on matters related to economic justice and climate change. Roman Catholics have the great benefit of Catholic social thought, which doesn't offer a specific political platform but clarifies the theological basis of and moral principles of a just economy. There is also a long tradition of commentary coming out of Protestant denominations and ecumenical organizations that calls Christians to love by advocating for fair wages and the rights of laborers to organize, emphasizing that economies should serve human needs, and underscoring the need for those who have enough to adopt simpler lifestyles. These documents and statements call Christians to act by embodying love through just economic policies and to see themselves as part of the commons. To paraphrase Cornel West, just economic policies, systems, and structures are "what love looks like in public."

In the twentieth century, personalist philosophy was an expression of disdain for the political and economic structures as they were evolving. Social and political structures could not be solely relied upon to create change. The only way for society to be transformed was from outside the established institutions and structures. One of the most well-known proponents of personalist philosophy in the United States was Martin Luther King Jr. King, who was educated at Crozer Theological Seminary and Boston University, developed two chief personalistic convictions: "1) that God is personal, and 2) that because human beings are created by and imbued with the image of God they necessarily should be treated with dignity and respect."[46] Near the end of his

---

[46]Rufus Burrow Jr. "The Beloved Community: Martin Luther King Jr. and Josiah Royce," *Encounter* 73, no. 1 (2012): 39.

life, King often spoke to organized labor groups. His last speech was delivered in Memphis, Tennessee, on April 3, 1968, regarding a sanitation workers' strike in that city. He was assassinated the next day.

At this point in his life and work, King had cultivated a consciousness that made him vulnerable because he could see life as a web of relationships as well as the connections between the history of conquest and colonization, racism, and economic injustice. He reflects on the parable of the Good Samaritan in that speech. The Good Samaritan story is placed in the Gospel of Luke within the context of Jesus's larger explanation of love; the story comes just after Jesus proclaims the greatest commandment: "To love the Lord your God with all of your heart, soul and strength" and "to love your neighbor as yourself." As King reflected on the meaning of love and the Good Samaritan, he called upon people of faith to develop what he called a dangerous unselfishness. He said, now the "question could have easily ended up in a philosophical and theological debate. But Jesus immediately pulled that question from midair and placed it on a dangerous curve between Jerusalem and Jericho. . . . And [Jesus then] talked about a certain man, who fell among the thieves." When someone falls among the thieves, King prophetically proclaimed, if we are to truly embody God's love, then we have to decide "not to be compassionate by proxy."[47]

Applying the Norm of Love within All Spheres of Life

The norm of love, *agape* love, the principle of *sola caritate*, has to be applied within all spheres of our life. Three-in-One is more about three than one and invites us to face up to the reality that the fullest expression of love is in "mutuality, reciprocity and totally shared life."[48] Love is not completely given on behalf of or completely received, but discovered in receiving and in giving for the benefit of the whole web of relationships. When God's mutuality becomes a lens through which to see and a norm for judging public life, the profound and urgent need to transform society's unjust systems and structures is unavoidable.

---

[47]Martin Luther King Jr., *"All Labor Has Dignity,"* ed. and with an Introduction by Michael K. Honey (Boston: Beacon Press, 2011; reprint of 1986 edition), 190–91.

[48]Letty Russell, *The Future of Partnership* (Philadelphia: Westminster, 1979), 35.

One of the images theologians used in recent years to reflect on the social meaning of the Trinity is an icon painted by Russian Andrei Rublev in the fifteenth century. Rublev was inspired by the story of Genesis 18, when three visitors come to announce that a child will be born to Abraham and Sarah, who were already very old. Three angels are depicted in the icon sitting together at a table as equals around a common cup. Theologians have commented on the movement that appears to be part of this image. Elizabeth Johnson observes that "what catches the meditating eye most is the position of the circles is not closed. What the image suggests is that the mystery of God is not self-contained or closed but . . . evokes the idea that this divine communion is lovingly open to the world, seeking to nourish it."[49] The icon invites the viewer beyond contemplating a God of immense hospitality to move toward and into, and to embody, the love that flows beyond the image.

Embodying love and entering into that movement toward, into, and beyond the image of the Trinity is a radically countercultural idea and may seem overwhelming. Allow me to close this chapter with a more personal example of how two real people of faith acted in and out of God's abundant overflowing love.

The two relatives of my father whom I knew best were Aunt Fleta and Uncle Ossie Marsh. They owned a small farm near Sullivan, Missouri, a town about fifty miles from St. Louis. I loved to visit their farm and that little town. It was so different from the city where I lived.

During our summer visits, Aunt Fleta spent most of her time tending the garden, putting up vegetables for winter, and cooking for the rest of us. On occasions, she would let me help with the canning. The dinner table usually had an incredible spread of dishes made from the season's harvest. One of the summers that we were able to stay for a more extended visit, Aunt Fleta and Uncle Ossie had a particularly abundant cucumber crop. I remember sitting down at the dinner table and surveying plates and bowls filled with pickled cucumbers—sweet pickles, sweet and sour pickles, pickle relish, chow chow made with corn and pickles; lettuce salads heavily laden with cucumbers; tomato, cucumber,

---

[49]Johnson, "Trinity," 299.

and onion salad marinated in homemade apple cider vinaigrette; and a cucumber salad made with sour cream and onions. There were probably other cucumber dishes. The problem for me during our extended visit was that cucumber dishes appeared at every meal. We ate cucumbers for every lunch and dinner that week. After a week, I resisted going to the table when I was called for dinner. Coming from a city where our food was purchased primarily at a grocery store, I complained about eating cucumbers so frequently and longed for more variety. Their table didn't seem to have enough options.

It wasn't until many years later that I realized how much Aunt Fleta and Uncle Ossie's household economy differed from my expectations. The practice of eating the food from their garden wasn't just about cost effectiveness or enjoying the food that they harvested from their own land; it was about ensuring that everyone had enough and being able to share with a larger community. They had lived through the Great Depression. There was a time when they were forced to migrate to a city in order to find work. They knew the reality of scarcity and recognized the importance of living by an ethic of enough. Even when times were better, they limited what they stored up in jars for themselves and other things that they would buy so that they would also be able to share with others—their money, their food, their talents, and other resources. During their lifetimes, their sharing went so far as to provide a home for my father and his brother, Gene, when their mother could not afford to raise her sons. Their sharing was also not limited to their own family. They opened their eyes to the see the faces of the people in their community who were hungry—some of them migrants—and they shared their food or often offered work opportunities on their farm.

I do not intend to present an overly sentimental and romantic portrait of the past by relating my memories of Aunt Fleta and Uncle Ossie. I am aware of many inequalities and injustices that were present during that era, as in our own. Neither Aunt Fleta nor Uncle Ossie had the opportunity to travel the world and encounter people living in very different cultures and circumstances. It would have been easy for them to turn in on themselves and to hoard what they were able to produce so that they could ensure their own nuclear family's well-being. But they chose a different path. They aimed to embody love and keep the values of mutuality, reciprocity, and community at the center of their economic activities. Aunt Fleta and Uncle Ossie did not let their personal and individual needs take priority over those of others, sometimes even chickens, cows, and dogs. Their response to the scarcity they confronted in their time was to love others by having the moral courage to recognize when they had enough.

CHAPTER 6

Extensive Roots

Ecocentric and Theocentric Visions of Economy from a Wider Variety of the World's Great Faith Traditions

Of all created things the source is one,
Simple, single as love; remember
The cell and seed of life, the sphere
That is, of child, white bird, and small blue dragon-fly,
Green fern, and the gold four-petalled tormentilla
The ultimate memory.
Each latent cell puts out a future,
Unfolds its differing complexity
As a tree puts forth leaves, and spins a fate
Fern-traced, bird-feathered, or fish-scaled.
       —"Prayer of Nature," *Gates of Prayer*[1]

The concept of the Social Trinity discussed in the preceding chapter is a uniquely Christian symbol and metaphor for God, but the Christian faith does not have an exclusive claim on defining what love is or how love should be embodied in our life together.

---

[1]"Prayer of Nature," Special Themes, *Gates of Prayer: The New Union Prayer-book* (New York: Central Conference of American Rabbis, 1975), 656.

Christian theologians have too often encouraged churches to impoverish themselves and their way of thinking and being in the world by focusing narrowly on sources of knowledge unique only to Christian tradition. We are living in an ever-challenging environment where confronting the problem of wealth requires listening to experiences far beyond our own. Trees inspire awe in many cultures as symbols of life and growth as they stand tall enough to connect earth and sky. One of the most influential communitarian groups in Kentucky, the Shakers of Pleasant Hill, chose a tree of life as their symbol to lead the way for a community aiming to bring heaven to earth. Pacifist activist Philip Berrigan observed that in the Jewish Haggadah and throughout the Hebrew and Christian scriptures, "trees are sensitive to moral dimensions. They give or withhold fruit in accord with just or unjust conduct."[2] In nature, trees naturally modify their root systems to adapt to their environments. Healthy trees need extensive root systems to adapt. In this chapter, I continue digging for roots and nurturing a more extensive root system by exploring the theological and moral imagination of a wider variety of the world's spiritualities and religions: Native American theological reflection, Buddhism, Judaism, and Islam. The richer and more textured understanding of human beings and our limitations, concepts of wealth and community, and definitions of love found in these traditions provide not only a greater understanding of the commons but also extensive roots for nourishing alternative visions of economy.

On two occasions I have team taught an international travel course for graduate students in Bellarmine's master of arts in spirituality program and taken them to Kerala, India. The goal of the course is to explore interfaith spirituality and to learn to reflect critically on life-transforming faith practices that tackle social, economic, and political inequalities in a cultural context quite different from the United States. One of the most important sites we visit in India is the Sameeksha ashram in Kalady, Kerala (see Figure 6.1). Sameeksha is a word and a name with origins in Sanskrit that mean "intellect," "deep insight," and "understanding." The Kerala Province of the Jesuit Society started the ashram in 1987

---

[2]Philip Berrigan, "Barren or Fruitful: A Sign for the Times," *Union Seminary Quarterly Review* 44 (1990): 160.

for the purpose of promoting a culture formed by the deep insight of interreligious harmony. Fr. Sebastian Painadath and Br. Varkey Manipilly, both Jesuits, have significantly formed and continue to influence the work and witness of Sameeksha. Painadath, director of Sameeksha, was trained as a theologian in Germany, teaches theology at the ashram, and introduces seekers to the pursuit of the divine in their daily life through Indian-Christian methods of contemplative prayer. Another resident of this community is Fr. Samuel Rayan, a theologian who has been an innovative voice in dalit theology from the beginning of the movement.

Figure 6.1. Interfaith Prayer Chapel at Sameeksha Ashram, Kalady, Kerala, India

Sacred texts surround a circular rug displaying symbols of the world's great faith traditions in the Interfaith Prayer Chapel at Sameeksha. Photo by Elizabeth Hinson-Hasty in May 2010.

The grounds of Sameeksha are shaded by a wide variety of trees and are rich in fauna and other forms of life, making it easy to identify with Rayan's reflections that "the earth is a symbol that sums up all the gifts of life and love which God shares with humankind and all living beings. It is not so much a thing or object as a relational reality, vibrant and alive, dynamically mediating life and love from heart to heart."[3] Those who live at Sameeksha and those who visit for shorter periods of time to study or go on retreat honor the life form of traditional ashrams in India. Visitors are welcomed to the community's table for vegetarian meals served on stainless steel plates, which can be easily cleaned and are long lasting. Buildings on the grounds are made out of bricks of clay from a nearby river and wood found in the local area. A thick foliage of trees and bushes deflects the sun's rays from the brick facades and tiled rooftops of each building.

A small interfaith prayer room stands in the center of the ashram. Large darkly stained wooden doors command your attention as you approach the building. I always find it irresistible to step inside and sit around the circular rug adorned with symbols of all the world's great religious traditions. Sacred texts housed in specially made wooden display boxes surround the rug's edge. There are no absolute claims to authority in this circle, but rather a challenge to open oneself up to listen to the sacred experiences expressed by others, both people and the trees.

Central to the understanding of spirituality and dialogue at Sameeksha is the call to interreligious harmony expressed in interfaith action and solidarity. The ashram provides space for retreats and hosts a variety of educational programs as well as a ministry to migrant workers in Kerala. God's life-giving force is palpable in the midst of such natural splendor, and honest conversations among people of faith reveal the oppressive social, economic, and political realities that cut across religious and national borders. Interreligious dialogue leads to the understanding that people of faith can't relieve eco-human travail and transform poverty-inducing economic systems and structures without working together.

Thus far in our conversation, I have argued that people of faith

---

[3]Samuel Rayan, "The Earth Is the Lord's," in *Ecotheology: Voices from South and North*, ed. David G. Hallman (Geneva: WCC Publications; Maryknoll, NY: Orbis Books, 1994), 140.

are uniquely situated to challenge US society's hyperindividualism and idolatry of the market, but I have kept my attention focused primarily on the rich store of resources within Christian thought. One reason to take this approach is that I am trained as a Christian theologian and ordained as a Presbyterian teaching elder. However, I have come to the conclusion that it is just as dangerous and problematic to compartmentalize and segregate religious sources of knowledge and traditions from one another as it is silo-ize economics in the Western academy or prioritize money and market-based logic within US society. Intellectual and religious compartmentalization can lead to the fragmentation of communities.

In this chapter I take a risk for both practical and methodological reasons to expand the conversation by listening to and exploring the rich and more textured understanding of human beings and our limitations as well as the visions of just and right relationships within the economy found across a religious spectrum. I won't presume to be a scholarly expert on all the traditions of faith described here, but rather a fellow seeker who is open to a "new consciousness, to wonder, to sorrow, to tears, to songs, to anger, to action."[4] Rayan writes, "In all faith traditions the divine—or God—is concerned as the absolute 'yes' or affirmation of goodness, justice, freedom, love and life, and as the absolute 'no' or the negation of evil, oppression, deprivation, and domination."[5] Partners in dialogue in this circle have the shared goal of embodying love in a just economy.

This chapter is by no means an exhaustive study but is intended to suggest the need for further investigation, dialogue, engagement, and cross-pollination. My effort here is to underscore key ideas to help people of relative wealth in my own US cultural context to envision their role as standing in interreligious solidarity with the most vulnerable peoples and regions of the planet. A great gift we can receive from Native American spirituality is becoming conscious of "the infusion of the sacred through all of life and all

---

[4]Samuel Rayan, *In Spirit and Truth: Indian Christian Reflections on Spirituality and Worship*, volume 2, ed. Kurien Kunnumpuram (Mumbai: St. Paul Press Training School, 2012), 130.
[5]Ibid., 129.

of creation"[6] and discovering the innate value of the natural spaces in which we live. The concept of Buddhist economics challenges the assumption that unlimited growth is an unquestionable good. Jewish practices of Sabbath-keeping and Jubilee invite us to reflect on God's covenant, which does not allow humans to own other people or the planet; God is the ultimate source of all life. Finally, a brief exploration of the principles of Islamic finance and banking allows us to think about how to build wealth without charging or collecting excessive interest. Together, these ideas, rituals, beliefs, and concepts form an extensive interreligious root system to nourish interreligious solidarity and to grow alternative definitions of wealth and poverty, a consciousness that humans are but one aspect of the commons, and a healthy engagement with markets.

Native American Reciprocity and Spatiality and the Tetrad

Indigenous peoples represent tremendous wealth in cultural diversity around the world and live in areas rich in natural resources, but these populations also experience some of the greatest material deprivation. According to the United Nations, indigenous peoples are "over-represented among the poor, the illiterate, and the unemployed . . . While they constitute approximately 5 percent of the world's population, indigenous peoples make up 15 percent of the world's poor."[7] Studies of indigenous peoples in Latin America show that the state of their poverty remains relatively static. The right of these people to sustain themselves is too often "denied by colonial and modern states in pursuit of economic growth."[8] These communities lack access in most countries to the dominant decision-making structures and often do not have full control of their land. What can those of us in positions of social and ecclesial privilege learn from the theology, rituals, and lifestyles of indigenous peoples that can produce harmony while transforming the economic, political, and social systems and structures that lead to poverty? Can we play an active role in breaking the cycle of the

---

[6]George E. Tinker, "Towards an American Indian Indigenous Theology," *Ecumenical Review* 62, no. 4 (2010): 345.
[7]United Nations, "State of the World's Indigenous Peoples," January 14, 2010, www.un.org.
[8]Ibid.

world's long history of colonization and conquest? The experiences of indigenous peoples are critical to any conversation about the problem of wealth because the perspectives and lifestyles of native peoples turn upside down the Euro-Western individualist mindset and definitions of poverty and wealth.

From the perspective of indigenous peoples, my theological traditions are defined by a colonialist mindset, and my white middle-class identity in both church and society is one of privilege. The writings of George Tinker—Baldridge Professor of American Indian Cultures and Religious Traditions at Iliff School of Theology, a Lutheran minister, and an enrolled member of the Wazhazhe (Osage Nation)—have challenged me in life-nurturing and mind-broadening ways as I examine my own theological tradition and social privilege and read about his work to decolonize his own thinking. I have chosen to be specific here about my exploration of Tinker's thought because I find it impossible to write about indigenous theologies in a general way. In addition, I want to be intentional about maintaining a focus on the problem of wealth in the US context.

For Tinker, Native American theology is inherently political because of North America's history of colonization and conquest and the reciprocity and spatiality that are central to Native American identity and tribal life. He says that the Euro-Western individualistic understanding of self as somehow separate from a larger community of living organisms is a "deeply foreign" idea for Native Americans. Tinker writes that claiming "life as a gift is more than just my life or even human life in general, but every rock and every tree and every stream is a part of life and has life in itself."[9] The world is not created by a single deity, but is itself in a continual process of creation.

For Native Americans, human beings do not enjoy some special privilege of dominion over other living things. The whole ecosystem—"two-legged," "four-legged," "winged," "flying ones," animate and inanimate objects—participates in world-balancing and harmony-producing activities. Reciprocity and spatiality are central to tribal life, shaping cultural values as well as social and political structures within different communities. In other words, space—the natural environment in which one lives—matters,

[9]George E. Tinker, "The Integrity of Creation: Restoring Trinitarian Balance." *Ecumenical Review* 41, no. 4 (October 1989): 532.

holding social and religious significance. Native traditions are land-based; therefore, rituals and ceremonies emerge in relation to sacred sites. For example, Tinker references the story of Corn Woman in his article "The Integrity of Creation: Restoring Trinitarian Balance." Corn has been a staple food for Native American peoples for thousands of years, so a variety of stories surrounding its origin are told within different communities. Among tribes living on the North American eastern seaboard, the First Mother, Corn Woman, or Corn Mother gives her life in love so that her children will have food to sustain themselves. In one version of Corn Woman's story, she tells her son to kill her and then to drag her body along the ground in a clearing. Tall, healthy green stalks of corn grow after her blood sinks into the earth. Her bones when they are buried are "reborn in beans, squash, and other staples."[10] Out of the gift of her body, her children are fed.

Reciprocity and spatiality for Native Americans extend beyond a notion of partnership among human beings to kinship ties with plants, animals, rock beings, spirit beings, and all sorts of other-than-human persons. Traditionally, Native Americans have appreciated distinctions in the ecosystems and what they contribute to specific regions. The ecosystem on top of a mountain may be very different than the valley below. If a particular space is no longer available or no longer exists, then a ritual or ceremony may no longer be able to be performed, therefore permanently altering the culture and practice of a particular community.

In contrast, Christian theologies, particularly in the Reformed traditions, state their mission in terms of proclaiming "God's reconciling act in Christ Jesus" and are oriented toward traditions emerging from a text held sacred. Creedal statements such as the Apostles' Creed begin with the idea of God as Creator, and explorations of the understanding of self and community are understood in relation to the sinfulness and fallenness of human beings and God's intervention for salvation and redemption. Historically, the majority of Christian theological reflection has focused on individual salvation. Tinker argues that this orientation and beginning point for Christian mission and theological reflection does not resonate with Native American experience because of the continual suffering "from the effects of conquest by European immigrants over

---

[10]Ibid., 533.

the past five centuries."[11] To ask Native Americans to begin with a concept of God and forgiveness of individual sin is to begin with Euro-Western concepts that cannot be imposed on Native American cultures. Tinker sees *god*, *creator*, and *believe* as problematic words.

Most importantly for my own arguments exploring the concept of the Social Trinity as God's oikosystem and as a model for alternative visions of human relationships, Tinker says that Native Americans can't be forced into Trinitarian thinking. Tinker is non-Trinitarian because concepts of God as Creator and the world as Creation and the Trinity continue to maintain an "up-down schema" that is "deeply embedded in the 'social imaginary' of euro-colonial people." The problem, in his perspective, is that Three always equals One. The whole idea of God in Oneness fails to capture the rich splendor of the world's biodiversity and has been used in ways that preserve the power of colonizers. Tinker writes, "This order-of-creation mentality then evolves politically into the valorization of 'meritocracy' as a norm in American political, intellectual, and socioeconomic culture. . . . Capitalist economies function with a clear up-down hierarchy of command, as do modern military 'chains of command.' "[12] The superiority of the concept of one maintains "a monolithic image of power . . . which is static—and superior."[13]

In contrast, the Native American worldview is reciprocal and spatial. Four is the sacred number and represents the paired manifestation of male and female in Native American community and reciprocity of God as Father, Mother, Son, and Holy Spirit. The schema of relationships for Native Americans is lateral and found in the harmony and balance of duality. Two halves are needed to make a whole; no superiority is attributed to light over dark, male over female, or day over night. Tinker describes Native Americans as "community-ists," rather than as a Euro-Western concept of communists.

I agree with Tinker that I could not defend a concept of Trinity used to support social or political hierarchies. In my mind, the

---

[11] Ibid., 531.

[12] George E. Tinker, "Why I Do Not Believe in a Creator," in *Buffalo Shout, Salmon Cry: Conversations on Creation, Land Justice, and Life Together*, ed. Steven Heinrichs (Waterloo, ON: Herald Press, 2013), 170.

[13] Ibid., 172.

Social Trinity is a useful metaphor as it conveys God's relational ecology, invites reinterpretation of the dominant Euro-Western understanding of the relationship of self to the commons, and reenvisions social and economic relationships. One is always only known in Three, never just as One. However, I also admit agreement with Tinker that the Trinitarian understanding of God is not a universal statement of faith naming the sacred experiences of all people in all places.

Additionally, Tinker's perspective presses and stretches me to consider more deeply the meaning of interrelatedness and to redefine the meaning of the words *poverty* and *wealth*. Neither poverty nor wealth can be fully quantified as numbers, statistics, charts, and graphs. Poverty is just as much a lack of consciousness of the commons and the interrelatedness of all things as it is a lack of access to basic necessities such as food, water, education, clothing, adequate housing, and so on. Wealth is embedded in the harmony and balance of the commons much more than in gross national product, individual bank accounts, and corporate budgets.

Growing Interest in Theologies and Lifestyles of Indigenous Peoples

Since the 1970s, interest among Euro-Western academics, religious leaders, and activists in the environmentalist movement has grown regarding the theologies and lifestyles of indigenous peoples. At that time, academics and religious leaders began to develop a consciousness of the active role played by churches in the conquest of native peoples and the potential for people of relative wealth to learn from others who always understood the sacred connection between human beings and the land. Early approaches to Christian dialogues, consultations, and programs were framed by Western, Euro-American, and classical Christian assumptions that were reflective of early missionary movements. For example, some of the first participants in consultations sponsored by the World Council of Churches were anthropologists rather than indigenous peoples.[14]

---

[14]See Maria Chavez Quispe, "Guest Editorial," *Ecumenical Review* 62, no. 4 (December 2010): 335. Indigenous theologies and issues first moved into the orbit of World Council of Churches with the Programme to Combat Racism and the Commission of the Churches on International Affairs. There were two consulta-

EXTENSIVE ROOTS

139

Creating space in Christian churches for indigenous peoples to set agendas for dialogues and consultations about indigenous issues remains a challenge but has evolved over time, largely due to pressures coming from within the ecumenical movement from indigenous peoples and churches in the Global South. Some significant recent examples of the way the churches are changing in their understanding of the importance of theologies and legitimacy of lifestyles of indigenous peoples include the 1986 apology issued by the United Church of Canada to First Nations Peoples, WCC involvement in the United Nations' process for adopting the Declaration on the Rights of Indigenous Peoples, WCC consultations held in 2008 and 2009 that involved indigenous peoples naming indigenous issues and ecclesial and social visions, and the Call to Action, "There's a New World in the Making," issued from the North American Regional Forum and Hearings held in November 2011 in Calgary, Canada, as part of the Poverty, Wealth, and Ecology project. "There's a New World in the Making" was written in the form of a prayer based upon a Cree ritual presented to the participants in the consultation as "Standing Stones" and includes the four primary quadrants representing the four directions—east, south, west, and north.

Interest in concepts such as *Sumak Kawsay* and *buen vivir* emerging from the ancestral knowledge of indigenous peoples of Latin America continues to grow in ecumenical circles. The terms refer to "living well." *Buen vivir* "reaffirms the cosmocentric and holistic conception of life and development in respect, harmony, and balance with mother earth. It is also a relationship of spirituality, of coexistence, instead of domination, that ensures the sustainability of life as God's creation."[15] *Sumak Kawsay* as a concept emerged from a resistance movement in Latin America in the 1980s. Carmen Seco Pérez describes the history of Amazonian peoples as one of being destroyed and disenfranchised by the state while mobilizing to "remain loyal to their roots."[16] The term

tions held in Barbados in the 1970s; Barbados I (1971) and Barbados II (1977). Participants invited to Barbados I were primarily anthropologists.

[15]Angelique J. W. M. van Zeeland, "The Changing Development Context," *Ecumenical Review* 66, no. 3 (October 2014): 313–23.

[16]Carmen Seco Pérez, "A Journey towards Wholeness: Sumak Kawsay and the Voice of the Ecuadorian Amazon," *Unidad de Información Socio Ambiental* (Quito: Universidad Andina Simón Bolívar, 2016), 3.

Sumak Kawsay "draws on various proposals, trying to crystallize something different, alternative in order to find common ways to resolve conflicts, forgiveness and above all, restoring harmony between humans and nature."[17] Pérez suggests a new translation of *Sumak Kawsay* as the "pursuit of wholeness: a way of walking that affirms in every step the vibration of life."[18] Four mantras—health, love, working, and wisdom—express the courage of Amazonian peoples to live how they want live, to maintain holistic relationships with people and the forest, and to fight for sovereignty over their own land. This idea of good living is now enshrined in the constitutions of Bolivia and Ecuador and represents a shift from institutionalizing indigenous peoples toward struggling for their own sovereignty, freedom, and autonomy.[19]

Pope Francis as an innovative leader of the Roman Catholic communion has become the first pope to ask for the forgiveness of indigenous people. In a speech given at the Second World Meeting of Popular Movements held in Santa Cruz de la Sierra, Bolivia, Pope Francis said, "I ask humbly for forgiveness, not only for the offenses of the church herself, but also for crimes committed against the native peoples during the so-called conquest of America."[20] The pope expressed his deep appreciation for what he called a "polyhedric" form of coexistence, "where each group preserves its identity by building together a plurality which does not threaten but reinforces unity."[21]

Buddhist Economics

The concept of the relational self is central to Buddhism. Prosperity in Buddhism is realized collectively and defined in terms of "more being." "More being," however, is not defined in material or monetary terms. Sulak Sivaraksa, a Thai social critic, plays a leading role in mobilizing people in Thailand. His work is fueled and grounded in what he calls "Buddhism with a small b." Among other accomplishments, he founded and edited one of the field's

---

[17]Ibid., 1.
[18]Ibid., 13.
[19]Ibid.
[20]"Read Pope Francis' Speech on the Poor and Indigenous Peoples," *Time*, July 10, 2015.
[21]Ibid.

most influential journals, the *Social Science Review*; started Thailand's indigenous NGO movement; and supported refugees after the 1988 uprising in Burma through activities such as the Jungle School for displaced students.

Sivaraksa believes that Buddhism offers the tools for mind training necessary to resist systemic and structural evil and the suffering experienced in consumer-driven societies. Capitalism may have some benefits, but Sivaraksa argues that those benefits "are largely unintended byproducts of the system . . . For maximum results capitalism alienates humans from their communities, families, and ultimately, their spiritual selves by attributing worth solely in terms of economic value."[22] Western societies, he observes, teach people to "compartmentalize" and never to be fully aware of themselves and their motivations. "Put differently," Sivaraksa writes, "consumerism is a perverse corollary of the Cartesian proof of personal existence: 'I shop, therefore I am.' "[23] Consumers are well-trained in the United States to believe that they increase their well-being by accumulating more goods. People become controlled by greed, unaware of themselves, and what they really want or need to be happy. Sivaraksa does not dismiss the importance of economics as a field of study. In his classic essay "Alternatives to Consumerism," Sivaraksa turns to the writings of German economist E. F. Schumacher to underscore an alternative approach to economics that champions low technology and sustainability.

Schumacher was a Rhodes Scholar, an economic advisor to the British Control Commission in postwar Germany, and the top economist and head of planning for the British Coal Board. Like most other economists, Schumacher focused early on in his career on growth as the means to thrive and flourish, but he grew to change his perspectives. He ultimately concluded that the real problem of Western society was not a technical and economic problem related to growth, but a deep philosophical one. Bigger is not always better, and growth is not always good. In *Small Is Beautiful: Economics as if People Mattered*, Schumacher observed that economists in the West were primarily urban intellectuals with little experience of the ways of traditional agricultural communi-

---

[22]Sulak Sivaraksa, "Alternatives to Consumerism," in *Liberating Faith*, ed. Roger Gottlieb (Lanham, MD: Rowman and Littlefield, 2003), 287.
[23]Ibid., 288.

ties. He identified one of the most fateful errors of our age as the mistaken belief that the problem of production has been solved. Economics has been allowed to become the primary measure of meaning in Western societies, a measure he saw as too fragmentary and narrow. Schumacher wrote, "If economic thinking pervades the whole of society, even simple non-economic values like beauty, health, or cleanliness can survive only if they prove to be 'economic.' "[24] He called for a nobler economics, unafraid to discuss spirit and conscience, moral purpose and meaning of life, with the aim of situating people within a larger web of life.

Schumacher underscored the importance of traditional agricultural communities that embraced handicrafts and village lifestyles. He pointed out, "Gandhi's scheme was to begin with the villages, to stabilize and enrich their traditional way of life by use of labor-intensive manufacture and handicrafts, and to keep the nation's economic decision making as decentralized as possible, even if this slowed the pace of urban and industrial growth to a crawl."[25] Small means free, efficient, creative, enjoyable, and enduring, whereas Western societies had an obsession with "giantism." The increase of wealth depended upon unlimited growth and making demands on natural resources available in the world without placing limits upon them. Schumacher insisted upon the scale of industry to be treated as a primary and independent problem and advocated for what he called "decentralist economics."

Buddhist economics, Schumacher argued, emphasized "right livelihood." The essence of civilization is not in the "multiplication of wants but in the purification of human character." The production of goods can never then be seen as more important than creative activity. According to the teachings of the Buddha, nonhuman nature is not reduced to passive matter that is instrumental in human production and wealth creation for the sake of enriching human life. The whole creation, the whole community of living organisms, is part of a larger cycle of creation and destruction that works together to sustain life.

Buddhist economics invites Western societies to rethink the function of work. The intention of work is not just to produce

[24] E. F. Schumacher, *Small Is Beautiful: Economics as if People Mattered* (New York: Harper and Row, 1973), 43.
[25] Ibid., 5.

goods and services. Work gives human beings the chance to use and develop our faculties, to overcome ego-centeredness by joining with others to work toward a common goal or task, and to bring forth enough goods and services needed for sustenance. Buddhist economics invites us to rethink the attachment to material things, to rethink the role of wealth, and to consider the scale and size of a viable economy. Simplicity and nonviolence are essential aspects of the Buddhist way of life. Consumption is not the ultimate purpose or goal for human life, but the means of human well-being. The beginning point for economic planning and production becomes ensuring that everyone has access to the way to express creative activity.

The problem that Schumacher identifies in mainstream economics is that the love of money and material wealth are given priority above all else. Markets then become the means to institutionalize "individualism and non-responsibility."[26] The dominant logic of the marketplace that gives everything a price does not allow for qualitative distinctions to be made that are of vital importance for the flourishing of the whole creation. One of the problems that informed Schumacher's shift as an economist from increased technology and growth to low technology and a steady state was the mismanagement of "developing" nations by wealthier, highly industrialized nations. Technology became good to him only where it was seen to be appropriate.

Sivaraksa is a strong critic of social developmentalism. He argued in a lecture given in April 2012 at the Berkeley Center for Religions, Peace and World Affairs that globalization, the term used today to describe the global economy and trade across borders, was coined after "development" became a dirty word.[27] The word *development* became sacred in 1960 when the United Nations adopted the term and introduced the Decade of Development. Development, Sivaraksa argues, never worked, in his examination of the experience of people living in Asian countries. "In ten years, the poorer countries became even poorer. The rich countries became

---

[26]Ibid., 42.
[27]Sulak Sivaraksa, "Buddhist Economics in the Age of Globalization," lecture sponsored by the Berkley Center for Religion, Peace, and World Affairs, April 12, 2012, berkleycenter.georgetown.edu.

richer."[28] From Sivaraksa's perspective, *development* is synonymous with *Americanization* and adopting US-style free markets.

Buddhist economics offers an alternative way of thinking by emphasizing a relational way of being in the world; both people and the Earth matter. From a Buddhist point of view, it is an illusion to suggest that technology can control nature. Mastering nature through technology is always an illusion. Sivaraksa makes an observation that may be startling to many US Americans. When we envision the future of the world, Sivaraksa thinks that we should not have in mind cities like New York, Washington, DC, or Chicago, but the poorest cities of India, Indonesia, and Thailand, where happiness is discovered in the commons and with a sense of belonging.

Sabbath Practice, Debt Release, and Jubilee as Resistance to the "Double Straits" of Economic Injustice and Environmental Destruction

Judaism grounds and centers its moral imagination in ritual laws, the *halakah*, a Hebrew word meaning the "path one walks." Many Christians continue to make the mistake of judging Judaism as a flawed and rigid religion that prioritizes law over grace. However, the purpose of *halakah* is not to create a set of rigid principles but to guide faithful people in ways that will make it easier to live in covenantal relationship with God and God's creation. Reconstructionist rabbi and director of the Shalom Center Arthur Waskow says that the laws and teachings of the Torah set forth "a time-tempered rhythmic process of economic, ecological, and political action that is intended to preserve abundance and that warns of utter disaster if the balance in undone."[29]

Justice, care for the most vulnerable, equality, and totally shared life are at the heart of Jewish ethical teachings regarding money and wealth accumulation. Stories and laws contained in the Torah make it clear that the problem faced by people living in poverty in the ancient world were the laws and practices of empires that drove them deeply into debt and forced them to turn over their

---

[28]Ibid.

[29]Arthur Waskow, "Jewish Environmental Ethics: Intertwining Adam with Adamah," in *The Oxford Handbook of Jewish Ethics and Morality*, ed. Elliot N. Dorff and Jonathan K. Crane (New York: Oxford University Press, 2013).

land and sometimes themselves to others already possessing tremendous wealth. Ulrich Duchrow and Franz Hinkelammert observe, "The basic contradiction appearing in Ancient Israel after the spread of the money-interest-property economy was between debtors and creditors. In real terms, this led to the concentration of land in the hands of the big landowners on the one hand and the over-indebtedness of the small farmers on the other."[30] Israelite rituals and laws emerge as a form of resistance to the stranglehold grip of ancient empires.

Egypt is the first among many ancient empires introduced in the Hebrew Bible. The exodus story arguably remains the most important event for Jewish people because it records God's involvement in history as a Liberator, Healer, and Transformer of life for the most vulnerable. Christian theologian Daniel Groody asserts that "symbolically, the empire represents any power that arrogates to itself the power that belongs to God alone, or any group that subjugates the poor and needy for its own advantage."[31] *Mitzrayyim*, the Hebrew word for Egypt, literally means "double straits," "narrow place," or "narrow confinement." We can think of this term as reference to the geographical location of Egypt—or more metaphorically, from the perspective of the Israelites who were held in the "narrow confinement" of slavery. The Egyptians "made their lives miserable with hard labor, making mortar and bricks, doing field work, and by forcing them to do all kinds of other cruel work" (Exod. 1:14). When the Hebrew people cry out to God for liberation, God responds through Moses.

Freeing oneself from bondage means much more in the story than a journey into the wilderness and making a home in a new physical space and territory. On the journey in the wilderness, the Israelites learn to depend upon God for manna, their daily food and daily bread. The manna could only be stored up and saved for the seventh day of the week, the Sabbath (see Exod. 16). Freedom from bondage required a fundamental reorientation of the understanding of self, the reliance upon God for sustenance, a commitment to life in covenant community, and resisting what

---

[30]Ulrich Duchrow and Franz Hinkelammert, *Transcending Greedy Money: Interreligious Solidarity for Just Relations* (New York: Palgrave Macmillan, 2012), 47.

[31]Daniel Groody, *Globalization, Spirituality, and Justice* (Maryknoll, NY: Orbis Books, 2007), 34.

Groody calls "the empire mentality." After Hebrew slaves escape from the ownership and oversight of Pharaoh in Egypt, the first thing that they discover is the Sabbath.

Sabbath practice in Jewish tradition provides time to detach oneself from things, an opportunity to reflect on the creation of human beings and the land in the image and likeness of God, and to mend tattered communities. Abraham Heschel, a social mystic and Jewish theologian, reflected on the significance of the practice of Sabbath-keeping in the modern world in his now classic book *The Sabbath*. Heschel described the Sabbath as a form of resistance to the fascination with conquering and owning space that is held in such high esteem in the most highly industrialized and technologi- cally driven societies. He writes, "To the biblical mind . . . labor is the means toward an end, and the Sabbath as a day of rest, as a day of abstaining from toil is not for the purpose of recovering one's lost strength and becoming fit for the forthcoming labor. The Sabbath is the day for the sake of life."[32] In the first creation story in Genesis, God's final act is not one that underscores unlimited growth and creative activity, but rather God deliberately chooses not to create and rests. The reason to keep the Sabbath is for the lives of individuals and the life of the commons so that nothing—people, plants, all living things—is held in bondage by human labor, just as the Israelites were freed from slavery by the greatest Liberator.

As part of Sabbath practice, debt codes outlined in Deuter- onomy 15 insist that not only is there a requirement of rest in the seventh year, but people shall be released from debt. Robert Wafawanaka, a biblical scholar teaching at the Samuel deWitt Proctor School of Theology, writes about the "humanitarian at- titude" toward people living in poverty adopted in Deuteronomy 15. Problems faced by people living in poverty are discussed within the context of *shemittah* or the year of release that required the remission of debts every seven years. Historical evidence suggests that there was an established tradition of debt in the empires of Mesopotamia, Egypt, Syria, and Canaan. These economies were agrarian, so most of the debt involved agricultural products. Debt was incurred through soft loans given by the wealthy, mainly royals, to people living in poverty. Some of the people took on

---

[32] Abraham Heschel, *The Sabbath* (New York: Farrar, Straus, and Giroux, 1951), 14.

debt in order to survive. Others were merchants needing loans for travel and the acquisition of goods. There are references in ancient documents to high rates of interest being charged, which made it difficult to repay the loans. As a result, some people were forced to sell themselves or other family members into indentured servitude or lost their land and property. Historians and archaeologists have found records of debt cancellations in Mesopotamian and Sumerian documents. But according to Wafawanaka, the "parts of the Hebrew Bible that deal with debt cancellation and release issues are the most documented in ancient Near Eastern literature."[33]

Debt release was required because people and the land were created in God's likeness and, therefore, could not be owned by other human beings. Other principles informing debt release ensured that loans would be interest-free. When garments were taken as a pledge or collateral for loans, they were to be returned each night before nightfall. Wages should be paid by employers to workers on a daily basis. Jesus, a faithful Jew, is remembered by Gospel authors for referencing Deuteronomy 15:11 when he says, "The poor will be with you always" (see Matt. 26:11; Mark 14:7; John 12:8). Jesus's statement should not be interpreted as a theological excuse for the persistence of poverty, but understood as a prophetic call to obey the teachings of the Torah to eliminate poverty.

The most radical social and economic transformation is called for after fifty years in the year of Jubilee, as announced in Leviticus 26:8–13:

> Count off seven weeks of years—that is, seven times seven—so that the seven weeks of years totals forty-nine years. Then have the trumpet blown on the tenth day of the seventh month. Have the trumpet blown throughout your land on the Day of Reconciliation. You will make the fiftieth year holy, proclaiming freedom throughout the land to all its inhabitants. It will be a Jubilee year for you: each of you must return to your family property and to your extended family. The fiftieth year will be a Jubilee year for you. Do not plant, do not harvest the secondary growth, and do not

---

[33]Robert Wafawanaka, "Is the Biblical Perspective on Poverty That 'There Shall Be No Poor among You' or 'You Will Always Have the Poor with You'?" *Review and Expositor* 111, no. 2 (May 2014): 111.

gather from the freely growing vines because it is a Jubilee: it will be holy to you. You can eat only the produce directly out of the field. Each of you must return to your family property in this year of Jubilee.

When I have spoken in churches about the meaning of authentic Sabbath practice and the Jubilee year, people have often asked who puts this day of reconciliation into practice. Rabbi Waskow says that scholars disagree as to whether Jubilee was ever carried out, but the ideal endured in the teachings of the prophets, including Jesus. Waskow insists that the concept of Jubilee remains relevant as an ideal toward which we should strive for the sake of people and the planet.

He argues that part of our contemporary problem with wealth is that we haven't taken a sabbatical from work for the last five hundred years, which leaves us on the verge of "decreating the world." The last three industrial revolutions made major impacts on our life together (economically, socially, and politically). World economic leaders now argue that we are on the verge of a fourth industrial revolution, the digital revolution, during which cyber-physical systems will shape our life together in ways that have no historical precedent.[34] Artificial intelligence will be able to master many of the tasks that people now perform. Klaus Schwab, founder and CEO of the World Economic Forum, suggests that in the future digital revolution, "talent, more than capital, will represent the critical factor of production. This will give rise to a job market increasingly segregated into 'low-skill / low-pay' and 'high-skill / high-pay' segments, which in turn will lead to an increase in social tensions."[35]

Waskow imagines at least three major structural reforms that could be part of a contemporary Jubilee. The first is wealth-recycling, which involves the transfer of massive amounts of investment and capital from the control of giant, long-standing corporations to grassroots and local businesses that are worker-owned, consumer co-ops, family-operated, or neighborhood-operated. If liquid assets are a problem for the corporation, the wealth of the

---

[34]Klaus Schwab, "The Fourth Industrial Revolution: What It Means, How to Respond," World Economic Forum, January 14, 2016, www.weforum.org.
[35]Ibid.

corporation could be recycled by turning over a portion of ownership rights to a community ownership trust that could transfer assets to workers. A second structural reform he suggests is taking a sabbatical from research and development every seven years to allow time to reflect on the environmental and social impacts of production and technology. A third possibility is to empower neighborhoods to encourage economic renewal, cooperative business ventures, and celebrate their life together one day a month.[36] Community celebrations could relate to a neighborhood venture such as an energy co-op that would gather money for, install, and manage solar collectors to reduce energy prices for surrounding homes and businesses.[37]

Islam's Prohibition of *Riba* or Usury

Much like the *halakah* of Judaism, the practices and disciplines of Islam are intended to guides one's actions toward the love of Allah. Mecca, Muhammad's first hometown, was situated on a lucrative trading route. Most of the inhabitants of the region surrounding Mecca were Bedouins, nomadic people. When Muhammad began to receive revelations from God in 610 CE, conflicts had already developed between nomadic tribes and rich class traders. Some tribes settled in small towns that were meeting points for the purpose of trade and pilgrimages. Traditional forms of hospitality, exchange, and trade were beginning to erode, and people started focusing on money as the primary means of exchange. The transition to a money economy, Duchrow and Hinkelammert suggest, was facilitated during Muhammad's lifetime by an increasingly popular belief that hoarding money leads to immortality. Muhammad opposed this belief and because of his opposition experienced persecution and ultimately was forced to flee to Medina. The revelations he received from Allah dealt extensively with money, interest, wealth, and building a just and egalitarian community.[38]

---

[36]See Arthur Waskow, "Toward a Jubilee Economy and Ecology in the Modern World," The Shalom Center, May 12, 2008, theshalomcenter.org.

[37]Arthur Waskow, "Healing America: Beyond Economics," The Shalom Center, March 27, 2016, theshalomcenter.org.

[38]I have been greatly aided here by the work of Duchrow and Hinkelammert. See *Transcending Greedy Money*, 85–86.

Five injunctions within Islam guide faithful Muslims toward appropriate ways to limit or restrain their behaviors within markets and to consider the accumulation of one's individual wealth in relation to a broader community. These injunctions include the following:

- The prohibition of *riba*, or usury.
- The practice of *zakat*, or almsgiving, which is an obligation for those who have the financial means to share, between 2.5 and 20 percent of one's resources.
- The division of *faraid*, or inheritance.
- *Waqf*, which literally means "to stop, contain, or preserve," refers to the endowment of personal wealth for the public good, such as giving land or other resources for a charitable purpose.
- Charity, *sadaqah* in Arabic, encompasses alms, grants, inheritance, loans, *waqf*, and so on.

An overarching objective of all five injunctions is "the equitable distribution of wealth and the reduction of social disparities."[39] The prohibition of *riba* has attracted a great deal of interest among academics in the aftermath of the economic crisis that became most evident in mid-2008. Islamic banking potentially offers an alternative to conventional banking and the finance industry in the West.

The current dominant model for the conventional banking and finance industry in the United States is that of debt finance and encourages financial speculation. Money in this model is a commodity that has value apart from human labor or resources provided for that labor from the natural environment. Chris Meyer, an entrepreneur, and Julia Kirby, an editor for the *Harvard Business Review*, observe that profits in today's conventional financial industry in the West are not "primarily generated from value-adding work of supporting investments in 'real sector' companies, but

---

[39]Lucas Andrianos, Edward Dommen, Bob Goudzwaard, Rosario Guzman, Clement Kwayu, Carlos Larrea, Konrad Raiser, Jung Mo Sung, and Michael Taylor, "The Report of the Greed Line Study Group of the World Council of Churches," comp. Athena Peralta, in *The Greed Line: Tool for a Just Economy*, ed. Athena Peralta and Rogate Mshana (Geneva: WCC Publications, 2016), 21.

from zero-sum work of trading financial investments."[40] Money understood as capital has lost its connection "to value creation of any non-financial kind."[41]

The alienation of capital from the real economy has had some disastrous consequences in recent decades. An example is easily found in the housing crisis beginning in 2008. Mortgage companies secured loans above house value frequently charging high interest rates and fees and then sold them to borrowers who did not have the ability to repay the loans. The bad loans were then bundled and sold in packages along with other risky mortgages as "mortgage backed" securities to investors. When borrowers defaulted on the loans, investors got back a fraction of the loan's value. About 85 percent of the mortgages that were part of the housing crisis were subprime.

The crisis emerged partly out of the ideology and mythology informing the American Dream as then-president George W. Bush argued that "Americans do best when they own their own homes" without pressing at the same time for tighter regulations on the mortgage industry and legislation to secure higher worker wages.[42] One of the ways that the US federal government contained the crisis was by creating the Troubled Assets Relief Program (TARP), which authorized the Treasury to spend up to $700 billion to bail out the banks.[43] Many commentators expressed a sense of indignation at the bank bailout, especially when banks that received the bailouts "awarded their top executives nearly $1.6 billion in salaries, bonuses, and other benefits."[44] In this case, monetary capital was captured by the lure of financial speculation, and the crisis radiated far beyond Wall Street. Mohammed Akacem and Lynde Gilliam make the observation that in the case of the US housing crisis, the current model of debt finance coupled with

---

[40]As quoted by Scott Bader-Saye in "Disinterested Money: Islamic Banking, Monti di Pietà, and the Possibility of Moral Finance," *Journal of the Society of Christian Ethics* 33, no. 1 (Spring/Summer 2013): 120.

[41]Ibid.

[42]See Mark Landler and Sheryl Gay Stolberg, "Bush Can Share the Blame for Financial Crisis," *New York Times*, September 20, 2008.

[43]For more detailed information, see "Emergency Economic Stabilization Act of 2008," www.congress.gov.

[44]CBSNews, "$1.6B of Bank Bailout Went to Execs," December 21, 2008, www.cbsnews.com.

federal deposit insurance resulted in "the socializing of loss and the privatizing of gain."[45]

Islamic principles of economics and finance are intended to offer some balance between an individual's freedom to create wealth in a market economy and the needs of a larger community. Islam is the only religion that recognizes a spiritual tradition identified with the story of Abraham, Sarah, and Hagar that still maintains a prohibition of charging interest, or *riba*, on money loaned. Prohibitions against *riba* are found in the Qur'an and Hadiths. The Hadiths include the following teaching of Abu Sa'id Al-Khudriy citing the conditions for exchanging money and goods: "Gold for gold, silver for silver, wheat for wheat, barley for barley, dates for dates, hand to hand, in equal amounts; and any increase is *Riba*."[46]

Islamic banking first emerged in the 1960s in Egypt as the banks began to apply the rules and norms of Islam, in particular Sharia law, to finance. However, it was not until the 1970s that the practice and institutions of Islamic banking took hold and begin to grow in Muslim countries.[47] In the last fifteen to twenty years, markets for Islamic finance have soared within Muslim countries, and Islamic banking is gaining increased attention in the Global North as well. Malaysia is one of the predominately Muslim countries where Islamic banking and finance have grown, and the industry now represents one-fourth of the Malaysian economy. Albaraka International Bank was the first Islamic bank established in the United Kingdom in 1982. London is the center of Islamic banking and finance in Europe. Today, the top five Islamic banks found in the West include Lariba (which literally means "no *riba*"), University Bank, Harvard Islamic Finance Program, Guidance Financial Group, and Samba. In the United States, federal regulations prevent Islamic financial institutions from being called banks, but you can find institutions such as Lariba, Devon Financial, and Guidance Residential in states with large populations of Muslim immigrants, such as California, Illinois, Ohio, Minnesota, and Virginia.

---

[45]Mohammed Akacem and Lynde Gilliam, "Principles of Islamic Banking: Debt versus Equity Financing," *Middle East Policy* 9, no. 1 (March 2002): 124.

[46]As quoted in Mahmoud Amin El-Gamal, "A Basic Guide to Contemporary Islamic Banking and Finance," June 2000, 3, *www.nubank.com*.

[47]Akacem and Gilliam, "Principles of Islamic Banking," 124.

With respect to the problem of wealth, the most important characteristics of the system include the belief that money is a means of exchange and not a commodity. Islamic banks only invest in real assets, do not charge interest on loans, and prohibit variable forms of interest and speculation. Other important prohibitions include not investing in gambling, pork, pornography, alcohol, drugs, and armaments. Islamic banking inverts the relationship between a creditor and debtor as it has been established and defined in the conventional Western banking system and does not consider money to be a commodity or capital. Rather, money is understood to be "potential capital" that can only be put into productive use through the labor and services of a human being. According to scholars of Islam, "The lender has nothing to do with this conversion of money into capital and with using it productively."[48] Furthermore, charging a variable or fixed rate of interest is forbidden because it fails to consider the profitability of the labor or business itself. Benefits and losses of a loan given for a business venture are always shared between the creditor and the borrower, according to a formula that reflects their level of participation in the labor or service performed. In an equity-based system, depositors are shareholders who essentially gain or lose along with profits gained or losses sustained by the bank.

In order to determine whether a loan meets the criteria of being "*riba*-free," Islamic scholars or Sharia advisory councils meet to arrive at a fatwa or opinion. Theoretically and theologically, it doesn't make a difference if you are a man or woman working in Islamic finance or participating in the advisory councils. Anyone, regardless of gender or religion, is able to apply for a loan or be part of the financial institution. However, none of the financial institutions that have offices in the United States that I researched or talked with had women on the Sharia advisory councils.

Islamic banks structure loans in different ways, and Islamic banking products in the United Kingdom offer an example. If someone is interested in purchasing a home and goes to the Islamic Bank of Great Britain, they might consider either the Ijara or Murabaha plans. Ijara is a leasing arrangement where home buyers essentially rent to own the property a bank purchases for

---

[48]As quoted in ibid., 125.

them. Murabaha offers a somewhat different approach in that the bank supplies the house at a margin above the cost. The customer then pays off the debt in installments. In one case, banks make money from the leasing agreement. In the other case, banks make money because the price agreed upon is more than the market value of the house.[49] Lariba, the oldest community-owned *riba*-free institution in the United States, determines the eligibility of customers for loans in a similar way as conventional banks with some important differences. The "*riba*-free" approach includes considering the activity that the person is proposing to enter and has some alternative means to determine worthiness of customers' applications if they have no credit score. Akacem and Gilliam assert that John Maynard Keynes would not have supported Islamic banking because of its emphasis on shared partnership. They also suggest that the Muslim approach can better handle macroeconomic shocks because it relies upon equity rather than debt. Malaysia has the largest Islamic banking industry in the world, and the country did not face the same degree of financial distress in 2008 as the United States, the United Kingdom, or Iceland. However, it is difficult to judge with accuracy whether that was the result of Islamic banking, because 75 percent of banking in Malaysia retains the Western conventional model.

An Extensive Root System for Interreligious Harmony, Solidarity, and Action

The ideas and religious teachings discussed in this chapter provide an extensive root system to nourish a different set of fundamental social values. In recent years, social, economic, and spiritual resistance to neoliberalism, market fundamentalism, and market idolatry has been growing in the United States and around the world. The concluding section of this book is intended to provide a narrative of hope by offering concrete examples of real people embodying differing values and new parables of the commons to inspire the theological imagination of middle-class US Americans to work for social change.

---

[49]Hilary Osborne, "Islamic Finance: The Lowdown on Sharia-Compliant Money," *The Guardian*, October 29, 2013.

PART IV

INCREASING THE THEOLOGICAL
AND MORAL IMAGINATION
OF THE US MIDDLE CLASS

Chapter 7

Real People Embodying Different Values

> To live under siege, with the equilibrium and the tranquility of inner peace: to prevent the springs of my being from being polluted by the bitter waters that flow as drainage from the table lands of violence and hatred: to do these two things in even the most limited and circumscribed way is to be strong enough to carry the heavy stones of the spirit.
>
> —*Howard Thurman*[1]

Social mystic and civil rights visionary Howard Thurman challenged with poetry and clarity the norms used in the twentieth century by the dominant white culture to define and divide people along lines of class, race, gender, and creed. There is much to learn about confronting the problem of wealth and creating systemic change from the moral courage and theological imagination of the nonviolent resistance of civil rights activists. Historically, white women and people of color in the United States have been excluded from the dominant strategies used to increase individual wealth and thus were forced out of necessity to orient themselves toward a different set of foundational economic values. Thurman, one of the founding pastors of the Church of Fellowship of All Peoples, held profound and radical commitments to personalist philosophy and the practice of nonviolence. *Jesus and the Disinherited*, a book

---

[1] Howard Thurman, "Mysticism and Social Action," *A.M.E. Zion Quarterly Review* 92, no. 3 (October 1980): 4.

written soon after Thurman led a delegation of friendship to India to visit Gandhi, laid the foundation for the nonviolent resistance movement and became a sort of sacred text for civil rights activists. Thurman began the book with the question of what religion, more specifically the Christian religion, teaches "people with their backs against the wall."[2]

He argued that many religions have been "born of a people acquainted with persecution and suffering has become the cornerstone of a civilization and of nations whose very position in modern life has too often been secured by a ruthless use of power applied to weak and defenseless peoples."[3] Thurman's statement implies that the Christian faith, like the other great world religions, arose from a very different set of values than those that built societies by exploiting the weakness of the most vulnerable. In Jesus's time, Jewish people confronted the same question that the disinherited face in every age. That is, "What must be the attitude toward the rulers, the controllers of political, social, and economic life?"[4] Other Jews who were Jesus's contemporaries were prone to see only two paths that they could take in response to the political, social, and economic control of the Roman Empire—either not to resist and become agents of empire or to resist by the use of physical force and be destroyed by the Romans. In contrast, what Jesus showed in his commitments and action is that there are many more paths of resistance. Most prominently in Jesus's teaching and preaching is the path of loving one's neighbor as much as oneself.

Today in the United States there is a swell of social, economic, political, and spiritual resistance to neoliberalism, market fundamentalism, market-driven logic, and market idolatry. Paths of resistance are evident in solidarity protest movements such as the Coalition of the Immokalee Workers' Campaign for Fair Food, the Occupy Wall Street movement in 2011, and the policies proposed by Senator Bernie Sanders in his 2015–16 campaign for the Democratic nomination for US president. A wide variety of ecumenical and denominationally related organizations

---

[2]Howard Thurman, *Jesus and the Disinherited* (Richmond, IN: Friends United Press, 1976; reprint of 1949 edition), 11.

[3]Ibid., 12.

[4]Ibid., 22–23.

have worked consistently for more than a century, and a strong interfaith movement is gaining traction. Offices for social witness within denominations and religious advocacy groups make prophetic statements calling people of faith to act and to lead the United States toward an economy that serves the commons. I have included a long list of documents, statements, and creeds made by interfaith, ecumenical, and denominationally related groups in the "Additional Resources" part of this text to give a sense of the theological basis and strong witness of communities of faith to the elimination of poverty, fair wages, worker rights, pay equity, economic justice, and sustainability. Moreover, grassroots ventures to work toward authentic alternative forms of wealth creation are creating new paths of resistance. We need all of these efforts and much more to confront the problem of wealth and to change the systems and structures accelerating wealth inequalities, creating poverty, and destroying our natural environment.

My intention in this chapter is to nurture your imagination for an economy that serves the commons by telling stories about real people in the United States who are acting as midwives for such an economy. When selecting stories to include as examples in this chapter, I have focused on real people who illustrate activities within economic life that have very different goals from neoliberal capitalism. I underscore a movement that motivates people to voluntarily renounce their wealth for the sake of a larger common good and highlight the efforts of people who historically have been excluded from the dominant strategies used to create wealth. Not all of these ventures will emerge from a specific religious conviction or mission, but many are grounded in religious commitments, and none could be successful without the support of people of faith. Stories told address the Catholic Worker movement; eco-holistic efforts to develop a local land economy; intentional communities transforming market-oriented approaches to church and reinterpreting the meaning of work and wealth; and cooperatives, particularly worker-owned businesses. I have chosen not to include in this chapter people committed to religious orders, primarily to keep the subject matter under control. However, I have a deep and profound respect for people who commit themselves to living in a monastic community. I do not intend to disregard the importance of the transformational practice of prayer and contemplation, the witness to simple living, the way they preserve communal life and provide hospitality for people living in poverty in urban and rural areas, and their activism.

A set of common characteristics emerges from these stories that lend themselves to a new vision of political economy. These stories are intended to give us new ideas for rethinking our middle-class economic activities, like home ownership, banking, and the mission of religious communities, and for addressing issues of economic justice such as food deserts, poverty wages, and lending practices. A fundamental distinction between the stories of real people told in this chapter and neoliberal capitalism described in chapter 4 is that these stories *begin with the understanding of self-as-radically-interdependent-and-formed-in-community. The ultimate purpose of human labor and the creation of wealth is for the sake of the commons*—feeding the hungry, clothing the naked, housing the homeless, providing chances for everyone to have meaningful work and play, nurturing creativity and collaboration, and balancing human consumption with the needs of the ecosystem. This means that wealth is made in the interest of the commons. The economy is understood as anything but morally neutral. *Six fundamental social values are held at the center of one's economic activities—reciprocity, cooperation/collaboration, interdependence, accountability to the commons, sustainability, and the inclusion of diverse peoples and experiences.* Maximizing profits and accumulating material goods and wealth for the sake of luxury are never the ultimate aims of these ventures even though they can be and many are profit-making.

Communities That Arise out of Need

The Catholic Worker movement is a way of life that represents an alternative to participation in and collaboration with the dominant economic, social, and political systems and structures. It is somewhat distinct among the examples of resistance that I offer in that Catholic Workers are not capitalists or socialists, and the movement does not intend to be market-oriented or market-driven. In essence, the Catholic Worker movement is about embodying an ethic of peace and ushering in what Peter Maurin, a French peasant and cofounder of the movement, described as a "society where it is easier for people to be good."

Some scholars would describe Catholic Worker communities as

intentional communities, but I am sensitive to an objection made to this term by Martha Hennessey, Dorothy Day's granddaughter and a Worker at Maryhouse in New York. Hennessey refers to the Catholic Worker communities as "communities that arise out of need." In other words, if there are hungry and homeless people on the street, the call is to respond to Jesus's teaching to "love your neighbor." Jesus didn't say wait until you have time or society made it easier for you to do so.

Catholic Workers seek to eliminate social distance and ensure that no one is valued more than another or receives greater privilege. No distinction is made between those who are "deserving" or "undeserving" of sustenance, concern, or care. Therefore, they oppose violence in all forms—attitudinal, conceptual, social, political, physical, and economic. Catholic Workers organize the economy of their households and activities in ways that ensure that there will be enough resources to provide for anyone who has needs.

Their activities and activism relate to issues emerging in specific contexts and are expressions of deep theological commitments. The Catholic Worker movement originated from and is grounded in a theological tradition that claims that people are created in the image of God to live together in harmony with one another and as faithful stewards of God's creation. The distinctive contributions made by all living things are valued as essential to common life, or to draw upon a Pauline concept, the body of Christ. "If one part suffers, all the parts suffer with it; if one part gets the glory, all the parts celebrate with it. You are the body of Christ and parts of each other" (1 Cor. 12:26–27). Catholic social teaching, the writings of early church fathers, lives of the saints, philosophies of personalism and distributivism, and theological concepts of the mystical body of Christ and corporal works of mercy inspired Dorothy Day and Peter Maurin to envision a movement that responded directly to the urgency of need all around them.

Origins of the Catholic Worker Movement

Day and Maurin cofounded the movement in 1932, the worst year of the Great Depression. No federal poverty line had been established at that time, but poverty was evident everywhere across the nation. By 1933, one-fourth of US residents were unemployed. Those who could find a job were often forced to work for the lowest possible pay without any benefits. Congress did not pass the Fair Labor Standards Act until 1938, despite many earlier efforts to regulate work hours and wages. Entitlements and safety nets such as social security, food stamps, and unemployment and disability insurance were not available, even after a good deal of advocacy and activism done by Catholics like John Ryan, Protestant Social Gospelers, and the strength of labor and socialist movements. Many people unable to find family-sustaining employment were forced to migrate. When weather destroyed crops all across the Great Plains, farmers and their families were forced to load up their household belongings on trucks and wagons as they made the exodus out of the plains states in hope of discovering more promising lands. The weather-beaten faces of Midwestern farmers symbolized the new economic migrant status.

At the other end of the spectrum, there was also the legendary wealth of industrialists, entrepreneurs, and philanthropists such as John Jacob Astor, Andrew Carnegie, and John D. Rockefeller. Some of the first articles that Day wrote for socialist newspapers were about the excesses of the robber barons, which she gave provocative titles to punctuate the contrast in the United States between the experience of the rich and the poor—"Mr. J. D. Rockefeller, 26 Broadway: Here's a Family Living on Dog Food" (*New York Call*, November 13, 1916).

Day was first and foremost a reporter. When she met Maurin she had just returned to her apartment in New York City from a trip to Washington, DC, where she was commissioned by the *Commonweal* and *America* to report on the Hunger March of the Unemployed and a farmers' convention that brought together small farmers and tenant farmers from all around the United States. Maurin introduced Day to what he called the "church's social dynamite" found within documents such as *Rerum novarum*, the writings of the early church, and the stories of the saints. Together, they developed a three-pronged program of action that included a newspaper to disseminate ideas, the creation of houses of hospitality, and farming communes.

Day was influenced by the socialist movement, but it is also critically important to emphasize that the Christian theological tradition enabled her to more fully comprehend the flawed understanding of human nature informing the US economic and political systems. Individual self-interests were valued at the expense of the common good and defended by the use of violent physical force. Dorothy Day and the Catholic Workers practiced the "little way," a term used by St. Térèse of Lisieux who thought of each act of love, resistance, and challenge to economic injustice, social exclusion, and violence as a way of embodying God's love. No effort was considered too small or insignificant.

She and Peter Maurin began a house of hospitality with an idea they borrowed from St. Jerome that every house should have a Christ room open to people in need of shelter. All of the workers who lived in the houses of hospitality had to do all of the jobs, from cleaning toilets to editing the paper they published, from making sure there was enough food for the evening meal to speaking to groups about their work. They started a farming commune for the purpose of "curing unemployment" and solving "the problem of the machine," and with the intention of reintroducing the connection between vocation and work. Practices of prayer and contemplation energized them for their work. Day attended daily Mass and followed a rule in the spirit of Benedict. As the movement grew, regular retreats were planned to sustain the Workers.

Houses of hospitality and Catholic Worker farming communes were not envisioned to be charities or institutions. The Catholic Worker intentionally defied the traditional approaches within churches and social organizations used to address the situation of people in poverty. Dialogue about poverty in the Catholic Worker community did not bear middle- or upper-class assumptions. They were trying to change the assumptions of the discussion of poverty from economic concerns to theological ones. All people who entered into a house of hospitality were treated as human beings created in the *imago dei* and essential to the mystical body of Christ. Houses of hospitality are conceived to be simply houses where people can go to live as long as they need. No proof of "need" was necessary. Socially defined distance between classes was of no importance. No one person deserved more care, preference, or privilege than another—regardless of race, gender, creed, or class.

Day thought that economic systems and structures that forced people into material poverty were abhorrent, but voluntarily renounced money she was paid for her labor by sharing with the community and individual ownership of other material things. Her commitment to voluntary poverty led her to reexamine money and the meaning of work. Money was a means of exchange, not a commodity to be traded. She thought that everyone should pray for the grace to give up any job that didn't serve the common good. Some of the jobs she specifically challenged were in advertising, insurance, and banking. In her perspective, the sole purpose of advertising was to increase one's desire to accumulate material things without examining one's motivations, considering what one actually needs, or the resources being taken from the environment to produce enough goods to satisfy one's desires at the expense of the ecosystem. Moreover, she thought the insurance and banking industries defrauded people living in poverty. Maurin and Day believed in the development of "small cottage industries" that were sustainable and connected labor and livelihood. Houses of hospitality are governed by consensus and supported by donations, cottage industries, shared income, or a combination of them. Day herself never took a salary, paid taxes, or voted. She thought that other human beings and caring for the earth were everyone's personal responsibility.[5]

Communities Form to Address the Needs of Different Local Contexts

There are about 216 Catholic Worker communities in the United States today, and 32 located in different countries around the world. Each of the communities organizes itself a bit differently so as to respond directly to specific needs of the surrounding local community and the ideas of Workers supporting them. Part of the beauty of the movement is that there is no central authority or headquarters. What is held in common, according to the website, is that "Catholic Workers live a simple lifestyle in community, serve the poor, and resist war and social injustice. Most are grounded in the Gospel, prayer, and the Catholic faith, although some houses . . . are interfaith." Maurin's Easy Essay on "A Radical Change" sums up well the alternative offered by the Catholic Worker movement to politically framed paths of resistance.

---

[5]Many excellent studies of Dorothy Day and her writings are easily available online on the Catholic Worker website, at www.catholicworker.org. This section summarizes a book-length project on Day. See Elizabeth Hinson-Hasty, *Dorothy Day for Armchair Theologians* (Louisville: Westminster John Knox Press, 2014).

A Radical Change

1. The order of the day
   is to talk about the social order.
2. Conservatives would like
   to keep it from changing
   but they don't know how.
3. Liberals try to patch it
   and call it a New Deal.
4. Socialists want a change,
   but a gradual change.
5. Communists want a change,
   an immediate change,
   but a Socialist change.
6. Communists in Russia
   do not build Communism,
   they build Socialism.
7. Communists want to pass
   from capitalism to Socialism
   and from Socialism to Communism.
8. I want a change,
   and a radical change.
9. I want a change
   from an acquisitive society
   to a functional society,
   from a society of go-getters
   to a society of go-givers.[6]

Intentional Communities Redefining the Meaning of Work and Wealth

Another effort at the grassroots level is found among people who form intentional communities. These intentional communities bear similarities to the Catholic Worker movement, but they are not always organized around distinctive faith commitments or voluntary poverty, and some would claim to embody a form of social capitalism. They hold in common the belief that the

---

[6]Peter Maurin, "A Radical Change," www.catholicworker.org.

creation of wealth is a collective communal goal as opposed to a path toward individual prosperity. Several different models of intentional communities are found across the country in response to needs in both urban and rural environments. People may form an intentional community as a new way of being church that counters the values of market-driven society; offers intentional living arrangements centered around ensuring access to affordable housing or sustainability of communities and the earth; creates centers for social innovation or social collaboration; or focuses on accompaniment and advocacy. Their primary missions are not market-driven or market-oriented. Intentional communities represent alternative forms of wealth creation by disrupting dominant norms of success, wealth, and power and reinterpreting the meaning of work and wealth as neighbor love known in community.

A Model of Congregational Life That Challenges the Values of Market-Driven Society

Gordon and Mary Cosby started the Church of the Savior in 1946 to address the racial and economic divide in church and society. One way to approach social, economic, and political change is to think about the great impact that you can make. Another way, the path that Gordon and Mary took, was to focus on belonging to and building community. The Church of the Savior began in restaurants and coffeehouses, and operated with a small headquarters in a brownstone near DuPont Circle in Washington, DC. The church never owned a traditional building. When the church legally incorporated in 1953, it purchased land that would later become a retreat center for the purpose of rest and what Gordon Cosby called "re-creation." Rather than focusing on realizing a specific and easily articulated statement of mission, the church emphasized and explored creating ways for people to connect the inward and outward journey of faith in smaller groups.

The beginning point of the Christian life is personally cultivating a relationship with Christ and others in a community. Journeying inward responds to the call to cultivate a life with Christ and others through the practice of daily spiritual disciplines, such as prayer, eating together, and reflecting on scripture. The personal relationship is only the beginning. Journeying outward is beginning to recognize the face of Christ in others, particularly those most vulnerable in society, and drawing one into more authentic community.

Elizabeth O'Connor, one of the founding members of the Church of the Savior, reflected on her experiences in *Journey Inward, Journey Outward*, published in 1968. O'Connor suggested that "the failure to maintain the tension between inward and outward may account now for the urgency of the church to be engaged in poverty programs and civil rights demonstrations, and community organizations, and its breathless seeking of God at work in the secular city."[7] The church's mission is to identify talented disciples, call forth their gifts, and prepare them to share those talents in a society where so many people are forced to live with their backs against the wall.

Early on, the Church of the Savior discovered its mission in places where needs were evident. They established a coffeehouse ministry at the Potter's House. Members of the Restoration Corps painted and repaired dilapidated buildings. An ecumenical group called For Love of Children (F.L.O.C.) aimed to close Washington, DC's Junior Village for children. A shop was founded to serve as an outlet for local artisans. The School for Christian Living prepared members for mission. The community also shared meals together at least three times a week. In the 1960s, a few members established an intentional living community called the Covenant Community where they committed to sharing housing for a year. Several of those who joined that intentional community gave up their living arrangements and their jobs. They considered a monastic model in a rural area at first, but then "discovered that they wanted to be in the inner city with the poor. They felt that the essential tasks would be to listen, to learn, and to give themselves—to be neighbors in a society that cannot afford neighbors."[8]

One of the ministries that emerged from the Church of the Savior is the Faith and Money Network. Originally called the Ministry of Money, the network was founded by Don McClanen to help people recognize "the relationship between money and fear

----

[7] Elizabeth O'Connor, *Journey Inward, Journey Outward* (New York: Harper and Row, 1968), 29-30.

[8] Ibid, 117.

and anger."[9] The Faith and Money Network offers workshops to help people connect their relationship with money to their spiritual beliefs and values and equips people "to transform their relationship with money, to live with integrity and intentionality, and to participate in creating a more equitable world."[10] An important practice in which the Faith and Money Network invites people to engage is writing a money autobiography that examines the formation of one's thoughts about money and the powerful feelings money evokes. In the 1980s the Faith and Money Network began "pilgrimages of reverse mission," which involve transforming US understandings of money and wealth by taking small groups to places of economic poverty such as India, Palestine, and Haiti.

Bev Cosby, Gordon's brother, founded a similar ministry to the Church of the Savior called Church of the Covenant in their hometown of Lynchburg, Virginia. My husband, Lee, and I were actively involved in that congregation while we lived in Lynchburg, where I worked for Interfaith Outreach Association and he served as the associate pastor of a local Presbyterian church. We frequently cooked and served dinners at the Lodge of the Fisherman and participated in evening prayer as we were able to do so. Lodge of the Fisherman welcomed anyone to the table for a weekly meal. After breaking bread, everyone gathered there discussed issues of political and social importance. One of the most important aspects of our time at Church of the Covenant was learning that the congregation was truly a meeting place that did not concern itself with boundaries of class, race, gender, or religion as they were imposed by the dominant society. Lee and I team-taught a Sunday school class at the church where he served as associate pastor, and we covenanted with them to take meals to the Gateway, a ministry established by Church of the Covenant for men who had recently been released from prison. A central aspect of that service was to build relationships across socially defined lines of difference.

Intentional communities implicitly and explicitly teach those who are involved that the ground of one's being is in God known in neighbor love, and therefore one's energies and activities should be focused on neighbor love in community. Moreover, they provide

---

[9]Mike Little, "Who We Are," Faith and Money Network, faithandmoneynetwork.org.
[10]Ibid.

unstructured and unprogrammed time that disrupts the tireless emphasis on efficiency that is a key element of neoliberal capitalism.

Intentional Community as Social Collaboratory

Covenant Community Church (CCC) in Louisville represents another type of intentional community that in forming its own identity by drawing upon the work done by the Church of the Savior, the resources of the secular Canadian Centre for Social Innovation in Toronto, and the practices of interfaith spirituality. Pastors Chip Andrus, Jud Hendrix, and Liz Kaznak did not want CCC to derive the identity or mission of the church from buildings or property, but rather to extend the church's mission beyond its own walls and nurture members of the congregation to determine their own sense of call and vocation in the world.

In contrast to a traditional church, the primary work of the people is in small intentional communities forming around a particular mission, not in worship. Weekly worship is the expression of people coming together for re-creation and reenergizing. The community as a whole is responsible for worship as several members meet once a week to determine the theme of the service and to determine who will write or create aspects of the liturgy. CCC has an open pulpit; anyone in the congregation can preach. The liturgy is free-flowing and includes weekly communion where everyone is invited to the table. After worship, the feast extends to a community potluck.

The importance of the Centre for Social Innovation in the original vision for CCC cannot be understated. Founded by a small group of entrepreneurs in Toronto, Canada, in 2003, the mission of the Centre is to create a model for shared workspaces for individuals and organizations working for social change. An observation of one of the founders is that organizations with a social mission face significant challenges due to limited financial resources, which means that they work in substandard facilities and are often isolated from a broader community of people with common interests. To foster collaboration, they create shared spaces or hubs for social innovation. The main goal of their activities then is to increase innovation by sharing resources, ideas, and their social imagination as opposed to fostering competition.

For about six years, CCC shared a building with another

church, James Lees Presbyterian Church. When the high costs of maintaining a building constructed in the early twentieth century threatened to drain the coffers of both congregations, they envisioned an alternative approach. Ultimately they concluded that identifying with a particular piece of property separated them from a larger community, their vision for their work in the world, and even from other Christians who met in their own buildings in various parts of the city. Together, Jud Hendrix and Phil Lloyd-Sidle, the pastors of CCC and James Lees, respectively, led members of the congregations to reach an agreement for the building to be repurposed as "1741 Social Collaboratory." The idea was to move out of a landlord/tenant relationship into a cooperative one. A vision statement named the group's deep core values of creating a space for mission and social innovation. Anyone in the local community could use the space as long as they covenanted to be part of the collaborator board. During board meetings, members made decisions about how to use the space by consensus. Ultimately, sixteen religious, justice, and arts groups met in the building. While working through this process, the congregations became aware of the way in which the walls of the church building not only kept out others who were different but also held in the congregation. They began a quarterly practice of inviting congregations across the city to worship together in a public space as a symbol of their broader connections.

Centered on Accompaniment and Advocacy for Immigrant Groups

Intentional communities are also created among immigrant groups in the United States on the basis of concepts of accompaniment and advocacy. St. William Catholic Church and the Catholic Worker in Louisville support La Casita, an intentional community for women who are recent immigrants to the United States.

One of the women I met at La Casita is Janet from Guatemala. Her native language is Mam. Janet works for a local cleaning agency and sends a good portion of her minimum-wage paycheck back to Guatemala to support her children and her aging parents. La Casita provides her a rent-free room at the local Catholic Worker house. In exchange, Janet does some minimal cleaning work in the house. When I visited her at the house, I asked her to describe what it is like to live in the United States. She said, "It is like being a ghost." "Being a ghost" for her meant that she lives unnoticed in the community. She wanted to stay under the radar, so to speak. She was afraid that if people noticed her, she would be held with suspicion. She couldn't afford to be sent back to Guatemala. Her family depends on her earnings for their survival.

The intentional community formed at La Casita supports women by creating a space where women can be visible in a culture where their contribution to a larger community remains hidden by economic deprivation and prejudice. The women write a covenant together to name the principles of their circle of support. Practicing "solidarity and justice" has emerged as a key theme in the covenants written by the women of La Casita. Women work on a personal level and advocate for others by assisting new immigrants entering their city, identifying opportunities for family-sustaining employment, providing a safe harbor for families entering the United States, and promoting awareness in the city of the invisibility of Latino/a people. It is worth mentioning that immigrant communities typically do not think that the creation of wealth is for one's own sake. Rather there is an expectation that wealth is created for a larger family. Family is defined in much broader terms.

Eco-Holism and Developing a Local Economy to Combat Food Apartheid

Another example of an alternative form of wealth creation is found in efforts to resist what Kentucky author Wendell Berry calls the "totalizing force of corporations." Berry writes, "There seems, really, to be only one way, and that is to develop and put into practice the idea of a local economy—something that growing numbers of people are now doing. For good reasons they are beginning with the idea of a local food economy."[11] Berry offers a vivid description in his 2012 Jefferson Lecture "It All Turns on Affection" of the importance of grassroots efforts to embrace eco-holism and return to a "land economy."

Berry's grandfather earned his living working on a farm in

---

[11]Wendell Berry, "The Idea of a Local Economy," *Orion Magazine*, orion-magazine.org.

the little town of Port Royal, Kentucky. As early as the 1920s, farmers and their families were confronted with the growing priority placed upon efficiency, productivity, and cost-effectiveness of farming subsumed under the slogan of making "every farm a factory."[12] Historian Deborah Fitzgerald observes that the entrance of industrial logic into farming meant that the farms were to reflect the ideals of "modern mass production" and decisions driven by the "industrial boardroom." Factory farms "linked capital, raw materials, transportation networks, communication systems, and newly trained technical experts. Interconnected and often sprawling, these systems of production and consumption functioned like grids into which fit the more identifiable components of industrialization—the tractors, paved roads, bank credit, migrant labor, and commodity markets."[13] Berry remembers this point on history's timeline in a more personal way.

His grandfather lived under the distress of debt for more than forty years after the small town in which he lived was forced to come face-to-face and toe-to-toe with an agribusiness executive and industrial Goliath—James P. Duke. Duke, in Berry's assessment of the situation, was a person who stood diametrically opposed to his grandfather; both in terms of the scale of Duke's wealth and the social measure of his achievements as well as regarding the difference between their understanding of how wealth and achievement should be measured.

A metaphor Berry learned from his teacher, Wallace Stegner, describes the essential difference between his grandfather and James P. Duke. Stegner thought that people in the United States could be divided into two kinds: "boomers" and "stickers": "Boomers . . . want 'to make a killing and end up on Easy Street,' whereas stickers are 'those who settle, and love the life they have made and the place they have made it in.' . . . The boomer is motivated by greed, the desire for money, property, and therefore power. . . . Stickers on the contrary are motivated by affection."[14] Stick-

---

[12]Deborah Fitzgerald, *Every Farm a Factory: The Industrial Ideal in American Agriculture*, Yale Agrarian Studies Series (New Haven, CT: Yale University Press, 2003).

[13]Ibid., 3.

[14]Wendell Berry, "It All Turns on Affection," National Endowment for the Humanities, 2012 Jefferson Lecture, www.neh.gov.

ers find a sense of belonging, belonging in the midst of a larger community of people that lives in symbiotic relationship with a much larger web of life. Berry's grandfather did not intend to increase his efficiency by harnessing and harvesting the land for his wealth and the wealth of his family, but rather he found his wealth by belonging to the land, the people, the place, the community it created and fed. In Berry's mind, what the majority of economists have ignored and failed to include in their definition of economy is the notion of land economy.

Efforts to develop a local food economy begin with a basic concern for preserving community, especially the quality of life in smaller rural communities, and for people in poverty living in neighborhoods in urban areas that are food deserts or food swamps. Sustainability is a value and norm that restores the prosperity of rural communities, eliminates poverty, and addresses racial and ethnic disparities in access to healthy food, which dramatically affects one's health and overall quality of life. Also, these efforts shorten the distance between producers and consumers and give consumers greater influence over the types of foods they eat.

Some Facts about Food Insecurity and Poverty

To gain a fuller understanding of the significance of developing a local food economy, consider the problem of hunger or food insecurity that persists in the United States. According to the US Department of Agriculture, 48.1 million people lived in "food-insecure" households in 2014—a statistic that had remained unchanged since 2012. Tracie McMillan, a researcher at the Schuster Institute for Investigative Journalism at Brandeis University, says that is "a fivefold jump since the late 1960s, including an increase of 57 percent since the late 1990s."[15]

One of the main reasons that people who are employed still live in food-insecure households is the decline in wages over the last forty years. In 2015 the official federal minimum wage was $7.25 an hour. With a forty-hour week, a family of four with one minimum-wage earner (working fifty-two weeks a year without

------

[15]Tracie McMillan, "The New Face of Hunger," *National Geographic*, www.nationalgeographic.com.

a vacation, paid or unpaid) would earn about $15,080. That is almost $9,000 less than the 2016 official federal poverty line. Keep in mind that the average minimum-wage worker is about thirty-five years old. More than one-third are at least forty years old, and almost half have some college experience. Women and people of color are more likely to work jobs for minimum wage, low wages, or poverty-level wages. This means that households with higher than the national average rates of food insecurity include those with children (19 percent), those with children headed by single mothers (35 percent) or fathers (22 percent), blacks (26 percent), Hispanics (22 percent), and/or seniors (9 percent).

Additional factors are the cost of housing and the lack of access to healthy foods. A report done by the National Low Income Housing Coalition concluded, "There is nowhere in the United States that people can afford to live on minimum wage."[16] If only about 30 percent of one's monthly budget should be designated to cover the cost of housing, then the rent or mortgage payment can only be about $419 a month. CBS Money Watch reported in 2013 that "rent prices across the country average about $1,231 a month, but the median rents in [the] most affordable places are about half that."[17] This fact forces many people working in minimum-wage or low-wage jobs to choose between paying for food, transportation, and other necessities and housing.

Creating "Oases in Food Deserts"

Let me offer two examples of organizations that are addressing the needs of communities of people who otherwise would not have access to healthy farm-fresh produce. The Black Church Food Security Network (BCFSN) in Baltimore, Maryland, and New Roots in Louisville, Kentucky, combat food apartheid in their cities through community organizing and cooperative economics.

Rev. Dr. Heber Brown III, pastor of Pleasant Hope Baptist Church in Baltimore, spearheads an effort that involves collaboration and support for pastors and members of black churches throughout the city and local black farmers. African American

---

[16]Kevin Matthews, "Minimum Wage Workers Can't Afford to Live Anywhere in the US," June 13, 2016, Truthout, www.truth-out.org.

[17]Ilyce Glink, "Top 10 Cheapest US Cities to Rent an Apartment," CBS Money Watch, July 20, 2013, www.cbsnews.com.

communities in Baltimore as in so many cities across the United States are disproportionately affected by lack of access to healthy, affordable food. City leaders and the food distribution system have failed black communities. According to a study conducted by the Johns Hopkins School of Public Health, more than one-third of African Americans in Baltimore live in food deserts.

Brown said that one of the reasons he started organizing community leaders for the BCFSN was due to multiple visits to members of his congregation hospitalized because of diet-related illnesses. What he recognized was the importance of the black church as one of the main economic resources of the black community. Brown said in an interview on the *Marc Steiner Show* that many of the same neighborhoods that are food deserts are also "job deserts," "health deserts," and "education deserts."

Pleasant Hope Baptist Church has responded by creating an "oasis." Along with other churches in the area they have organized community leaders to find spaces for small gardens where fruits and vegetables can be grown on their grounds. Maxine's Garden sits in the front yard of Pleasant Hope Baptist Church and is named after one of the oldest members who grew up on her family's farm in South Carolina. Maxine is the "mother" of Pleasant Hope's garden and can often be seen working diligently in the garden shortly after sunrise. The garden produced 900 pounds of produce in 2015 and more than 1,000 pounds in 2016. At first the produce was given away to anyone who needed it, but, over time, the church changed to a donation-based structure. In 2016, Maxine's Garden transitioned to selling the produce at prices that beat the local markets. All profits are reinvested back into the garden.[18]

The BCFSN works with intentionality to connect black churches with black farmers to provide access to healthy food for the most destitute communities and support local farmers. There are far fewer black farmers than white farmers, though the number of black farmers is on the rise. Journalist Leah Pinneman reported, "For decades, the US Department of Agriculture discriminated against Black farmers, excluding them from farm loans and assistance. Meanwhile, racist violence in the South targeted

---

[18]Updates regarding this project were provided via email correspondence with the Rev. Dr. Heber Brown III on February 14, 2017.

land-owning Black farmers, whose very existence threatened the sharecropping system. These factors led to the loss of about 14 million acres of Black-owned rural land—an area nearly the size of West Virginia."[19] One of BCFSN's partners is the Black Dirt Farm Collective located on Harriet Tubman's ancestral land. Partnerships with black farmers are especially significant because the ultimate goal is to free the black community from dependence upon dominant forms of wealth creation and a food industry driven by the interests and financial investments of whites.

New Roots in Louisville offers another example worthy of attention. Karyn Moskowitz founded the organization with two of her friends in 2009. In 2011 the city published a study on "The Social Determinants of Health in Louisville Metro Neighborhoods" that reported, "Louisvillians in the poorest neighborhoods have lower life expectancies sometimes by as much as ten years shorter than the overall Louisville Metro life expectancy; Louisville residents ages 40 to 65 who earn less than $20,000 annually are significantly more likely to report that they have had a heart attack, and neighborhoods that have been labeled as 'food deserts' have diabetes mortality rates that are two to three times higher than the total Louisville Metro."[20]

Moskowitz's advocacy and activism are fueled and informed by her Jewish faith. When presenting the model to churches and synagogues she cites Deuteronomy 16:20, " Justice, justice shalt thou pursue." She says, "the Hebrew word for charity—*tzedakah*—literally means justice. In Jewish tradition, *tzedakah* is not an act of condescension from one person to another who is in need. It is the fulfillment of a mitzvah, a commandment, to a fellow human being who has equal status before God." Pirkei Avot, *The Ethics of the Fathers*, also guide her. When she has the feeling that she is getting overwhelmed, she remembers the teachings of Rabbi Tarfon, "It is not your responsibility to finish the work [of perfecting the world], but you are not free to desist from it either" (Pirkei Avot, 2:16).

---

[19]Leah Pinneman, "After a Century in Decline, Black Farmers Are Back and on the Rise," *Yes! Magazine*, May 7, 2016.

[20]Patrick Smith, Margaret Pennington, Lisa Crabtree, and Robert Illback, "Louisville Metro Health Equity Report: The Social Determinants of Health in Louisville Metro Neighborhoods," Louisville Department of Public Health and Wellness, Center for Health Equity, 2011, 5. https://louisville.edu/cepm/westlou/louisville-wide/lmph-health-equity-report-2011/.

Moskowitz is "motivated by the thought of Justice, as opposed to Charity. . . . The Jewish response to hunger cannot stop at giving a can to the food pantry on Yom Kippur. We have to be part of this movement, as allies with the families that are struggling with food insecurity. We cannot give a can to a faceless 'needy' person or say, 'Canned food is better than nothing.' . . . We all should be able to access the same food regardless of income, race, zip code."[21]

Moskowitz's vision for New Roots is to provide every family in Louisville with access to "fresh, local food in their neighborhoods, integrate cooking from scratch into their daily routines, reduce diet-related illnesses and enjoy long, healthy lives." New Roots' works to develop a just and thriving food system through community organizing, by improving education, and creating access to fresh and local food for urban residents. Seventy-five percent of New Roots' shareholders are low-income. Families or shareholders work together to pool their money and SNAP benefits on a sliding scale so that they can gain the money they need to purchase enough volume of produce from local farmers. New Roots intentionally pulls together people of different ages, backgrounds, racial/ethnic, and income groups to overcome food insecurity, childhood hunger, and health disparities. Those who can afford to buy shares for twenty-five dollars pay that amount; everyone else pays twelve dollars. One way that churches and synagogues provide support is by offering space for Fresh Stop farmers' markets and food justice development classes, cooking demos, potlucks, and festivals.

These projects and other similar ones emerging in cities across the United States undermine neoliberal capitalism as they bring together communities that have been fragmented, undervalued, and excluded from the food distribution system. They also improve the urban landscape and make an impact on crime rates. Journalist Alex Kotlowitz reported that "urban farming and greening not only strengthen community bonds but also reduce violence."[22] In Philadelphia, for example, taking over vacant lots and cultivating gardens resulted over ten years in the reduction of shootings in the areas surrounding those lots.

---

[21]Email correspondence with Karyn Moskowitz, June 17, 2016.
[22]Alex Kotlowitz, "Plant Tomatoes, Harvest Lower Crime Rates," *Mother Jones*, July/August 2012.

Cooperatives and Worker-Owned Businesses

Cooperative economics, which is foundational to the work of both the BCFSN and New Roots, should be explored in greater depth. UN secretary-general Ban Ki-moon reminded "the international community that it is possible to pursue both economic viability and social responsibility" when the United Nations declared 2012 the International Year of Cooperatives.[23] There are a variety of different forms of cooperatives, including consumer cooperatives, producer cooperatives, purchasing cooperatives, and worker-owned businesses. In the United States, more than 130 million people are members of a co-op. Nearly thirty thousand cooperatives in the United States account for 2 million jobs, $75 billion in wages and benefits, and $500 billion in total revenue.[24] Cooperatives are mechanisms for wealth creation that operate by democratic decision-making. They are profit-making, but they do not intend to be profit-maximizing.

One of the most well-known models for cooperative business is the Mondragón Corporation in the Basque region of Spain. Mondragón would not have been founded without innovative work done by a priest named José María Arizmendiarrieta, who sought to bring together humanist models of solidarity with Catholic social teaching and first began to create change by setting up a polytechnic school open to all people. The Mondragón Corporation is a group of cooperative enterprises that include industry, finance, retail, and education. The first factory opened in 1950 to produce gas stoves. Today, the corporation employs about seventy-four thousand people in 257 firms, subsidiaries, and joint ventures in sixty counties in Spain.[25] Co-op members

---

[23]United Nations, International Year of Cooperatives 2012, social.un.org.

[24]Marjorie Kelly, "The Economy: Under New Ownership," *Yes! Magazine*, February 19, 2013.

[25]Sharryn Kasmir, "The Mondragón Cooperatives and Global Capitalism," *New Labor Forum* 25, no. 1 (Winter 2016): 53. Kasmir also points out that it is worth raising difficult questions when examining Mondragón's model. The co-op has not been completely shielded from profit maximization, and there are subsidiaries of the corporation in countries such as China paying wages as low as other corporations. These are important issues to name and should be considered

own and direct each enterprise. Workers vote and make decisions by social councils that affect the whole corporation. They "retain the power to make all the basic decisions of the enterprise (what, how, and where to produce and what to do with the profits)."[26] Each co-op sends representatives to a Cooperative Congress that makes decisions that affect the whole system. Profit is considered important to the corporation, but not given the utmost priority over putting people to work. Income is distributed more equally, and the corporation is loyal to the community. There is a limit placed on the salaries of managers. At Mondragón, managerial salaries can be no more than nine times the lowest-paid worker. The ratio between CEO and worker pay in Spain in 2014 was 127:1.[27] Unemployment in the Basque region of Spain is about 12 percent, less than half of the rest of the country.[28]

In the United States, cooperatives are often assumed to be the projects of liberal hippies, but there is a much longer history. Cooperatives have always been essential to the survival and accumulation of wealth for those pressed into the most marginal and precarious positions. The vision of a Cooperative Commonwealth in which no one would be dependent upon wage labor was central to labor and democratic socialist movements of the late nineteenth and early twentieth centuries. Some of the early US cooperatives were among women's groups and organizations founded by people of color.

Economist Jessica Gordon Nembhard points out in her book *Collective Courage: A History of African American Cooperative Economic Thought and Practice* that people who are the most vulnerable are forced to find ways to create a living or fund something that they need by doing alternative work. Many African Americans survived during slavery by collectively raising money to buy a family member's freedom, sharing food, or through mutual aid societies that supported things like funerals

as the model continues to evolve and be applied in other contexts.
[26]Richard Wolff, "Yes, There Is an Alternative to Capitalism: Mondragon Shows the Way," *The Guardian*, June 24, 2012.
[27]Ibid.
[28]Lauren Frayer, "While Spain Struggles, The Basque Region Shines," *All Things Considered*, October 25, 2012, www.npr.org.

and doctor's visits. During the civil rights movement, activists frequently found themselves in positions similar to that of Fannie Lou Hamer as they were forced out of their jobs because they tried to register to vote or participated in demonstrations. The question then became, what is the alternative means to generate wealth and money to sustain oneself and one's family? One of the main ways white women and African American people responded was through cooperative economics. W. E. B. Du Bois argued at the turn of the twentieth century that cooperatives were a good way for people of color to earn a living. Finding alternative means of wealth creation becomes an option forced upon people who have their backs pushed against the wall and who are prevented from participating freely in the dominant white economic structure.

Cooperative Banking

The majority of US Americans who are involved in co-ops are shareholders at a credit union. Historically, credit unions, savings and loans, and Morris banks were institutions created to serve underserved populations and business networks and communities of people that were "underbanked," meaning that they had little access to credit.[29] The Knights of Reliance, an organization formed in Texas in the 1800s, presented early opposition to "the concentrated banks of the East and the power of Wall Street" and advocated farming cooperatives as an alternative solution.[30] Later called the Farmer's Alliance, the organization became the model for the credit union industry. Credit unions, savings and loans, and Morris banks were designed with a democratic structure that included open and voluntary membership, democratic control (one

---

[29]Arthur J. Morris founded Fidelity Savings and Trust Company in 1910 in Norfolk, Virginia. Other Savings and Trust companies later emerged across the US under the Fidelity Corporation of America. Morris Plan Banks offered loans at high interest rates with repayment on installments to those who did not qualify at mainstream banks. One feature of the Morris Plan was that they also included a certificate for savings sold to borrowers at the time they took out their loans. The Morris Plan was popular through the Great Depression, but then declined as the economy improved. See Louis N. Robinson, "The Morris Plan," *American Economic Review*, vol. 21 (June, 1931): 222–224.

[30]Mehrsa Baradaran, "How the Poor Got Cut Out of Banking," *Emory Law Journal* 62 (2013): 498.

share, one vote), and policies against any form of discrimination. If the credit union operated with a surplus, it was distributed to all members.

While there are still more than 130 million people who are members of a credit union, Mehrsa Baradaran, a professor of law at the University of Georgia, argues that the United States essentially has two forms of banks, "one for the rich and one for the poor," but that since the 1980s they both have more similar goals and both pursue maximizing profits for shareholders. She argues that a distinct shift in the credit union industry occurred in the 1980s as changes in public policies forced them to begin competing with other banks. Baradaran points out that the way the market responded to the void created by changes in banking policies was to fill the gap with "fringe banks." Payday lenders and check cashing institutions existed only in a few urban areas before the 1970s, but since the mid-1990s the number of payday lenders grows at the rate of about 10 percent each year.[31] In the past, credit unions were organized to address the needs of people in poverty, and advocated for the general well-being of the underserved and underbanked. There were also government-backed savings systems for recent immigrants and people living in poverty, such as the Postal Savings System and state banks. Many of the state banks were chartered to meet the needs of farmers. At this time the Bank of North Dakota is the only state bank that remains in the United States.

There are some good examples of credit unions that hold true to their original mission. One is the Self-Help Credit Union in Durham, North Carolina, which started the largest Latino credit union. Further, Baradaran references some innovative movements led by people in poverty to avoid fringe banks, including informal lending circles that resemble the microloans given by the Grameen Bank and formal lending circles such as the Mission Asset Fund in San Francisco, California. Many of the people involved in these ventures are immigrants. For example, Baradaran estimates that 80 percent of Korean immigrants belong to at least one informal lending circle.[32]

---

[31]Ibid., 491. Baradaran is referencing research done by Christopher L. Peterson in *Taming the Sharks: Towards a Cure for the High-Cost Credit Market* (Akron, OH: University of Akron Press, 2004).

[32]Baradaran, "How the Poor Got Cut Out of Banking," 541.

Connecting Faith and Money on a Personal Level

Another aspect of considering alternative forms of banking relates to investments. For decades, religious communities and institutions have advocated for socially responsible, community-oriented investing.[33] However, Andy Loving, a financial planner and adviser at Just Money, says that seldom do local congregations intentionally think about the financial institution they choose for their own churches' banking. Loving challenges local congregations to ask how a bank reflects the "values of the kingdom of God" before opening accounts there.

In addition, it can be extremely difficult to begin a conversation in a local congregational setting about how individuals connect money and faith. To bring this issue to the forefront of his church's agenda, Loving worked with others at Jeff Street Baptist Community Church at Liberty in Louisville to challenge members to think beyond stewardship in terms of the amount they give to the church's budget toward how they personally invest their money and profit from their investments. Together they researched different financial institutions and decided to create a "common purse" that would be invested through Oikocredit, a worldwide cooperative and social investor that provides "funding to the microfinance sector, fair trade organizations, cooperatives and small to medium enterprises."[34] Many members invested in their name and received a personal return of about 2 percent. Others invested in the church's name and the congregation received the return. They surprised themselves when the small congregation with only about sixty people present for Sunday worship raised $180,000 for the common purse.

Loving observes that congregations should practice more than the spiritual discipline of sharing wealth. People of faith should

---

[33]Examples include but are not limited to the following: the Mennonite Creation Care Network; the Mission Responsibility Through Investment (M.R.T.I.) committee of the Presbyterian Church (U.S.A.) that advises individuals, congregations, and the Presbyterian Foundation about responsible investing; the United Methodist Church Foundation, which follows the Book of Discipline's guidelines for responsible investing; and the US Conference of Catholic Bishops' guidelines for Socially Responsible Investing.

[34]Oikocredit's mission statement is available at www.oikocredit.coop.

also practice "showing wealth." The communities that make up the Church of the Savior practice "showing wealth" by sharing tax returns once a year with members in order to overcome the social taboo of keeping income and wealth a secret from the larger community. For Loving, keeping financial information and one's income and assets a secret is an expression of the dominant society's individualistic approach to wealth creation. In an age where identity theft is prevalent, sharing tax returns is a dangerous practice. However, the point should not be missed that one's income and wealth are not private matters. The practice Loving describes reflects the early Christian belief that income and wealth are for sharing.

Shared Power, Shared Equity, and Worker-Owned Businesses

Author Marjorie Kelly writes that "the seeds of a different kind of economy" are being planted to grow "on a foundation of ownership . . . But this economy doesn't rely on a monoculture of design, the way capitalism does. It's as rich in diversity as a rainforest is in its plethora of species—with common ownership, municipal ownership, employee ownership, and others."[35] Shared equity and worker-owned businesses envision and practice alternative economic strategies and collective ownership. Their interest and investment are in local wealth creation, democratizing capital, and redistributing wealth. Many city governments inspired by the success of the Mondragón Corporation have promoted cooperative businesses and offered loans or grants in recent years to fund start-up co-ops, including, among others, the municipalities of Richmond and San Francisco, California; Cincinnati and Oxford, Ohio; Minneapolis and Northfield, Minnesota; New York City; and Burlington, North Carolina.[36]

Profit-Making, Not Profit Maximizing

Turning toward shared equity for all workers not only transforms a company but can also be incredibly profitable. For ex-

---

[35]Kelly, "The Economy."
[36]Philadelphia Area Cooperative Alliance, "Local Government Support for Cooperatives," Democracy at Work Institute, June 24, 2012, http://institute.coop.

ample, New Belgium craft brewing company became 100 percent worker owned in 2013. Kim Jordan founded the brewery with her former husband, Jeff Lebesch, in 1991 in the basement of their home in Fort Collins, Colorado, after they took a trip to Belgium and enjoyed the local beers.

Jordan began her career as a social worker. In an interview with the *Denver Post*, she reflected on the importance of being raised in a liberal household and educated in a Quaker high school for the way she views her sense of business leadership. The profit motive was held in suspicion by Jordan's family. Jordan's parents took her to "political things" and marched with César Chávez in California. Jordan says, "So there is that George Fox, 'let your light speak' thing. For me, that was profoundly important—this notion that you get this opportunity to choose who you want to be, and that is true of the corporate life as well. The confluence of those things was pretty important for me in terms of my thinking about New Belgium. And then I started to attract people like me. It's the virtuous circle, an upward spiral."[37]

In interviews, Jordan almost seems surprised to be CEO of a company the Brewers Association ranks the fourth-largest brewery in the United States. One of the main reasons that she sold the company to her workers was due to her concern about the widening gap in our society between the "haves and the have-nots" and belief that "you can choose what you do with profits." Jordan didn't want New Belgium to lose its identity as a company or a community of workers. When the workers were interviewed for the PBS news story they continued to reference their sense of interrelatedness: "The better I do, the better we do," and "I am not just working for myself, I am working for us all."

Nonprofits Connecting the Local and Global by Design

When Colleen Clines first traveled to India she was a student at the Rhode Island School of Design wanting to learn more about design in the two-thirds world. While there she learned about the experience of women who had been either kidnapped or sold

---

[37]Douglas Brown, "New Belgium Brewery's Kim Jordan Talks about Beer, Business, Quakers," *Denver Post*, January 23, 2013.

into sexual slavery. Nicholas Kristof and Sheryl WuDunn estimate in their book *Half the Sky* that there are "3 million women and girls (and a small number of boys) worldwide who can be fairly termed enslaved in the sex trade."[38] In the words of Kristof and WuDunn, "Capitalism created new markets for rice and potatoes, but also for female flesh."[39] Globalization made the transportation of human bodies more economically efficient.

After returning to the United States, Clines wanted to do something about the situation. She developed a project along with other women friends that would help women who had been victims of human trafficking to prove their own economic worth and ensure their freedom from sexual slavery. The name of the Anchal Project is taken from a term in Hindi referring to the edge of the sari as providing safety for loved ones. Collaboration and cooperation are at the heart of Anchal. Clines began with the intention to create a project led by the local community and to develop a human-centered design approach. Anchal provides women with the education and technological means (a sewing machine and computer access) to make beautiful scarves, blankets, and other marketable goods. The wonder of this project is that it not only gives some practical tools but also draws upon a native form of art to stitch the scarves and is also environmentally sustainable. Wearable or usable art is created from something women have access to in abundance in India, used saris that are recycled and repurposed.

Anchal's ultimate goal is to combat the global sex trade by providing enough work to support women full-time. Women must be paid more than they could make as prostitutes and prove their economic worth to their families. Anchal ensures consistent, sustained employment and that the women make 30 to 75 percent more than they would in the sex trade. Training and employing the women has a ripple effect. Women are most likely to use the money to support other family members or to create change for an entire community.

In 2015 Anchal began a pilot project called DyeScape that connects the local Louisville community where the project is

---

[38]Nicholas Kristof and Sheryl WuDunn, *Half the Sky: Turning Oppression into Opportunity for Women Worldwide* (New York: First Vintage Books, 2009), 10.
    [39]Ibid., 11.

based to the women working in India. DyeScape provides a natural dye initiative that offers opportunities to train exploited women in Louisville in the design and production of eco-friendly textiles. Community gardens have been cultivated in the Portland neighborhood on vacant lots that are used to grow plants for the production of naturally dyed products.

The Anchal Project is incredibly innovative but not without challenges. Clines is well aware that they will "never be able to come close to what a corporation can produce more cheaply." But the purchasing power, desire, and demand of consumers in the West for transparency concerning how the products they buy are produced and with a growing awareness of the damage that can be done by the textile industry, the organization has strong support. Other noteworthy and smart business ventures have emerged that connect local communities to larger global issues, such as Indego Africa, based in New York, and Krochet Kids International, based in Spokane, Washington.

Sustainable and Affordable Housing for the Creation of Community Wealth

Home ownership is touted as the means to increase the wealth of people living in poverty. However, for those working for low wages, minimum wage, or poverty-level wages, affording a home may be untenable, and taking on the responsibility as an individual could prove risky. Scholar and community organizer John Emmeus Davis observes that the current housing crisis in the United States is one of affordability.[40] Alternatives are needed to the traditional approaches to home ownership. There are a variety of ways people have and continue to respond to ensure not only access to affordable housing for lower-income individuals and families, but also different ways to build equity through shared-equity homeownership in the form of community land trusts, limited equity cooperatives, deed-restricted housing, townhouses and condominiums, and housing co-ops.

Two general principles that unite these efforts are the idea that

---

[40]John Emmeus Davis, "Homes That Last: The Case for Counter-Cyclical Stewardship," in *The Community Land Trust Reader*, ed. John Emmeus Davis (Cambridge, MA: Lincoln Institute of Land Policy, 2010), 8.

only part of a property's unencumbered value is generated by individual investment and the assumption that the land as a whole is owned by a community. Shared-equity homeownership limits the profits made by an individual. The emphasis is placed on what is shared between an individual and the community. A larger community contributes equally, sometimes more, to individually owned property by supporting city infrastructure; making concessions to private developers, in the form of public grants and tax credits; or making charitable donations. Thus, the community has the right also to increase its common wealth. Specific types of agreements vary but are designed to ensure access to a long-term solution to affordable housing when rising values are pricing lower-income people and their families out of the market. Shared-equity housing also places homeowners in a community-based support system.

Community land trusts offer a dual-ownership model where the owner of the land is a nonprofit community-based corporation. Housing can be built upon the land by individuals, but the trust retains ownership of the land itself. In the United States, community land trusts trace their origins to Ralph Borsodi, a pioneer in the back-to-the-land and self-sufficiency movement. Borsodi started the first leasehold community at his School of Living called Bayard Lane in Rockland County, New York, in 1936. Borsodi drew upon the cultural traditions and practices of other peoples and communities that preserved land for the common good, including "tribal lands among the native peoples of North and South America, the Ejidos of Mexico, the 'commons' of England, the Crofter System in Scotland, tribal lands in Africa, [and] the Gramdan movement in India."[41] The relationship to the land emphasized by these peoples was used to inform Borsodi's intellectual arguments and vision for communal life. The School of Living became a model adopted by other communities, including Common Ground in Alabama; Deep Run Farm, Downhill Farm, Julian Woods, and Seven Sisters in Pennsylvania; Deer Rock in Virginia; Heathcote Center in Maryland; Lane's End Homestead in Ohio; and Van Houten Fields in New York.[42] The first inner-city

---

[41]John Emmeus Davis, "Shared Equity Homeownership: The Changing Landscape of Resale-Restricted, Owner-Occupied Housing," National Housing Institute, 20, www.nhi.org.

[42]For a more complete listing, see Timothy Miller, *The Encyclopedic Guide*

community land cooperative formed in Cincinnati, Ohio, in 1980. At this time, more than one hundred community land trusts have been established across the United States, in cities from Burlington, Vermont, to Santa Fe, New Mexico.[43]

Co-housing communities and ecovillages offer more options through the formation of intentional collaborative neighbor-hoods built around balancing individuals' and families' needs for privacy and community support, encouraging participation and community decision making, and typically adopting green approaches to living. Co-housing communities grew in popular-ity at the end of the twentieth century and trace their origins to a model developed in Denmark in the 1960s. They are typically apartments or row houses that include small private living ar-rangements with some shared facilities and responsibilities such as community kitchens and weekly common meals, laundries, recreation areas, and workshops, and most also include shared maintenance, childcare, or elder care.[44] Ecovillages adopt green living practices, focus on sustainability, and sometimes combine co-housing models. They typically cultivate and farm communal organic gardens and construct high-energy-efficiency buildings that make use of alternative energy sources.[45]

The world's largest example of co-housing or private homes centered around a common space is located in Ithaca, New York. EcoVillage Ithaca was founded in 1991 by Liz Walker and now is comprised of three 'neighborhoods' with more than 200 residents from toddlers to seniors living there.[46] In addition to the village, this community has a vibrant educational mission offered through a non-profit partner program called Learn@EcoVillageIthaca. Their programs and publications introduce, educate, and mentor others with an interest in an integrated approach to sustainable community planning, green building design, and land-based livelihoods.

---

to *American Intentional Communities* (Clinton, NY: Richard W. Couper Press, 2015), 509.

[43]Preface to Davis, "Shared Equity Homeownership."

[44]See "Cohousing," in Miller, *Encyclopedic Guide*, 91.

[45]Ibid., 134.

[46]Christina Nunez, "How These Communities Save Energy—and Time for What Matters," *National Geographic* Online (December 22, 2015).

According to estimates made by the National Association of Housing Cooperatives, there are more than 1 million units of cooperative housing in the United States (limited- or zero-equity and market-rate).[47] Cooperative housing has been much more successful in other countries, including Sweden, Norway, Germany, Turkey, and Canada.[48]

Problematizing the Problem of Wealth

All of the efforts, particularly those at the grassroots level, contribute to an alternative social and economic vision and create systemic, structural, and attitudinal change. The stories of people told in this chapter illustrate collaborative decision making, provide a variety of ways to eliminate social distance created between and among human beings, and aim toward healing fragmented and divided communities. Each example embodies values of reciprocity, cooperation/collaboration, interdependence, accountability to the commons, sustainability, and the inclusion of diverse peoples and experiences. However, despite all of these wonderful examples, a lacuna remains in my argument that must be addressed.

We all remain dependent at least to a certain extent upon the current system and dominant forms of wealth creation for our own livelihoods and financial security. On a more personal level, those who are middle-class are largely aware of our wealth in comparison to others with lower incomes and within the global community. But at the same time, we know the heavy yoke of responsibility placed upon the shoulders of individuals in US society to provide for our own basic necessities. Considering alternative forms of wealth creation carries with it the fear of loss—loss of social standing, stability, financial security, health care, and the ability to educate children. This means that middle-class people of faith live in a state of tension between indignation and longing for a more humane, just, and loving economy, and feeling overwhelmed in the face of the current outcomes of economic policies and practices that are accelerating the wealth divide.

Further, middle-class people of faith often fail to grapple with

---

[47]Davis, "Shared Equity Homeownership," 27.
[48]Ibid.

the fact that wealthy decision makers and the social, economic, and political systems and structures depend upon members of what ethicist Mary Hobgood calls "the professional managerial sector" to keep the system going and maintain the status quo.[49] Professionals and managers are part of the working class and constitute a bit less than 20 percent of the US workforce. The working class, Hobgood says, is "divided by gender" and "deeply conditioned by race."[50] A large majority of those constituting the professional managerial sector are white. Professionals and managers have access to some social benefits and cultural institutions as those who are most wealthy but "receive higher income and status only if they produce, control, and disseminate knowledge and sources supportive of the status quo."[51] There is little doubt that those within "the professional managerial sector," the middle and upper middle class, have a vital role to play in movements for change and much to contribute from our experiences in terms of a broader social imagination. Theologians and ethicists such as Gloria Albrecht, John Cobb, Gary Dorrien, Ulrich Duchrow, Franz Hinkelammert, Mary Hobgood, Sallie McFague, Cynthia Moe Loebeda, Rebecca Todd Peters, Stephen Ray, and Joerg Rieger, along with many others, have commented on the need for a much more robust response from the middle class through engagement in nonviolent solidarity protest movements, alliances with labor organizations, and work to bring about alternative forms of wealth creation. What shifts in middle-class consciousness and commitments still need to occur to more vigorously engage in movements for social change?

In the United States, one reason for a less than robust engagement of middle-class people of faith in resistance movements is the broad perception that an undifferentiated group of people known as the "middle class" still exists, coupled with the belief that today's economy provides good conditions to facilitate upward social mobility. The old perception that people who want to do so can "pull themselves up by their bootstraps" and make opportunities for themselves is still heavily influential in church institutions and charitable organizations, even though it is not fac-

---

[49]Mary Hobgood, *Dismantling Privilege* (Cleveland: Pilgrim Press, 2000), 74.
[50]Ibid.
[51]Ibid.

tually based. When I presented some of my research about grow-ing wealth inequalities and people living in poverty at a women's church conference in 2013, one of the participants stopped me in the hallway and accused me of "trying to destroy the American Dream." The reality is that now even most middle-class people in the United States are one tragedy away from living in poverty.

Moreover, scholars suggest that many middle-class people are far from realizing the precariousness of their own economic situation. Duchrow and Hinkelammert observe that the majority making up the "mainline churches in the West, whose members are mostly middle-class, are far from realizing the dangers of the situation. Europeans still believe we are living in a social market economy."[52] Ironically, the shrinking of the middle class pre-sents churches and other religious organizations with a critical opportunity to educate their members and call them to action. Today, two-thirds of the US public believes that there are strong conflicts between the rich and the poor. The distinct shift in public consciousness of ongoing class struggles in recent years opens up the opportunity for raising new questions concerning middle-class identity, social stratification, and the relationship of class to race and ethnicity, and has potential to stimulate widespread interest and investment in economic activities with a different set of social values in mind. Raising tough questions about the role that social class, race, and sex and gender play in the formation of individual identities and understanding of mission is a critical undertaking for communities of faith on all levels. For example, how do middle-class social identities play a role in the mission of US congregations primarily composed of middle-class people? Are congregational identities formed more by the social standing of their members than a faith tradition's teachings about poverty, money, and wealth?

I think there is an additional important reason for a less than robust engagement of the middle class in resistance movements that goes beyond a lack of knowledge or sense of urgency about the situation. Our most holy sacred texts and stories offer very little guidance on matters that address the complexities of our

---

[52]Ulrich Duchrow and Franz Hinkelammert, *Transcending Greedy Money: Interreligious Solidarity for Just Relations* (New York: Palgrave Macmillan, 2012).

current economic systems and structures. Biblical stories are too often personalized and related to individual devotional practice. Those who attend church hear readings from the Bible at least on a weekly basis if not more, but reflections on the narrative by pastors and other preachers as well as in church school classes seldom break out of the paradigm established in the stories themselves, where class is defined almost solely in terms of a contrast between "the rich" and "the poor." It is impossible to find a replica of today's economy in stories coming out of ancient experiences of people living in a predominately agrarian society.

I reflected on this fact with a pastor in my local community whom I greatly admire and who reads the stories, particularly parables, as if US middle-class people are the rich. There is no doubt that in the larger global economy, middle-class US residents would be defined as the rich. It is also important to note that there should be distinctions made within the middle-class. For example, upper middle-class incomes do not reflect the "middle." Hobgood observes that "those whose incomes have been steady or rising, whose households in 2006 earned as much as $97,000 or more thought of ourselves as middle class even though almost 80 percent of US households earned less than we did."[53] But, at the same time, in US society, the middle class are not usually the owners or captains of industry or decision-makers within their places of work. The middle-class comprises primarily workers and middle managers—chefs, mechanics, accountants, bakers, teachers, professors, nurses, police officers—dependent on the system for our own well-being yet not fully in control of our own work, schedule, pay, retirement, and sometimes even our work-oriented goals. Middle-class workers are also indoctrinated in a system intended to uphold the power and privilege of the wealthiest elites. Institutions form our cultural and social values. Most alarmingly, our "socially constructed identities oblige most people in the society to act against their long-term interests so that [the wealthiest] can enjoy short-term benefits."[54] Defining middle-class experience in terms of those with the most privilege and economic power fails to get at the places where people with middle-class incomes

---

[53]Hobgood, *Dismantling Privilege,* 17.
[54]Ibid.

may make the greatest impact in movements for social change. Religious social activists and other leaders, pastors, priests, and laity must work together to cultivate a broader, more socially engaged theological imagination.

Similar questions to those raised by Howard Thurman in *Jesus and the Disinherited* should be at the forefront of our minds: What will be the attitude of the middle class toward the rulers, the controllers of political, social, and economic life? What will motivate us to play a larger role as agents of change? How do people dependent upon the system imagine something beyond the current economic system? It is easy to skewer the rich and sanctify people living in poverty, but when considering the context of the global wealth divide the US middle class still has difficulty fitting through the eye of the needle to enter into the biblical vision of the reign of God.

The Jesus movement of the ancient world drew upon sacred teachings and spoke directly into the economic, social, and political problems of their time. How then do we draw upon the depth of our traditions, rituals, and religious and social commitments to step into a creative, sometimes anxiety-producing space where we can imagine our identities as formed by those ideas and beliefs rather than our social standing? Authentic systemic and structural change will happen much more rapidly with a robust response from the middle class. In the next chapter I intend to inspire readers' theological imagination and invite you to begin writing your own story into the growing movements of nonviolent resistance and solidarity through imaginative parables of the commons that speak out of and into the complexities of middle-class US experience.

CHAPTER 8

Parables for Sharing

But Zacchaeus stopped and said to the Lord,
"Look, Lord, I give half of my possessions to the poor.
And if I have cheated anyone,
I repay them four times as much."

—*Luke 19:8*

Zacchaeus offers one of the most intriguing stories in the canonical Gospels for people of relative wealth when compared to the vast majority of the world's people. In my mind, it is one of the only biblical stories that compares somewhat easily to the experience of contemporary middle-class readers. Thus, reflecting on the story of Zacchaeus as told by the author of Luke (19:1–10) can deepen our understanding of the ancient context in which Jesus's parables were told and heard and underscore the importance of writing parables and stories for contemporary readers.

As a tax collector, Zacchaeus was a sort of middle manager in the Roman Empire. Tax collectors have never been known for their popularity in society. Justo González observes, "Taxation was always a problem in the Roman Empire, for the ancient notion persisted that freedom was incompatible with direct taxation."[1] There were times when the wealthy showed their support of the state through voluntary donations. When the state was in need of new sources of income, the Romans depended upon taxes and people like Zacchaeus to keep the system running. The Romans

---

[1] Justo González, *Faith and Wealth: A History of Early Christian Ideas on the Origin, Significance, and Use of Money* (New York: Harper and Row, 1990), 37.

believed in localized government, except in the cases of high judicial authorities and the army. Often the landowners within particular regions were given positions of authority and would then serve as tax collectors with the duty of gathering resources to bolster the empire. González says, "They contracted with the government to raise the taxes of a particular area and to collect a fee for this service. This fee, however, was only part of their profit. Since many agricultural taxes were collected in kind, publicans made large profits by reselling the goods collected or by hoarding them until prices rose."[2] Those given the responsibility for collecting taxes on behalf of imperial authorities would have been able to keep some of the proceeds for themselves.

Biblical scholar Robert Tannehill argues that "the indication that Zacchaeus is rich complicates the story and produces uncertainty in expectations."[3] In the synoptic tradition, tax collectors were usually those who could not find any other work.[4] Luke 5:27 refers to Jesus going out to see Levi while he was sitting at his toll booth collecting money. Average tax collectors played a key role in maintaining the bureaucracy of the Roman Empire. Zacchaeus was more than average. He was "the ruler of tax collectors" in Jericho and "in a position to make big profits."[5]

Wealth at that time wasn't created through stocks, bonds, or trade. In a predominately agrarian economy, wealth was primarily created by the labor of those who cultivated the land. Historian Peter Brown says that rich landowners converted the money they made from the food produced by the land "into privilege and power."[6] The peasants who didn't own the land that they worked made one of three arrangements with the landowner: "fixed rent, payment of a predetermined portion of their produce to the owner, or the status of *colonus*."[7] Biblical scholars think that Rome's economy moved in a downward spiral during Jesus's lifetime, so

[2]Ibid., 38.
[3]Robert C. Tannehill, "The Story of Zacchaeus as Rhetoric: Luke 19:1–10," *Semeia* 64 (1994): 202.
[4]See ibid.
[5]Ibid.
[6]Peter Brown, *Through the Eye of a Needle: Wealth, the Fall of Rome and the Making of Christianity in the West, 350–550 AD* (Princeton, NJ: Princeton University Press, 2012), 3.
[7]Gonzalez, *Faith and Wealth*, 72.

wealthy landowners introduced a tax on the farmers who worked their land. Taxes were levied at harvest time and drove many of the farmers into debt. If a farmer couldn't pay taxes, tax collectors "would often lend him money at annual rates that varied from 12 to 48 percent."[8] Many farmers were forced off of their land or were forced to work land owned by the wealthy to pay off their debts. Both the wealthy and those who were poor depended upon the harvest, which was vulnerable to the unpredictable changes in weather conditions. Only a small portion of each harvest stayed with laborers. Later, after taxes were collected, the collectors returned to the laborers to ask for the rent due to them on their land. The wealth and privilege of landowners enabled them to build granaries to ensure their own sustenance during times of famine. Heavy gates secured by lock and key protected stored food within the granaries and stood tall as symbols of the economic exploitation of people living in poverty.

Remember the debt codes and year of Jubilee described in Deuteronomy and Leviticus? Jesus and his followers would have been familiar with these teachings, too. No wonder the crowds grumble in the story when Jesus insists on visiting Zacchaeus in his house. Zacchaeus was "small in stature" as he was looked upon by the impoverished crowds. In other words, he stood between the rich and the poor and at first seemed more like a gatekeeper who guarded the granaries than an agent of change. In the minds of the crowds, Zacchaeus sank to the lowest of the low in social standing by being willing to enforce the oppressive and exploitative policies of the Roman Empire. Tax collectors would have been thought of by the crowds as individuals who increased their wealth by removing themselves from the common welfare. Seeing oneself as part of the commons and working for the common welfare was central to living in covenant with God. However, there is also a disruptive undercurrent throughout this story.

Zacchaeus holds a position of social honor within the empire, yet at the same time he is marginalized. He has been pushed to the margins of the community. What is the attitude toward Rome that he adopts? Zacchaeus breaks the social rules established by the landowners to keep people in their place. He disrupts the

---

[8]Ibid., 38.

dominant social logic and looks out for the commons instead of just himself. Like a child, he climbs a tree so that he can look above the crowds and catch a glimpse of Jesus as he enters the city. None other than the chief tax collector wants to try to see Jesus. Jesus also shows himself to be a rule breaker by publicly crossing well-established social boundaries and resisting the approval of the crowds; he insists on going to the tax collector's house to stay. There Zacchaeus reveals what he intends to do: "half of my possessions, Lord, I will give to the poor; and if I have defrauded anyone of anything I will pay him back four times as much" (Luke 19:8). This form of Zacchaean economics restores him to community. He conveys his willingness to renounce some of his own wealth, social status, and self-interest to do justice for a larger common good. He takes a different path.

Zacchaeus refuses to be trapped into and held in bondage by the position or narrative created for him by the Romans or other residents of Jericho. He has a larger social imagination as he steps into a difficult place, a creative space, where he is unafraid to generate tension with landowners and the crowds in order to eliminate the social distance that the empire has placed between him and those most vulnerable in his ancient society. Now you know why Zacchaeus, in Greek, literally means clean or innocent! Jesus, by crossing well-established social boundaries and barriers, shows the consistency of God's faithfulness in covenant even when human-made systems and structures fail, and he embodies God's love by welcoming Zacchaeus into the community. Faithful people who heard this story in the ancient world would not have had to dig beneath the surface of the text to unpack the material deprivation and unjust Roman policies that they faced. They lived the experience. The story named their anger and need while cultivating their faithfulness, moral courage, and imagination for new ways to live in covenant together.[9]

Parables represent another form of storytelling found in the biblical text that invites readers and hearers to identify and step

---

[9]My reflections on Zacchaeus' story were first introduced at a meeting on "International Calvinism: A Unity in Diversity?" Conference proceedings are published in *Reformed Churches Working in Unity and Diversity: Global Historical, Theological, and Ethics Perspectives*, ed. Ábrahám Kovács (Budapest: L'Harmattan, 2016), 180–182.

into a creative and imaginative space that exists between the present reality and that which could be. Storytelling has been used over centuries to speak directly to the most pressing social, economic, political, and theological problems of different eras and to inspire social imagination. Of course, many of the most well-known and timeless parables are those recorded in the canonical Gospels.

Contemporary biblical scholars emphasize the value of reading Jesus's parables in their ancient Jewish context. In her book *Short Stories by Jesus*, Amy-Jill Levine observes that parables have always been open narratives intended to leave multiple impressions over time. She writes, "What makes the parables mysterious or difficult is that they challenge us to look into hidden aspects of our own values, our own lives."[10] The origin of parables is found in the stories told in the Hebrew Bible. Levine cites Judges 9:8–15; 2 Samuel 12:1–7; and 2 Samuel 14:5–8. These stories were part of the culture and would have first been "told at home in the evening at dinner or in the workshops and the fields and the synagogues."[11]

Levine encourages readers of ancient parables to look for the challenging messages in Jesus's teachings. Parables are not platitudes intended to make us feel better about our own social reality; they are designed to draw us in and leave us feeling uncomfortable. Imaginative stories allowed their hearers to break free from the determinism of traditional ancient societies and called them to play a role in healing the world. Recall that Jesus prioritized economic justice in his teachings, as his story is told in the synoptic Gospels. There are thirty-one parables that Jesus tells in Mark, Matthew, and Luke, and nineteen of them refer directly to social class, indebtedness, the misuse of wealth, the distribution of wealth, and worker pay. Levine reminds us that Jesus told parables because they serve as "keys that can unlock the mysteries we face by helping us ask the right questions: how to live in community; how to determine what ultimately matters; how to live the life that God wants us to live."[12] What Jesus's parables helped people in the ancient world to express was the feeling of what it was like to live between anger and hope in the Roman

---

[10]Amy-Jill Levine, *Short Stories by Jesus: The Enigmatic Parables of a Controversial Rabbi* (San Francisco: HarperOne, 2015), 3.

[11]Ibid., 7.

[12]Ibid., 297.

Empire. Parables as a form of storytelling remind us that "the best teaching is not spoon-fed data or an answer sheet, but found in narratives that challenge, provoke, and inspire."[13] Contemporary readers are invited to experience inner tension and resistance as they read, hear, and reflect upon ancient parables, rather than just find calm acceptance.

Social reformers have continued this tradition by drawing upon their interpretation of parables in the Gospels and writing their own stories to inspire social imagination. Parables became particularly important for social reformers in the late nineteenth to the mid-twentieth centuries as they recognized the true cost of rapid and largely unregulated industrialization. For example, Clarence Jordan, the religious social activist who founded Koinonia Farms with his wife, Florence, wrote *The Cotton Patch Gospel* "to help modern readers have the same sense of participation in them which early Christians must have had."[14] *The Cotton Patch Gospel* recorded the story of a modern-day God movement. Jordan stripped away the "fancy language, the artificial piety, and the barriers of time and distance . . . [to] put Jesus and his people in the midst of our modern world, living where we live, talking as we talk, working, hurting, praying, bleeding, dying, conquering, alongside the rest of us."[15] Jesus tells the crowds "comparisons" to let them in on the "secrets of the God Movement" as he travels throughout the countryside in the US Southeast.

The long history of imaginative storytelling and parables in Christian thought and used by social reformers made me wonder what parables would cultivate theological imagination for middle-class people of faith, particularly those who identify as white, as I do, to have the moral courage needed to speak directly into and out of the most pressing problem of our time—the problem of wealth and how we create it. How would parables of the commons be told today? The parables and stories that are told below find inspiration in the biblical text and are intended to begin to write those teachings into our contemporary experience. They

---

[13]Ibid.

[14]Clarence Jordan, "A Note on The Cotton Patch Gospel—Matthew and John," in *Clarence Jordan's Cotton Patch Gospel: The Complete Collection*, Introduction by Jimmy Carter (Macon, GA: Smyth and Helwys, 2012; reprint of 1957 edition), 3.

[15]Ibid.

emerge primarily out of my own white middle-class experience, something missing in the ancient stories, and are also informed by a deep consciousness of and connection to a much broader community. The parables of the commons are intended to raise questions and wonder in your mind and to help you consider new ways to ally yourself with solidarity protest movements and other grassroots efforts to create systemic social, economic, and political change. Some of the settings and events within the parables will seem familiar and allude to real events, but these stories are about everyone and no one in contemporary US society. These stories are true in the sense that they convey and aim to call into question the dominant white middle-class values of US life and invite people of faith to think about transforming them so as to live into an economy that serves the commons.

As you read, reflect, and respond to the parables of the Commons and the others, I invite you to keep several questions in mind and to consider how you can tell and write new parables of your own. How is the stereotypical US middle-class experience described, challenged, and changed in each of the stories? What means are used to transform fragmented communities? How are the commons defined and redefined?

Parable of the Commons

The people of the city gathered at the amphitheater of a nearby park to talk together about how to sow the seeds of community. They shared stories and listened to each other until these things came to mind.

The commons are the ground of shared life and the oikosystem of the One called Love.

The commons are a household where all know and embrace their creation in the image of Love, sharing by day and night, gathering water to drink from the lakes and rivers under the sky, eating foods produced by the rich humus of the land, and seeing the wealth in the fish in the sea, the birds in the sky, and in every living creature that moves on the ground.

The commons are like the people who identify with no name and every name—diverse, varied, dynamic—loving their own needs and wants as much as their neighbors and nature.

The commons are like a treasure hidden beneath paved parking lots, garbage dumps, flattened mountaintops, fenced yards, gated communities, exclusive schools, private clubs, and technology used only to satisfy and protect individual wants and desires.

The commons are the means and ends of profits and governed by shared life rather than efficiency, production, and the bottom line.

The commons are like tables spread with food, and everyone is welcomed to dine regardless of their ability to pay; instead, the price of their meal is determined by the truths they are willing to share.

The commons are an expression of Love, the basis of all that is and that which is yet to come.

(Origins: These sayings and parables about the nature of the commons are inspired by Matthew 13.)

The Parable of the Neighborhood Buddha

Two men lived in a house on a corner lot on a street that was planned long ago to stand as a visible reminder of the connection between the city and the land. The houses were different sizes on the street, but all mimicked the terrain. They were built out of bricks made of clay and painted with colors reflecting the splendor of nature. The lines of the roofs on their houses were in full symmetry with their gardens, and large eaves shielded the windows from the summer sun. The street was beautiful. The homeowners were excited to live there.

When the homeowners moved in, they discovered a Buddha statue sitting in a corner of their yard. The statue was made out of cement and had weathered over the years. The Buddha appeared to be happy, laughing, and very well fed. For several months the homeowners paid no attention to the statue in their yard. Their garden's stone visitor sat there appearing to be alone. They were unaware of the Buddha's community.

While the homeowners were working during the day, many people walked by the Buddha. Children passed by on bikes, scooters, or foot on their way to school. Homeless people walked by on their way to the local park. Dogs walking with their owners were sometimes allowed enough freedom on the leash for a sniff of the statue. Squirrels and cats wandered near Buddha with much more freedom. Babies in strollers whizzed by as they were pushed by moms and dads out for their daily jog. Some of them would interrupt their busyness to stop and sit in front of the Buddha.

As good homeowners, the residents carefully tended their yard. During one evening, the homeowners decided that the task of clearing out weeds around the Buddha was becoming too much of a chore. They began to remove the statue. Just as they lifted the statue into a wheelbarrow, one of the neighborhood kids walked by and asked them what they were doing with his Buddha. Thinking that the kid didn't understand the rules of personal property, the homeowners tried to explain how tired they were of clearing out the weeds around the Buddha. The neighborhood kid responded, "Every time I walk down this street on the way home from school I never feel afraid because Buddha is there. Sometimes I stop and sit down so that I can look directly at Buddha and think about what happened during the day. I don't know why but I am drawn to him and I wish you would leave him there." Somewhat irritated by the kid's intrusion in their yard, one homeowner thanked him for his story and said, "We'll take that into consideration." The kid went home, and the homeowners proceeded to remove the statue.

Later, the homeowners were talking together and remembered that the kid only had one parent at home and often spent several hours home alone after school. The next day they put the Buddha back in its rightful place. In the weeks that followed, they planted flowers around the Buddha as a visible reminder of a sacred space in the city. Some days the men noticed that those passing by brought gifts to the Buddha—flowers, candles, fruit, water, and their mindfulness.

(Origins: The parable of the Neighborhood Buddha is inspired by two neighbors who live down the street from me.)

The Parable of the Porches

This is a story of two neighborhoods, one in the north and the other in the south.

North Place was planned by developers and builders to remind the city of the glorious communities of the past. Every street had sidewalks. A grocery and other stores as well as a movie theater were built within walking distance of the community so that people could easily go there. Developers and builders worked with the local school board to build an elementary school there. Neighbors and visitors entered the streets of North Place by checking in with a guard at a gate. Once permission was given to pass through the gate, the Main Street was easily seen—well-planned, designed, and landscaped only with native plants and trees. The homes held great value to people in the north.

One of the heads of the household in North Place lived in a house on Main Street. The house was impressive—two stories, sided with beige cedar shakes, and the wood trim was painted white. Built in a nineteenth-century style, the house boasted an expansive porch to welcome everyone who entered. There was a great deal of work to do to care for the house. Having to care for three children, the head of the household hired a gardener and a cleaner to keep the inside and outside neat and tidy.

The gardener and the cleaner were from a neighborhood in the south. They worked very hard. In the yard, the gardener kept the bushes neatly pruned, planted flowers in harmony with the seasons, and cut the grass as often as needed. The cleaner was equally industrious inside the house. She picked up clothes left on the floor so quickly that the fabric still held to the form of the body that wore them. She washed, dusted, and mopped until everything was neat and tidy. Once in a while, enough time remained in her day to cook for the family. Often she made her favorite dishes, rich casseroles filled with corn, rice, and beans.

The head of the household was pleased with the work of the gardener and cleaner, so she decided to reward them with a raise for their fine work. The head of the household invited them to sit on the porch and talk for a while. Near the end of the conversation, the head of the household revealed that she would increase the pay for the gardener and cleaner 10 percent—quite a handsome raise. The gardener thanked the head of the household, and the cleaner expressed a sense of joy. She began sharing a story about her family and told the head of the household how much the extra money would help her three children back home. Having never seen the cleaner's family, the head of the household asked more questions.

The cleaner talked for some time about her three children who lived in South Place. South Place was an unplanned neighborhood constructed primarily of cement block, tin, and rebar. Each house was small and shared water from a spigot nearby. Porches outside the front doors were made of tightly packed dirt swept often to keep the inside of the house clean. Most of the people who lived in this neighborhood of South Place squatted on land of little value to their city because of the steep incline of the terrain. The land was highly valued by the people there. People of South Place lived with the land, cultivating rich soil to grow fruits and vegetables to eat. They welcomed chickens into their homes and thanked them for providing eggs and honored the goats for their milk and labor they gave to keep the grass on the hillside neat and trimmed.

South Place prized community. They elected their own mayor. The mayor worked hard for South Place and pressured the city to build a school at the top of the hill. The cleaner's children lived with their grandmother, aunt, uncle, and two cousins. Whenever she was paid, she sent back money to help with her family's needs. The more she could send, the better all of their lives would be.

As the head of the household listened, awareness began to grow of connections between North Place and South Place. There was much more to learn, and so the head of the household began to ask even more questions and listened for a long time. The gardener said little in the conversation, but the cleaner shared a great deal. The three stayed on the porch for several hours, until it was time for the cleaner and gardener to return to their apartments in the city.

Over the coming weeks, the head of the household learned even more by talking to family, neighbors in North Place, and community leaders; meeting local friends of the cleaner and the gardener; and reading about the history of the south. Soon the head of the household and other neighbors of North Place began thinking about what they could do to help and how they could learn from South Place and the cleaner's family.

They began to meet at the North Place Common House to talk about what each family really needed to sustain themselves. Some decided to sell one of their family cars. Some of the proceeds were given to North Place and used to create a tool library and a car library, so that all residents had access to tools and a minivan when they were needed and more money could be shared. Others decided to speak to the developers and ask for other workers—roofers, painters, builders, gardeners, and cleaners—of North Place to be paid more. Several neighbors who worked in banks used some of the money to create a Common Fund that provided loans at very low interest for neighbors in South Place.

Neighbors of North Place began to meet with the cleaner, roofer, painter, builder, and gardener to learn about what it is like to live with the land more than to master it. They learned to cultivate their soil to be rich enough to grow fruits and vegetables to eat. They built chicken coops so that they could share fresh eggs. They opened their windows and doors and began to hear the sounds of neighbor and nature.

Over time, both of the neighborhoods in the north and the south grew in their beauty.

(Origins: The parable of the Porches is inspired by the parable of the Workers in the Vineyard and the connection between middle-class neighborhoods in the United States and Santa Faz, a community outside Guatemala City, Guatemala.)

The Parable of the Lost Assets

An owner of a family business sat down one day with an accountant and financial planner to review their growing assets. The business made coatings that prevented metals from rusting. Together, the three counted how much product they made and the employees' and the owner's growing assets—property, stocks, and a 401(k).

Over time, the owner had amassed a great deal of wealth. The planner advised the owner to keep the wealth in one place to help the business during lean times, because surely some assets would be lost and the owner should consider his children's inheritance. The owner counted again. Counting all of the assets he could, the owner determined just what he and his family needed to live a simple yet comfortable life and invested the rest in the commons.

(Origins: The parable of the Lost Assets draws upon biblical scholar Amy-Jill Levine's interpretation of the parables of the Lost Sheep, Lost Coin, and Prodigal Son, as well as the story of industrialist and philanthropist Charles Grawemeyer.)

The Parable of the Professor's Epiphany

The full professor was smart. She took teaching seriously, wrote as much and as often as she could, and worked to get promotions as soon as the university would allow her. She felt like she knew, understood, and was respected by the university.

After teaching for several years, the full professor began to notice that there were many more faces of teachers at the university whom she didn't see at meetings, events, or professors' assemblies. Always busy, she walked by classroom after classroom determined to be on time to teach, but missing the opportunity to stop and find out the teachers' given names. But she felt like she knew, understood, and was respected by the university.

One fall, the full professor noticed a teacher who consistently chose the same classroom nearby. The teacher left quickly after class so that the full professor could not easily greet her. She asked other full and associate professors if they knew the teacher's given name. The full and associate professors seemed surprised by the question. No one knew her as anything other than "teacher." The full professor wondered then how well she knew and understood the university.

The full professor looked for the teacher in the faculty lounge and the course listing, and read the names on office doors, but it was hard to find the teacher's name. The full professor moved on for a while to another task.

One day she was driving to the university, and the full professor decided to stop for a coffee. The line was long. As she waited, the full professor checked her email so that she could keep up with university business. She was looking down when she got to the head of the line. As the full professor ordered coffee, she realized in looking at the barista's face that the barista was the teacher. The full professor read the teacher's given name on her nametag, and they talked for a few moments until the next customer was anxious to be served.

The full professor walked onto the university campus, hot cup of coffee in hand, and began to talk to other full and associate professors about helping teachers. Professors, associate and full, talked, debated, and discerned. Over time, they decided that now they knew the university better and they would do what they could to help teachers. They began by inviting teachers to meetings, assemblies, and events and opening their offices for sharing. And then all the given names of teachers and professors could be found on their office doors.

(Origins: The parable of the Professor's Epiphany is inspired by James Keenan's book University Ethics *and his observations about the invisibility of contingent faculty on college and university campuses.)*

The Parable of the Loving Woman
and the Neighborly Police Officer

A woman named White who lived in the Midwest read one morning on the website of her church that a demonstration in response to the death of a man named Brown had been organized on the courthouse steps in her city that same afternoon. She was responsible for the care of her young daughter on that day. On most days she volunteered a great deal at her daughter's school, and she wondered if she had the time and energy to go. Many thoughts came to her mind. If she went, would she be asked to take on another leadership role to help people in the city? Most importantly, was it even appropriate for her to take her six-year-old daughter to a demonstration?

She lived in a neighborhood nearby the city center. The tree-lined streets shaded her house from the summer sun. It was hot that day, and staying inside the house seemed most appealing. The man named Brown lived across the city in a neighborhood with far fewer trees. There was once a bustling center for shopping there, but most of the shops had closed and buildings were torn down for parking lots, empty black slabs absorbing the hot sun.

While she was thinking, White felt her daughter pull the hem of her shirt to ask if they could go outside and splash in the small blowup pool in their yard. White welcomed the distraction. She helped her daughter pull on her bathing suit, and the two went outside to play. When they got outside, her daughter jumped into the pool joyfully with a huge splash that wet White's face. She dried her face with a towel. White watched her daughter play, but couldn't get the man named Brown, his mother, and his family out of her mind.

The sermon that week was titled "Loving Your Neighbor: An Inconvenient Truth." She remembered that love is patient, does not dishonor others, and is not self-seeking. Love always protects, always trusts, always hopes and perseveres. Had it ever been easy to live into God's covenant in the city? White gathered up her daughter and their things and drove from her neighborhood across town to the courthouse.

After parking their car, they walked toward the courthouse.

They met many other people on the sidewalk going to the demonstration on the steps. Each person who came to the courthouse
increased the crowd and, like a cell, joined together with others
to form a new system. The leader, a young woman from Brown's
church, welcomed White to the Crowd. White was glad to join
with the others who came to follow the leader. When the leader
shouted, the crowd learned to respond as one body.

The leader yelled, "Our streets?"

The crowd responded, "Whose streets?"

"Our streets?"

"Whose streets?"

One person in the crowd noticed that an officer wearing a flak
jacket and helmet was stationed on the roof of a nearby building holding a rifle. He had been charged by the captain of the
department and the city to watch the crowd. For a moment, the
spirit of the crowd changed. They felt afraid and wondered what
was happening. Seeing others looking up at the building, White
used her hand to shade her eyes from the afternoon sun, and she
looked up to see the officer.

The leader yelled, "Why are you in riot gear? We don't see no
riot here."

The crowd responded, "Why are you in riot gear? We don't
see no riot here."

In the same call-and-response as before, they chanted, "Why
are you in riot gear? We don't see no riot here. Why are you in
riot gear? We don't see no riot here."

And then the leader stopped the chanting to read a story about
the man called Brown and asked if anyone in the crowd wanted
to share why they were there. Women named Black and Brown
told stories about their sons. Later, another woman also called
White stepped into the center of the crowd and said, "Not enough
Whites are speaking up to say, 'This is about our humanity, too.
This gathering is a prayer for the sake of loving our neighbor as
ourselves.'"

The leader yelled, "This is our humanity, too. Love us as all
neighbors do!"

The crowd chanted back, "This is our humanity, too. Love us
as all neighbors do!"

From the top of the building where he was stationed, the officer
heard the shouts and stories of the crowd. Every day he drove

throughout the city and knew well the stark contrast between the neighborhood streets lined with trees and yards embellished with flowers and those made up primarily of dilapidated houses and flat parking lots adorned with dumpsters. As he looked down on the demonstration, the officer saw how the crowd was one body. For a moment he hesitated, and then he took off his helmet, set down the rifle, and walked down the stairs of the building to join the crowd. Soon the other officers followed.

When the demonstration ended, the crowd dispersed, knowing there was still much work to be done.

(Origins: The parable of the Loving Woman and the Neighborly Police Officer is inspired by the many people of faith who supported the Black Lives Matter movement after the shooting of Michael Brown and in the summer of 2016 as demonstrations to break white silence were planned all across the nation in response to the killings of Alton Sterling, Philando Castile, and five Dallas police officers.)

The Parable of the Good Felons

On a rainy day in the city, three felons in a halfway house woke up early to get ready for work. They showered, ate breakfast, and then walked to the door together and asked the guard to push the buzzer so that they could open the front door. Once outside, the felons walked briskly to the bus stop. Two felons waited for the Number 17 bus. The other felon had to take Number 41.

Across town, a teen was pulling on his rain slicker and backpack and putting on his bike helmet. He mounted his bike in the garage and then rode out of the driveway to head toward school. The rain slowed to a drizzle, and the traffic was light in the teen's neighborhood. He quickly made it to the stop sign at the big road. After looking right and then left, he turned onto the big road that led toward the city. Just as the teen wheeled across the yellow line, the bumper of a car speeding down the road met his bike's back wheel. The teen was thrown forward into the ditch on the side of the road.

The driver sped on.

The teen lay unconscious for about thirty minutes. Neither the teen nor his bike were visible from the road. Drivers hurrying to work passed by the ditch. Some were reading texts on their phones.

When the teen regained consciousness, he heard footsteps approaching in the gravel on the side of the road. The two felons who rode Number 17 were walking from the bus stop near the factory where they worked.

One felon saw the teen in the ditch and called out, "Hey, man. You okay?" The teen couldn't say anything in response. He shook his head, and his face grimaced in pain. The other felon noticed that the teen's pants were ripped and his leg was bleeding. He looked at the first felon and said, "We have to help, but we'll be late for work." The felon nodded his head. "We don't have a choice. This guy is hurt."

The two felons quickly ran down into the ditch. One felon took off his T-shirt and tied it around the teen's leg. The other felon took off his T-shirt and wrapped it around the teen's head. Both felons knew they couldn't leave the teen.

Shirtless, chest exposed, the felon climbed his way out of the ditch to get back up to the road. The felon tried to wave down a car for help, but the drivers seemed afraid. They passed by. Soon the felons heard sirens wail and hoped that help was on the way.

(Origins: The parable of the Good Felons is inspired by the story of the Good Samaritan and visits to Dierson House, a halfway house for people transitioning out of prison.)

The Parable of the Just Office Manager and the Righteous Business Owner

In the city, there lived an office manager. She took care of people who worked in the office, making sure they were paid on time, sending them information about their benefits, and helping them understand their goals and manage their time. Office employees would often come to her with their problems, and most of the time she would keep a distance as she had been taught to do as a good manager.

But one day, an employee, a single mother of three, went to the office manager asking for a raise. The employee was a good worker who had served the company well for years, and after years of service she had worked her way up from the mailroom to an office employee. Her daughter needed braces, her other children needed school supplies and uniforms, but she was already just barely scraping by. She had been falling behind on her mortgage payments. The office manager had always been taught that good managers keep it clean; keep a distance from those whom they manage. But when the employee came to the office manager, she knew that she couldn't keep her distance. The office manager knew that determining the employee's wages was outside her job description, but she did have access to a small travel fund for her own professional development. She knew that the employee really needed the help and decided to use that money to give the employee a small bonus.

The next week, another employee came to her. This employee had worked for the company for twenty years, but the position that he was in didn't allow for him to get any more raises. His wife had become ill, and even with the company insurance, the bills were piling up. He pleaded with the office manager to raise his salary. The office manager felt responsible even though she didn't have the power to change the way salaries were determined. Still, she just couldn't keep it clean. The employee really needed the help. From time to time, the office manager received gifts from vendors who wanted her to consider using their goods in the office. She saved them all and gave them to the employee so that he would be able to feed his family.

A week later, another employee arrived at the office manager's door. The employee was always late and had been written up several times for his inefficiency. He lived out in the suburbs, and the public transportation was never on time. The employee told the office manager that he needed a raise so that he could buy a car and then would be able to be on time for work. But the office manager had used all of the resources available. Even though she knew that this employee also needed help, she had to turn him away.

When the office manager drove home that evening, she was unable to forget about all three employees and all of the other people who worked in the office. Their stories stayed with her, but she was also aware that her own resources were limited. After a night of fitful sleep, the office manager drove to work and called a meeting of all the office employees. Together they decided to create an office emergency fund that each of them could use when they had a need. They began meeting together to determine other ways they could help each other.

Some time passed until one day the office manager was called to see the owner in his office. She could tell by the look on his face that he was outraged by her insubordination. She listened to him for some time and feared that she would lose her job. When she was allowed to speak, her words came from the depths of her heart about the employees' lives. "I know I was supposed to keep my distance. But when someone asks me for help they really *need* it."

By this time, employees had gathered outside the large glass window of the owner's office. As the owner listened to the office manager, he had never heard the stories of such hardship. Then he saw the employees through his office window. His face cooled. The owner sat down in his chair and asked the office manager to leave him alone for a while.

A few hours later he left the office. Rather than taking his usual route home, he spent the evening riding the bus around the city. Because he spent most of his time in his office, gathering around the table in the boardroom, and sitting with clients at restaurants downtown, he didn't see the decay evident in the city—abandoned buildings and neighborhoods and desolate landscapes—that he saw on the bus. Early the next day, the owner gathered everyone in the company for a meeting. The owner gave the company and all of its property to the company's employees for the sake of the city.

(Origins: The parable of the Just Office Manager and the Righteous Business Owner was inspired by the stories of real choice made by many middle-class people that are recorded in Lisa Dodson's book The Moral Underground: How Ordinary Americans Subvert an Unfair Economy. *This parable is revised and updated from an article titled "The Problem of Wealth" in* CrossCurrents.)

The parables above are somewhat limited by my own experiences and the context in which I live. My hope is for you to consider them in light of the issues you are facing in your own community. These parables and stories are based upon the assumption that contemporary people of faith of the Christian variety are still called to participate in the God movement by living in the tension between anger and hope, speaking to the most pressing issue of our time, and embodying God's love in the total social realm. How can you expand the stories and write your own imagination for the commons into a larger narrative with the aim of using the power and privilege you have to love others by working for just economic policies?

Concluding Observations
and a Call To Action

The social and political circumstances in the United States have changed dramatically since I began writing this book. When I started, the Occupy Wall Street movement was at its peak, and I visited with people living in tent communities in Calgary, New York, and my own hometown. Demonstrations organized by the Black Lives Matter movement were being held across the country, and Senator Bernie Sanders's proposals for free college, single-payer health care, and a living wage were making traction in the 2016 US presidential debate during the last few weeks I finished my work on the original manuscript. Nonviolent solidarity protest movements and a swell of interest in just economic policies gave me great reasons for hope. But by the time this book moved into production in January 2017, I, like many other liberals and progressives, was bracing myself for the inauguration of Donald J. Trump as the forty-fifth president of the United States and the appointment of the wealthiest cabinet of leaders ever in US history. New diagnoses of the problems we face were emerging on an hourly basis. What became very clear was how many white conservative Christian voters supported Trump. Calls to action made by liberals and progressives at this time are endless in anticipation of what may happen in the coming years. Why add one more call to action?

We are facing so many problems as a society—the increasing wealth divide; cancers of sexism and racism; mass incarceration; effects of drug abuse; lack of access to healthy food, clean water, and good quality public education for many; an epidemic of gun violence; caustic and corrosive rhetoric pervading political discourse; and more. Equally important, US society and the problems we face are not distantly related to what happens in the larger global community; rather, we are linked to it. As a global community we are confronted with the specters of nationalism, isolationism, terrorism, an increasing wealth divide, poverty, climate change, and the desperate need for economic migrants and refugees to have a place to call home.

We have arrived at another point in time when asking the right questions will be essential to understanding the connections between all of these problems and envisioning systems and structures that will lead to authentic change for the commons rather than preserving power and privilege for the few at the expense of the many. Moreover, I have argued that raising the right questions about how our current dominant forms of wealth creation accelerate poverty, divide neighbor from nature, and submerge people into poverty matters not only for human communities and the planet but also to a God who is the essence of Love, Mutuality, and Relationship. God's very nature is a relational ecology. What if we begin to see ourselves as created in God's relational image? For US Americans, that will be a very countercultural thing to do. Jesus said, "Our God is the one Lord, you must love the Lord your God with all your heart, with all your being, with all your mind, and with all your strength. The second is this, You will love your neighbor as yourself. No other commandment is greater than these" (Mark 12:29–31).

If the ultimate Christian vocation or calling is to love our neighbors as ourselves, how do we make that love public and take it out into the streets, into the boardrooms, and the legislatures? Many US Americans are prone to think that hyperindividualism, competition, and keeping self-interest and our own national interests at the center of economic activities will lead to the "blessing of our nation," alleviate poverty, and increase community. This is a false promise and hope. Our relationships, communities, nation, and world would look much differently if we consistently embodied love through the values of reciprocity, cooperation/collaboration, interdependence, accountability to the commons, sustainability, and the inclusion of diverse peoples and experiences. The wisdom of faith traditions invites us to live by an alternative social logic that is informed by a much richer picture of human beings—our limits and responsibilities—as part of a larger web of life. There are some glimpses in stories told here about the real potential for greater peace, stability, happiness, and justice in our society and for the larger global community, but the changing times evidenced in widespread support for the Trump campaign and Brexit may seem like I am trying to plant seeds on rocky soil.

I want to leave you with the challenge to reframe the debate in your own local context about wealth inequalities, poverty, and environmental destruction in terms of the way we create wealth and how our current dominant forms of wealth creation impact people who are the poorest as well as the planet Earth, our home. Ask the critical questions that hold self-interest and the interests of a larger community always in careful balance. Most importantly, this call to action is not only to embody love by working for just economic policies, but is also a call to live with a new social imaginary rooted in relatedness. An image of aspen trees flourishing in the mountains of Colorado comes to my mind. Aspens are the most widespread tree on the North American continent. Individual trees stand tall in large clusters, their slight round trunks sometimes shivering with a heavy wind. Aspens can grow and flourish in rocky soil. What is not so easily seen as one looks at a group or stand of trees is that aspens are one organism, connected by their extensive root system. People of faith and the communities we serve have a rich store of resources and wisdom to draw upon, leaving us uniquely situated to dig deep into our roots, and inspire and envision much-needed attitudinal, systemic, and structural change—that is, *if* we are willing to take it.

PART V

ADDITIONAL RESOURCES

Prompts for Further Thought, Reflection, and Discussion

This book is intended to be a resource for personal and communal reflection and discussion about the crises we are facing related to the increasing wealth divide, poverty, and the exploitation of our natural environment. You might use the prompts and questions for the purpose of journaling or as a beginning point for dialogue in a classroom setting, study group, or church school class.

Chapter 1

1. Do you think that the way we create wealth matters to God and to others? Why or why not?
2. How do you understand the "problem of wealth"? What are the theological reasons offered in the first chapter to begin, name, and define a discussion of poverty, wealth inequalities, and environmental destruction from the perspective of the problem of wealth as opposed to poverty?
3. If you have not explored wealth inequalities in your own city, take some time to investigate your own context. Are there areas of your city or town where the wealthy are geographically segregated from people living in poverty? How do you think this impacts and forms attitudes toward people living in poverty?
4. At this point in your reading, do you agree that it is important to reframe the broader public discussion about poverty and wealth inequalities in terms of the problem of wealth? Why or why not?

Chapter 2

1. What stories and teachings in the biblical text suggest that economics has always been central to Christian theology? Are there other stories and teachings in the biblical text that are not included in this chapter that come to your mind? If so, which stories?

2. Reflect on your understanding of economics as the managing of right relationships in God's household. How do early Christian ideas of the way people of faith should think about their economic activities challenge the patriarchal ordering of the household?

3. After reading chapter 2, what role do you think religious leaders should play in debates about wealth inequalities, economic justice, fair pay, workers' rights, and so on?

Chapter 3

1. How has religious thought—more specifically, Christian thought—played a crucial role in the formation of the discipline of economics in the Western academy?

2. When was a solid boundary established between the disciplines of theology, moral philosophy, history, and economics in the Western academy? How were the debates and disagreements leading to the creation of economics as a stand-alone discipline theological in nature?

3. How do you understand the impact of economism on the attitudes of people in the US toward money, wealth, and community? In the past, economics was taught in relation to moral philosophy, history, and theology. Do you think that this relationship should be reemphasized and restored in educational contexts? Why or why not?

Chapter 4

1. Clearly define and briefly describe in your own words the two dominant approaches to wealth creation and their consequences as they are outlined in this chapter.

2. The importance of using the term "neoliberalism" in reference to conversations about poverty and wealth inequalities

is debated by scholars and some religious social activists. Do you agree or disagree with the historians, anthropologists, leaders of financial institutions, and religious leaders who think that the term is too diffuse to serve as an analytic category? Explain your position.

3. Why do you think people in the United States, even those involved in a faith community, are reluctant to or fail to demand better economic alternatives?

4. Consider the story of Sarah and Hagar as it is told at the end of the chapter. What theological reasons are given in support of naming neoliberalism as the root cause of the growing wealth divide and for framing the debate in terms of the problem of wealth?

Chapter 5

1. How does the concept of the Social Trinity deepen your understanding of the essence of God's relatedness? What language is used throughout chapter 5 to name the three persons of the Trinity? Reflect on these metaphors.

2. This chapter explores how the Trinity is a way of describing God's nature as love. Take some time to return to the biblical text and think more about the biblical stories of Ruth and Naomi and Mary at the wedding of Cana. How is God's love expressed in these stories?

3. Do you think that the concept of the Social Trinity can enable Christians in our contemporary world to reenvision the shape of social, economic, and political systems and structures? If so, in what ways?

4. Consider the story of Aunt Fleta and Uncle Ossie told at the end of chapter 4. What examples come to your mind of people who have embodied love and lived in mutuality and relationship, and practiced an ethic of enough?

Chapter 6

1. How does the Native American worldview of reciprocity and spatiality challenge the social imaginary of people formed by and who benefit most from the dominant white cultures of the West? What does the Native American per-

spective of George Tinker outlined in chapter 6 contribute to contemporary debates about climate change?

2. British economist E. F. Schumacher explored the concept of Buddhist economics in his book *Small Is Beautiful*. How does the concept of Buddhist economics stand as a challenge to consumerism in the highly industrialized countries of the Global North, particularly the United States? How does Buddhist economics invite you to rethink your own relationship to material things and the purpose of work?

3. Reexamine the discussion of the Jewish practice of Sabbath-keeping outlined in chapter 6. How is Sabbath-keeping a prophetic practice? Consider the connection between Sabbath-keeping and liberation.

4. Why do you think that Islam is the only faith tradition identifying with the story of Abraham, Sarah, and Hagar that continues to prohibit usury? Consider the theological basis for Islamic banking. What potential do you think the practice of Islamic banking has for transforming banking in the United States?

Chapter 7

1. What concepts, traditions, and social teachings provided the theological basis for the Catholic Worker movement? The Catholic Worker movement defies the traditional charitable approaches supported by churches and social organizations that are intended to address the needs of people in poverty. Take note of the ways the Catholic Worker movement defies traditional approaches to charity.

2. The Church of the Savior is a model of congregational life that challenges the values of market-driven society. Reflect on the spiritual disciplines and practices of that community. What are other examples are included in the chapter for ways that intentional communities redefine work and wealth?

3. Reexamine the principles of cooperative economics. Are there examples of cooperative businesses or banks in your area? How are these ventures supported by your local community? How do they support your local community?

4. To what extent is access to affordable housing an issue in your area? Do you think the alternatives to traditional home ownership presented in chapter 7 are viable options to address needs for affordable housing present in your local community? If so, in what ways?

Chapter 8

1. One of the claims made in this chapter is that Zacchaeus is one of the only stories in the biblical narrative that compares somewhat to contemporary middle-class experience. Respond to this claim. Are other stories in the biblical text comparable to contemporary middle-class experience? If so, which ones?
2. Reflect on the origins of parables. How would the ancient hearers of Jesus's parables have understood his intentions in using short stories to address issues that they faced?
3. Whom do you identify with in the parables included in this chapter? How do the parables affirm the way you live? How do the stories challenge you to think or live differently?
4. After reading the chapter, reflect on your own context. Write on your own or imagine with others in a group a parable to challenge you or others in your community to hold six fundamental social values at the center of your economic activities—reciprocity, cooperation/collaboration, interdependence, accountability to the commons, sustainability, and the inclusion of diverse peoples and experiences.

APPENDIX 2

Documents of Catholic Social Teaching

The Roman Catholic Church has a long tradition of social teachings that form a body of doctrine on social and economic justice. Catholic social teaching is grounded in the prophetic tradition of the Hebrew Bible, the writings of the early church fathers, and in Jesus's teachings in the Gospels. The US Conference of Catholic Bishops emphasizes seven themes that emerge from the papal, conciliar, and episcopal documents: (1) the life and dignity of the human person; (2) the call to family, community, and participation; (3) rights and responsibilities; (4) the option for the poor and vulnerable; (5) the dignity of work and workers; (6) solidarity; and (7) care for the creation.[1]

Documents of Catholic Social Teaching			
1891	*Rerum novarum*	"The Condition of Labor"	Pope Leo XIII
1931	*Quadragesimo anno*	"After Forty Years"	Pope Pius XI
1961	*Mater et magistra*	"Christianity and Social Progress"	Pope John XXIII
1963	*Pacem in terries*	"Peace on Earth"	Pope John XXIII
1965	*Gaudium et spes*	"Pastoral Constitution on the Church in the Modern World"	Second Vatican Council

[1] "Seven Themes of Catholic Social Teaching," US Conference of Catholic Bishops, www.usccb.org.

1965	*Dignitatis humanae*	"Declaration on Religious Freedom"	Second Vatican Council
1967	*Populorum progressio*	"On the Development of Peoples"	Pope Paul VI
1971	*Octogesima adveniens*	"A Call to Action on the Eightieth Anniversary of *Rerum novarum*"	Pope Paul VI
1971	*Justitia in mundo*	"Justice in the World"	Roman Synod
1975	*Evangelii nuntiandi*	"Evangelization in the Modern World"	Pope Paul VI
1981	*Laborem exercens*	"On Human Work"	Pope John Paul II
1987	*Sollicitudo rei socialis*	"On Social Concern"	Pope John Paul II
1991	*Centesimus annus*	"On the Hundredth Anniversary of *Rerum novarum*"	Pope John Paul II
2015	*Laudato si'*	"On Care for Our Common Home"	Pope Francis

Documents Related to the US Context

1983		The Challenge of Peace: God's Promise and Our Response	US Conference of Catholic Bishops
1986		Economic Justice for All	US Conference of Catholic Bishops

Appendix 3

Selected Statements
on Just Economy
and Wealth Inequalities
by Protestant Denominations
and Ecumenical Organizations

Many denominations and ecumenical organizations continue to maintain offices (even if they are shrinking) that keep social witness on the agendas of churches. A broad network of denominational, ecumenical, and interfaith organizations brings issues of poverty and wealth inequalities to the forefront of the public forum by providing educational programming, waging letter campaigns, encouraging participation in and training people for advocacy, and drafting creedal or confessional statements.

Examples of denominational offices include the Presbyterian Church (U.S.A.)'s Advisory Committee on Social Witness Policy, the United Church of Christ Justice and Witness Ministries, the United Methodist General Board of Church and Society, the Social Action Commission of the African Methodist Episcopal Church, and the Episcopal Network for Economic Justice. Ecumenical organizations include collaboration between denominational offices at the United Nations Church Center, the National Council of Churches, the World Council of Churches, and the World Communion of Reformed Churches. The list below provides examples of important documents that could be considered part of a Protestant or ecumenical tradition of social teaching.

1908	Social Creed	Federal Council of Churches (Later the National Council of Churches)
1938	Resolution on the Church and Labor	Christian Church (Disciples of Christ)
1946	Social Principles	The Evangelical United Brethren Church
1967	The Confession of 1967	United Presbyterian Church in the United States of America (UPCUSA) and now within the Book of Confessions of the Pres-byterian Church (U.S.A.; PCUSA)
1971	Income Maintenance	UPCUSA
1972, 1976, 2012	Social Principles	The United Methodist Church
1973	State and Local Tax Reform	UPCUSA
1976	Economic Justice within Environmental Limits	UPCUSA
1978	Human Rights	Presbyterian Church in the United States (PCUS)
1980	On the Crisis of Pri-orities in the National Budget	PCUS
1980	Labor Relations—Theo-logical Affirmations from Biblical Perspectives	PCUS
1980	International Economic Justice	PCUS
1981	Resolution on Labor	American Baptist Church, USA
1995	God's Work in Our Hands: Employment, Community, and Chris-tian Vocation	PCUSA
1997	Affirming "Democratic Principles in an Emerging Global Economy"	United Church of Christ

1999	Social Statement on Sufficient Sustainable Livelihood for All	Evangelical Lutheran Church of America
2000 (revised and adopted from a statement first made in 1988)	Economic Justice for a New Millennium	United Methodist Church
2003	A Faithful Response: Calling for a More Just, Humane Direction for Economic Globalization	United Church of Christ
2004	The Accra Confession	World Alliance of Reformed Churches (now World Communion of Reformed Churches)
2006	Alternative Globalization for People and Earth	World Council of Churches (WCC)
2007	The Social Creed for the Twenty-First Century	National Council of Churchs (NCC)
2011	"There's a New World in the Making"	North American Regional Hearings and Forum, Poverty Wealth and Ecology Project, WCC
2011	Speaking Out for a Faithful Budget	NCC Poverty Initiative
2012	Economy of Life, Peace, and Justice for All: A Call to Action	WCC
2012	Sao Paula Statement: International Financial Transformation for the Economy of Life	WCC
2012	Together Towards Life: Mission and Evangelism in Changing Landscapes	Commission on World Mission and Evangelism
2014	Together Building a Just Economy: A Manifesto for People of Faith	Seminary Consortium for Urban Pastoral Education (SCUPE) Congress on Urban Ministry

APPENDIX 4

Selected Statements on Just Economy, Worker Rights, and Wealth Inequalities Made by a Wider Variety of Religious Traditions and Interfaith Organizations

Interreligious harmony calls people to act in solidarity and to transform the social, economic, and political systems and structures into an economy that serves the commons. A selected list of recent statements on just economy, worker rights, and wealth inequalities appears below.

2008	Ecclesial and Social Visions of Indigenous Peoples	World Council of Churches (WCC) Consultation in Baguio, Philippines
2008	Ethical Employment Practices	Union for Reformed Judaism
2011	Muslims and Christians Engaging Structural Greed	Lutheran World Federation (LWF) Conference on Muslims and Christians Engaging Structural Greed
2010	Buddhist-Christian Common Word on Structural Greed	WCC and LWF Conference on Buddhists and Christians Engaging Structural Greed Today
2012	The Vision and Mission Statement of the NPS	The Network of Spiritual Progressive (NPS)
2013	Resolution in Support of Paid Sick Days	Union for Reformed Judaism

2015	Resolution in Support of Paid Family Leave	Union for Reformed Judaism
2015	Declaration on Income Inequality and the Widening Wealth Gap	Parliament of World Religions
2015	Indigenous Peoples Declaration	Parliament of World Religions
2015	Ending Extreme Poverty: A Moral and Spiritual Imperative	The World Bank
2015	Reducing the Gap—Interfaith Riches	WCC Common Message from Building an Interfaith Community Summer Course in Chateau de Bossey, Switzerland
2015	Interfaith Call for Justice and Compassion in Finance	WCC Workshop on Faith and Finance in Bangkok, Thailand

Glossary of Alternative Theological and Other Terms for Envisioning an Economy That Serves the Commons

Ashram. A monastery or spiritual retreat center where people go to seek wisdom from religious sages and to listen to the prayers of the trees. Ashrams are an integral part of the Hindu and Christian spiritual heritage of India.

Cooperatives. The United Nations defines a cooperative as "an autonomous association of persons united voluntarily to meet their common economic, social, and cultural needs and aspirations through a jointly owned and democratically controlled enterprise." (See 2012 International Year of Cooperatives, "About Cooperatives: International Co-operative Alliance Statement on the Co-operative Identity," www.un.org.)

Distributivism. An economic philosophy emerging from the social teachings of the Catholic Church, particularly *Rerum novarum* and *Quadragesimo anno*. The basic idea is to distribute wealth as widely as possible among citizens, rather than supporting systems and structures that allow wealth to be concentrated in the hands of a few individuals.

Eco-holism. The commitment to sustainability as a value that will eliminate poverty, increase the well-being of smaller rural communities, satisfy hunger, and eliminate racial and ethnic disparities in access to healthy foods.

Economism. A term used to describe the assumption or viewpoint that economics, market-based logic, and money itself are of utmost and decisive importance in determining the route to human flourishing.

Ecodomy. Refers to building life in its fullness.

234 *ELIZABETH HINSON-HASTY*

Economy. The Greek root of the word *economy* is *oikos*, which literally means household. From a Christian theological perspective, *economy* refers to the way in which we manage right relationships in God's household.

Ecumenical movement. A movement aimed at promoting unity in understanding and cooperation in mission for justice among Christian denominations.

Intentional communities. Communities that organize their religious ritual and practice, economic affairs, living arrangements, or other aspects of daily life around cooperative or communal principles.

Interreligious solidarity. A methodology for interreligious engagement that moves beyond only dialogue about the convergence of values or morals found in the world's great religious traditions on matters of economic and social justice to constructing theory in the midst of transformational action.

Oikosystem. An alternative term used in reference to God's economy of salvation that associates the Social Trinity with the commons. *Economy* is derived from two Greek words: *oikos*, meaning household, and *nemein*, meaning management, dispensation, ordering. "Oikos" is partnered with "system" to address the deficiencies of the ancient patriarchal ordering of the household and to emphasize the interdependence of God with the whole creation and the contingency of human existence.

Parable. The *Oxford English Dictionary* (*OED*) notes multiple origins of the word *parable*, including French and Latin. The *OED* defines a *parable* as a metaphorical saying or narrative; an enigmatic or mystical saying. Biblical scholar Amy Jill Levine observes that the etymological root of this term can be found in Greek words *para*, meaning alongside or together with, as in *parallel* or *paradox*, and *balo*, which means to cast or to throw.

Political economy. According to the *OED*, économic politique first came into use in French in 1611; earlier as *oeconomie politique*. Political economy refers to the branch of economics dealing with economic problems of government. Adam Smith used this term in *The Wealth of Nations*, as he proposed the means to "provide a plentiful revenue or subsistence for the people . . . and . . . to supply the state with a revenue sufficient for the publick services."

Postcolonial, postcolonialism. Relating to the social, cultural, economic, and political conditions of a nation that has freed itself from colonial rule.

Poverty. There are a range of definitions of poverty related to particular contexts. The primary manner in which poverty is defined in heavily industrialized and technologically advanced countries in the Global North is lack of access to material resources and money needed to live life in a way that is acceptable to the dominant social group. According to mystical traditions, the poverty experienced as a result of the voluntary renunciation of worldly goods is a religious mystery that deepens one's encounter with the divine. From the experience of Native American peoples, poverty can also be defined as a lack of consciousness of the commons and the interrelatedness of all things—two-legged, four-legged, six-legged, winged ones, and inanimate and animate objects.

Resistance. Concrete action taken as the result of an inner awareness of the sacredness of all things.

Riba. An Arabic term that can be translated in English as *usury.* Yahia Abdul-Rahman, founder of Lariba, an Islamic financial center, defines it as "the act of taking advantage of those who need money to meet their basic necessities through the act of renting them money at a price called 'interest.' " (See Yahia Abdul-Rahman, *The Art of RF [Riba-free] Islamic Banking and Finance* [Hoboken, NJ: John Wiley and Sons, 2010], 2.)

Social and solidarity economy. A concept of economics that refers to forms of production and exchange that aim to satisfy human needs, build resilience, and expand human capabilities through cooperative and collaborative social relationships. The role of labor in sustaining the livelihood of individuals and families is recovered as opposed to accentuating the role of capital.

Social mysticism. A "double vision" or consciousness cultivated by one's openness to encountering the underlying unity of all things in the midst of daily activities. Social activities are not seen as an end in themselves, but as expressions of one's resistance to social and political artifices that create tangible yet false boundaries between human beings, God, and the natural world. Consciousness of the underlying unity of all things compels social mystics to examine critically the economic, political, and social environment that surrounds them and to address the sense of moral incoherence they experience through purposive action. Examples of significant US social mystics include Dorothy Day, Thomas Merton, and Howard Thurman.

Social Trinity. Social concepts of the Trinity emerge from an understanding of God's creative work in the world and how human beings participate, collaborate, and work in partnership with God.

Sola caritate. In Latin, "love alone." Reformed theologians and ethicists in Europe and North America are calling for this new sola to be added to the principles that defined the sixteenth-century Protestant Reformation.

Solidarity. The French term *solidarité* was derived from the Latin *solidum*, meaning whole sum. Solidarity is the unity or agreement of a feeling that leads to concrete action for social, economic, and political change.

Sumak Kawsay. A concept of the good life emerging from the experiences of indigenous peoples in Latin America. It is the pursuit of wholeness in every aspect of one's life by seeking and embodying harmony-creating and world-balancing wisdom.

Ubuntu. An African concept that is difficult to translate directly into English. Desmond Tutu says that the idea is, "My humanity is caught up, inextricably bound up in yours." Other commentators and religious leaders translate Ubuntu to mean "I am because you are. You are because I am," "collective personhood," and "collective morality."

Usury. The excessive charging of interest on money loaned by people of relative wealth.

Wealth recycling. The transfer of massive amounts of investment and capital from the control of giant long-standing corporations to grassroots and local businesses that are worker-owned, consumer co-ops, family-operated, or neighborhood-operated.

Zacchaean economics. Restoring oneself to community by practicing giving back resources, money, and goods that were received because of unjust economic policies and unfair, unearned social privilege.

Index

Abraham, 92, 126
Africa
  pollution problem, 119–20
  poverty concerns, 5
  South Africa, 61, 120–23
  sub-Saharan Africa, 87, 88
  tribal lands used for the common
    good, 187
  ubuntu concept, 122–23, 236
African Americans
  black farmers, 175–76
  decline in wealth, 85
  Fannie Lou Hamer as advocate
    for, 17
  food insecurity, families living with,
    174
  incarceration rates, 7, 121
  low-wage jobs, overrepresentation
    in, 82
  poverty rate, 6
  slavery, surviving through collective
    efforts, 179–80
  wealth divide, black Protestant
    views on, 21
agape, 111, 114, 125
Akacem, Mohammed, 151–52, 154
Allegretto, Sylvia, 85
American Economic Association
  (AEA), 60–61
American Indians. *See* Native Ameri-
  cans
Ames, Elizabeth, 27–28
Anchal Project, 185, 186
Andrus, Chip, 169
Appalachia
  folk remedies of, 24, 94
  social developmentalism in, 69–70
  Tennessee Valley Authority project,
    67, 70–77
Aquinas, Thomas, 42, 58, 102
Arius, theology of, 101–2
Arizmendiarrieta, José María, 178
Asia

slum populations, 5
social developmentalism in, 143–44
South/Southeast Asia, 53, 87
sweatshops, 4
Assisi Shanthi Kendra ashram, 105
Augustine, Saint, 40–41

Ban Ki-moon, 178
Baradaran, Mehrsa, 181
Barger, William, 60
Barton, Bruce, 89
Beck, Glen, 28–29
Berrigan, Philip, 130
Berry, Wendell, 171–73
Biss, Eula, 11
Black Church Food Security Network
  (BCFSN), 174–76, 178
Black Lives Matter movement, 209,
  213
Boesak, Allan, 120, 121, 123
Boff, Leonardo, 99
Bondi, Roberta, 114
Borsodi, Ralph, 187
Bretton Woods conference, 73–74
Brookings Institute studies, 6–7, 13,
  21
Brown, Heber, III, 174–75
Brown, Michael, 209
Brown, Peter, 37, 39–40, 195
Brueggemann, Walter, 31, 32
Buddhism
  being *vs.* having, 20
  Buddha Christ statue of Kerala,
    105
  Buddhist economics, 134, 140–44,
    222
  parable of the neighborhood Bud-
    dha, 201–2
buen vivir concept, 139
Buffett, Warren, 50, 86
Burks, Flossie (Momo), 64–65
Bush, George H. W., 85–86
Bush, George W., 151